THE AUTHOR'S INTRODUCTION

A journey is defined as traveling from one place to another or a trip. This book entitled "True Israel (What African American's Need to Know)" is a compelling reality of a journey from Christianity to being a true Hebrew Israelite of the bible.

After nearly 32 years of being part of the modern-day Christian church (Christianity), a shocking awakening took place in my life and that was discovering I was a descendent from the lineage of Abraham, Isaac and Jacob.

Surely, many questions came to mind concerning this new discovery. The first question was what do I do next? Does it make a difference? How could this have happened to me and to all the other so called African Americans and people of color around the world? What is the story?

The religion of Christianity has missed the mark on many of the biblical doctrines and this book will explore and test some of those doctrines against the bible itself. This book "True Israel" will be informative, controversial, shocking, thought provoking and hopeful.

This book is dedicated to all of the so-called African Americans that are still sleep and will awaken in the near future. This information will be a good start into understanding who you are and what is your purpose. The modern-day Christian church teaches that the so-called African Americans are Gentiles and True Israel does not matter anymore. This information is far from the truth and the bible does not teach it.

The fact that the church does not teach this truth lends room for much more deception in the doctrines of Christianity. Once you realize who you are and read the bible from that perspective the scriptures make more sense and lines up perfectly. The African Americans and other people of color who have been scattered around the world are the true Israelites of the bible and this book will explore that truth using scriptures and history to validate that claim.

My Awakening Story

I became very restless in church, directing the dance ministry and being part of other church auxiliaries faithfully. I was very dedicated in reading my bible thinking I had some understanding, however when I would listen to the pastors or ministers preach, I had difficulty making the connection from their sermons to what I was reading in the bible.

I ignored this for years and went along with my church routine; however, the urge to know more about the truth of the bible grew along with some discomforts in the church that I was attending. I had no biblical basis why I was feeling this way but I knew I needed to do something.

I thought maybe I grew beyond the church I was attending and this led me to search for another church. I did eventually find another church and joined. Shortly thereafter, this feeling I didn't belong came over me again. I would sit in the pew and look at the pulpit and there was a huge stand up cross and a Christmas tree (It was Christmas time).

Immediately I felt uncomfortable as I stared at the cross and Christmas tree in the pulpit. I didn't understand what was happening to me and suddenly these things made me uncomfortable. During this time, I was discovering who I was as an Israelite of the bible so I needed to see if I could find scriptures to match how I was feeling about the church at this time.

I believe the Most High God was trying to wake me up for a few years prior and it finally hit me why I was feeling this way due to the Laws, Statutes and Commandments of the Most High God. I found scriptures to support my feelings concerning the Christmas tree and the cross and it was history from there. I left the church and began seeking the truth of the matter and this book is a manifestation of my Journey toward the truth. (Jeremiah 10:1-6 / Exodus 20:4).

Of course, there is much more to my awakening story but this short testimony is for those who may be wondering why they are feeling disconnected from the church during these last days. The Most High God is calling his people out of religion and back to his Laws, Statutes and Commandments. The scripture says "Come Out of Her My People" (Revelation 18:4). Henry Barton

Table of Content

Chapter 1

Chapter 2

Chapter 3

Chapter 4

Chapter 5

Chapter 6

Chapter 7

Chapter 8

Chapter 9

Chapter 10

Chapter 11

Chapter 12

Chapter 16

Chapter 17

Chapter 18

Chapter 1

THE BIBLE

Many people around the world own bibles, but how many people actually read it? How many people actually study it? The bible is an amazing book of history and prophecy. But whose history does the bible speaks about? How does one study the bible? How should one read the bible? Answers to these questions and many others will be presented here in this chapter.

Many have assumed that the bible is a book for and about Christians or those who practice modern day or Roman Christianity; however, the bible had a beginning before Roman Christianity was even created. The whole entire bible centers on the Nation of Israel and its descendents which are Israelites. The Israelites did not identify themselves as Christians but as brethren, saints and /or elect. The disciples were called Christians in Antioch by others not of themselves.

Acts 11:26 (KJV)

[26] And when he had found him, he brought him unto Antioch. And it came to pass, that a whole year they assembled themselves with the church, and taught much people. And the disciples were called Christians first in Antioch.

Also read Acts 26:28 and I Peter 4:16.

As a matter of fact, if one does the research on the word "Christian" it was actually used as a derogatory term during the biblical days.

Every book of the bible was written by an Israelite for Israelites and all those who intend on following the God of the Israelite nation should treat it as such. When one reads the scriptures, they should read it from an Israelite perspective and receive the proper interpretation. The bible itself reveals the writers were indeed Hebrew Israelites.

Paul wrote 13 Epistles (books) in the bible and he was an Israelite:

Romans 11:1 (KJV)

1 I say then, Hath God cast away his people? God forbid. For I also am an Israelite, of the seed of Abraham, of the tribe of Benjamin.

Philippians 3:5 (KJV)

5 Circumcised the eighth day, of the stock of Israel, of the tribe of Benjamin, an Hebrew of the Hebrews; as touching the law, a Pharisee;

The books Paul is responsible for writing are:

Romans	I Corinthians	II Corinthians	Galatians
Ephesians	Philippians	Colossians	1 Thess
2 Thess	I Timothy	II Timothy	Titus
Philemon			

- Biblical scholars speculate that Paul wrote the book of Hebrews but this information is not confirmed.

Moses wrote five of the Old Testament books known as the Torah or Pentateuch. He also was a Hebrew Israelite:

> **Exodus 2:11(KJV)**
>
> [11] And it came to pass in those days, when Moses was grown, that he went out unto his brethren, and looked on their burdens: and he spied an Egyptian smiting an Hebrew, one of his brethren.

The books Moses is responsible for writing are:

Genesis	Exodus	Leviticus
Numbers	Deuteronomy	Psalm 90

- Biblical scholars speculate that Moses may have written the book of Job or at least some of it but this information is not confirmed.

Although Abraham is not noted for writing any of the books of the bible, however he is an important figure or patriarch in the bible who was also a Hebrew Israelite.

> **Genesis 14:13 (KJV)**
>
> [13] And there came one that had escaped, and told Abram the Hebrew; for he dwelt in the plain of Mamre the Amorite, brother of Eshcol, and brother of Aner: and these were confederate with Abram

All of the Apostles/Disciples were also Hebrew Israelites; one in particular was called an Israelite by the Messiah himself. (Bartholomew or Nathanael).

> **John 1:47 (KJV)**
>
> [47] Jesus saw Nathanael coming to him, and saith of him, Behold an Israelite indeed, in whom is no guile!

Since all of the Twelve Tribes of Israel were Israelites due to them, being descendents of Abraham, Isaac and Jacob. This would make the "MESSIAH" himself an Israelite from the tribe of Judah.

Hebrews 7:14 (KJV)

[14] For it is evident that our Lord sprang out of Juda; of which tribe Moses spake nothing concerning priesthood.

The question of the day would be: When did the bible become a Christian book? Those who chose to follow the ways of the Messiah should have just followed the ways of the Israelites who chose to follow the Messiah and the Messiah chose to follow his Father in heaven. We should remember, The Messiah was the king of the Hebrew Israelites and not the Gentile nations. The bible should be read from an Israelite perspective and the interpretation of scriptures will become clearer.

Matthew 27:37 (KJV)

[37] And set up over his head his accusation written, THIS IS JESUS THE KING OF THE JEWS

Mark 15:2 (KJV)

[2] And Pilate asked him, Art thou the King of the Jews? And he answering said unto them, Thou sayest it.

John 19:19 (KJV)

[19] And Pilate wrote a title, and put it on the cross. And the writing was JESUS OF NAZARETH THE KING OF THE JEWS.

No new religion (Roman Christianity) was necessary because when the Messiah purposely died by the shedding of his blood to redeem the Nation of Israel (Israelites) (Acts 5:30-31); that same mercy and grace spilled over to the Gentile nations by way through the Israelites. Salvation is of the Hebrew Israelites or Jews according to scripture and the Gentile nations was grafted into the fold by Israel's fall (Romans 11:11).

John 4:22 (KJV)

[22] Ye worship ye know not what: we know what we worship: for salvation is of the Jews.

Romans 11:11 (KJV)

[11] I say then, Have they stumbled that they should fall? God forbid: but rather through their fall salvation is come unto the Gentiles, for to provoke them to jealousy.

Notice in Romans 11:11 Paul is making a point to say just because True Israel fell does not mean the Most High God is done away with them. "God Forbid" (means no) they are not done away with but rather Gentile nations have the opportunity to be part of the natural branches of the Olive Tree with True Israel.

All of the promises in Romans 9:4 belong to the Israelites (True Israel). This includes the future Kingdom to come in which Israel will be the ruling nation again.

Romans 9:4 (KJV)

[4] Who are Israelites; to whom pertaineth the adoption, and the glory, and the covenants, and the giving of the law, and the service of God, and the promises;

Remember, when the Messiah was crucified, then resurrected and before he ascended into the heavens. He had a conversation with the disciples and a question was asked; **"Lord, wilt thou at this time restore again the kingdom to Israel".** Why would this question be asked? The disciples knew the next kingdom would belong to them (The Israelites) (True Israel).

HOW TO STUDY THE BIBLE

The Bible could be a long and complex book to understand but yet plain and simple at the same time. Most people will try to read the bible like a novel and that works only if one is reading it to get a historical background. However, if one is trying to read the bible to receive a deeper understanding or for a spiritual revelation, there are certain criteria's one must follow.

Here is a list of bible study rules that will help one completely and thoroughly study scriptures to get the best interpretation or understanding there is to get. The bible says in all thy getting get understanding.

Proverbs 4:7 (KJV)

[7] Wisdom is the principal thing; therefore get wisdom: and with all thy getting get understanding.

---

1. **Ask The Most High God for guidance**: Always before studying or doing any biblical or historical research work, one should **pray** to invite the Most High God to help provide direction towards the truth. Anyone praying and studying the bible for truth will be made free.

John 8:32 (KJV)

[32] And ye shall know the truth, and the truth shall make you free.

> **John 16:13 (KJV)**
>
> [13] Howbeit when he, the Spirit of truth, is come, he will guide you into all truth: for he shall not speak of himself; but whatsoever he shall hear, that shall he speak: and he will shew you things to come.

2. Study The Bible For Correction: The bible offer ways for all to walk in righteousness and walking in righteousness is keeping his commandments. As we study the word of God, we should study it in a way that will correct our behavior into righteousness.

> **John 16:13 (KJV)**
>
> [13] Howbeit when he, the Spirit of truth, is come, he will guide you into all truth: for he shall not speak of himself; but whatsoever he shall hear, that shall he speak: and he will shew you things to come.

> **2 Timothy 3:16 (KJV)**
>
> [16] All scripture is given by inspiration of God, and is profitable for doctrine, for reproof, for correction, for instruction in righteousness:

3. Prove All Things: The bible says we should prove all things and this should not be limited to just the scriptures. The bible is considered to be a book of actual history and can be aligned with other historical materials that can validate its truth and existence.

> **1 Thessalonians 5:21 (KJV)**
>
> [21] Prove all things; hold fast that which is good.

4. God's Word Never Contradicts Itself: If you are studying the bible and you came across two or more scriptures that seem to contradict each other then there's a problem. When this happens, one should find out why. It could be a variety of reasons such as context, added scriptures, scriptures removed, translation issues, division breaks, punctuation and verse divisions etc. For Example: A contradiction or is it?

Romans 3:20 (KJV)

[20] Therefore by the deeds of the law there shall no flesh be justified in his sight: for by the law is the knowledge of sin.

Romans 2:13 (KJV)

[13] (For not the hearers of the law are just before God, but the doers of the law shall be justified.

The two verses above appear to be contradicting each other, however when read in its context you'll notice the meaning of the two verses.

Romans 3:20 focuses on those who are just going through the motion of keeping the law (some say the sacrificial law) without ever changing on the inside. They have no connection with the Most High God.

Romans 2:13 are those who are keeping the law through the faith of the Messiah and desiring to be obedient to The Most High God.

5. Find Out What The Bible Really Says: When reading or studying the bible we should remove our own opinion or bias as much as possible. This will help us face the truth of what the bible is really saying. Our own human philosophy can cloud the truth of the scriptures. No prophecy of the scripture is of any private interpretation.

> **2 Peter 1:20 (KJV)**
>
> [20] Knowing this first, that no prophecy of the scripture is of any private interpretation

6. Examine The Context: The most difficult task most people have when studying or understanding scriptures is context. So many misinterpretations of scriptures have been a result of not understanding the context of the scripture(s). For example: Let's look at a very popular passage from the book of Philippians.

> *Philippians 1:6 (KJV)*
>
> *[6] Being confident of this very thing, that he which hath begun a good work in you will perform it until the day of Jesus Christ:*
>
> For many years it was taught Philippians 1:6 was associated with the sanctification / salvation process. This scripture has nothing to do with sanctification or salvation at all. Putting this verse in its proper context changes the meaning entirely. When Paul states **"Being confident of this very thing"** he is referring to the **Fellowship/ Partnership** in the gospel he had with the church of Philippi. The work was the spreading of the gospel that both Paul and the church of Philippi shared in the ministry together and this work was to continue until Christ return.

Paul is worth mentioning concerning his epistles or letters when studying scriptures. Paul's writing style is very complicated and can lead one to destruction if not careful. His brethren Peter warned and said:

> **2 Peter 3:16 (KJV)**
>
> [16] As also in all his epistles, speaking in them of these things; in which are some things hard to be understood, which they that are unlearned and unstable wrest, as they do also the other scriptures, unto their own destruction

Paul epistles or letters must be read in its entirely to fully understand his message, especially if you are unlearned in the scriptures and have no understanding of God's laws, statutes and commandments. Many false doctrines have been created by those who did not understand Paul epistles or letters.

7. **Let The Bible Interprets Itself**: It is highly recommended when studying the scriptures or bible that you allow it to interpret itself as much as possible. This works well especially when studying specific topics or defining words in the bible. For example: The word "Egypt".

The word **"Egypt"** is not only a place located in Africa. The bible associates the word "Egypt" with the word "bondage". This appears in many scriptures throughout the bible.

> **Exodus 13:3 (KJV)**
>
> [3] And Moses said unto the people, Remember this day, in which ye came out from Egypt, out of the house of bondage; for by strength of hand the LORD brought you out from this place: there shall no leavened bread be eaten
>
> **Exodus 13:14 (KJV)**
>
> [14] And it shall be when thy son asketh thee in time to come, saying, What is this? that thou shalt say unto him, By strength of hand the LORD brought us out from Egypt, from the house of bondage:

Exodus 20:2 (KJV)

² I am the LORD thy God, which have brought thee out of the land of Egypt, out of the house of bondage.

Also Read: Deuteronomy 5:6, Deuteronomy 6:12, Deuteronomy 7:8, Deuteronomy 8:14, Deuteronomy 13:5, Deuteronomy 13:10, Joshua 24:17. Judges 6:8, Jeremiah 34:13 and Micah 6:4

8. Start With Clear Scriptures: When studying any teachings or doctrine in the bible one should start with clear scriptures and build from there. For example: If I wanted to find out **"What Is The True Gospel"**. The first verses I'll start with is Mark 1:14-15.

Mark 1:14-15 (KJV)

¹⁴ Now after that John was put in prison, Jesus came into Galilee, preaching the gospel of the kingdom of God,

¹⁵ And saying, The time is fulfilled, and the kingdom of God is at hand: repent ye, and believe the gospel.

Now, according to this verse the gospel is **"The Kingdom of God"** not the "The Messiah" himself. The next step is to build upon this verse to confirm it with another scripture or two such as Matthew 4:23

Matthew 4:23 (KJV)

²³ And Jesus went about all Galilee, teaching in their synagogues, and preaching the gospel of the kingdom, and healing all manner of sickness and all manner of disease among the people.

It seems as thou Mark 1:14-15 and Matthew 4:23 appears to be supporting The Messiah preaching about the Kingdom of God. Did the Messiah tell anyone else to preach that message? Let's see...

Luke 9:1-2 (KJV)

1 Then he called his twelve disciples together, and gave them power and authority over all devils, and to cure diseases.

2 And he sent them to preach the kingdom of God, and to heal the sick.

In Luke 9:1-2 the Messiah also told his disciples to preach the same message of The Kingdom of God. So, it is safe to say the true gospel is the **Kingdom of God**. This was the gospel of The Messiah.

This process should continue until some clarity of the doctrine in question is clear using plain and simple scriptures first.

Now, should we deny preaching about the Messiah? Absolutely not, because the bible teaches, we should preach about him as well but he is not the Gospel, his message is the Gospel.

Acts 8:12 (KJV)

12 But when they believed Philip preaching the things concerning the kingdom of God, and the name of Jesus Christ, they were baptized, both men and women.

---

9. Use Multiple Bible Translations: Using more than one translation of the bible is extremely important because what one scripture says in one bible may say something totally different in another. Most people prefer reading and studying from the King James Version; however, the King James Bible does have errors as all bibles do. This is why it's very important to use different translations. Where one version may incorrectly interpret a word the other may interpret it correctly. For example:

Luke 17:37 (KJV)

[37] And they answered and said unto him, Where, Lord? And he said unto them, Wheresoever the body is, thither will the **eagles** be gathered together.

Luke 17:37 (NIV)

[37] "Where, Lord?" they asked.

He replied, "Where there is a dead body, there the **vultures** will gather."

Luke 17:37 (NASB)

[37] And answering they *said to Him, "Where, Lord?" And He said to them, "Where the body is, there also the **vultures** will be gathered."

Luke 17:37 (AMP)

[37] And they asked Him, "Where, Lord?" He answered, "Where the corpse is, there the **vultures** will be gathered."

Notice the King James Version of this verse says "Eagles", however the New International Version, New American Standard and the Amplified says "Vultures". The correct interpretation is Vultures because in the context of the verse, "Vultures" gather around dead bodies not Eagles.

10. <u>Read Here A Little and There A Little, Line Upon Line</u>:

The bible is very clear about how we should study the scriptures.

---

2 Timothy 2:15 (KJV)

[15] Study to shew thyself approved unto God, a workman that needeth not to be ashamed, rightly dividing the word of truth.

One must be able to rightly divide the word of truth so that all the pieces fit and make sense. A scripture in the book of Isaiah sums it up perfectly how one should study the bible.

Isaiah 28:9-10 (KJV)

[9] Whom shall he teach knowledge? and whom shall he make to understand doctrine? them that are weaned from the milk, and drawn from the breasts.

[10] For precept must be upon precept, precept upon precept; line upon line, line upon line; here a little, and there a little:

The bible is saying in order for one to teach knowledge and have an understanding of doctrine or teaching; one must be weaned from the milk and drawn from the breast, meaning one should understand the basics of the bible before one can receive any deep or hidden understandings of the scriptures.

The basics of the bible are the Laws, Statutes and Commandments that was given to the Israelites. This is the key to getting the understanding of the scriptures. The fear of the Lord is the beginning of wisdom and following the Most High God Laws, Statutes and Commandments leads to getting biblical understanding.

There is much more to be said about the bible and its fascinating history. The many translations, the removal of books (The Apocrypha), the chapter breaks, the verse breaks, the punctuations, the adding of scriptures and the removal of scriptures and still the bible survives.

We must not be fooled to think that no bibles have errors in them. We just need to be diligent in studying to show ourselves approve realizing the issues are there. It is amazing that through all the tampering with the bible the Most High God still preserved it enough for his people to find and follow him.

We must always search the scriptures for ourselves to make sure what's being said or preached to us is true. In these last days many are being a strayed due to the many false prophets lurking about with false doctrines.

Acts 17:11 (KJV)

[11] These were more noble than those in Thessalonica, in that they received the word with all readiness of mind, and searched the scriptures daily, whether those things were so.

We must remember the bible has many applications but only one interpretation with few exceptions. We must remember not to apply all scriptures to everyone and everybody at all times. The bible has a few consistent messages from Genesis to Revelation and they are:

- The Most High God Laws, Statutes and Commandments (Righteousness)
- The Nation of Israel (The people of the Book)
- The Next Coming Kingdom of God

As we continue on this journey in studying God's word and seeking the truth, let's be mindful of all the tips in this chapter that will help us get some understanding in the things of the Most High God. (Matthew 6:33).

Matthew 6:33 (KJV)

[33] But seek ye first the kingdom of God, and his righteousness; and all these things shall be added unto you.

Chapter 2

TRUE ISRAEL (PEOPLE OF COLOR)

How many people know who the true descendents of Israel are? How many people know, but choose not to admit it? What difference does it make? Does it really matter today?

In today's society the true descendents of the Israelites are rarely spoken about. In fact, the majority of the true descendents of Israel do not even know their Israel. Why? What people fail to understand is that Israel was once a nation on the earth in the ancient of days and the lead kingdom on the earth. What happened? Why is True Israel not the lead nation anymore today?

Many have come to believe that True Israel became a nation again on May 14, 1948. Is that true? Or was that a political strategy to deter away from the true people of the land? There are many questions to be asked and answers needed concerning the facts of True Israel from a biblical and historical point of view.

The bible has a lot to say concerning True Israel along with documented and other historical evidence that cannot be denied. The bible can actually be lined up with world history if one knows where to look. The Israelites of the bible are the so-called African Americans and other people of color that has been scattered around the four corners of the earth.

In spite of the overwhelming evidence to prove this fact many people choose to ignore this claim, even True Israel themselves. This chapter will be dedicated to shedding some light on this ordeal with biblical scriptures and other resources if necessary.

The true children of Israel are alive and are awakening everyday to their true heritage and identity. According to scriptures the children of Israel are not done away with and truth must be told because without knowing the true people of the book many can be misled into dangerous territory in this world in the near future. Please keep an open mind as we explore the truth.

THE TRUE COLOR OF ISRAEL
(THE OLD TESTAMENT)

The first exploration is to make a connection with the true color of Israel. Those would be people with melanin in their skin. Melanin is a dark brown to black pigment occurring in the hair, skin, and iris of the eye in people and animals. It is responsible for tanning of skin exposed to sunlight.

This point is not to say that the Most High God care about black people because of their skin color, however it is used as a marker to identify True Israel on the earth today. There are many believing True Israelites thinking skin color is all there is to this awakening, however there is much more to consider than one's skin color.

Another misconception is that True Israel is a religion. The fact of this matter is True Israel is a nation or nationality of people that was governed by the Most High God Laws, Statutes and Commandments which happens to be a dark race of people then and still today. Religion has absolutely nothing to do with being a True descendent from the nation of Israel.

In the bible the Israelites had dealings with other nations of people that looked just like them and was often mistaken for other nations of people that also had melanin in their skin.

There are many examples of this portrayed in the bible. First, let's establish the skin color of the Egyptians whom the Israelites often dwelled with and then later became captive to them.

The Zondervan Compact Bible Dictionary, page 213 describes the color of Ham (One of Noah's son) and he is described as being the progenitor of the dark races. The definition reads like this:

> *HAM – The youngest son of Noah, born probably about 96 years before the flood; and one of eight persons to live through the flood. He became the progenitor of the dark races;* **NOT THE NEGROES**, *but the Egyptians, Ethiopians, Libyans and Canaanites (Gen, 10: 6-20). His indecency, when his father lay drunken, brought a curse upon Canaan (Gen 9: 20-27).*
>
> (This definition came from the Zondervan Compact Bible Dictionary Pg. 213)

As one can see from this definition of HAM, the Egyptians were of the lineage of Noah's son HAM, a dark race of people but not the Negroes, meaning there was another lineage of people that were dark just as the Egyptians but they weren't Egyptians.

The other lineage of people came from HAM's brother Shem, Noah's other son. The Israelites stems from the lineage of Shem not HAM.

Genesis 6:10 (KJV)

[10] And Noah begat three sons, Shem, Ham, and Japheth.

Genesis 9:18-19 (KJV)

[18] And the sons of Noah, that went forth of the ark, were Shem, and Ham, and Japheth: and Ham is the father of Canaan.

[19] These are the three sons of Noah: and of them was the whole earth overspread.

Genesis 10:1 (KJV)

1 Now these are the generations of the sons of Noah, Shem, Ham, and Japheth: and unto them were sons born after the flood.

There are many biblical and non biblical scholars who have access to this truth and will agree that the Israelites are from Noah's son Shem and they both were a dark race of people. The modern-day Christian church teaches that the so-called African Americans and other people of color scattered around the world are under the lineage of HAM not Shem. The churches even teach that African Americans are Gentiles and are not TRUE ISRAEL. If those who occupy Israel today are the true so-called Jews; when did they lose their color or melanin in their skin? Let's explore some examples of this color debate in the bible.

Example #1 (Old Testament):

Genesis 50:7-8, 9, 11 (KJV)

7 And Joseph went up to bury his father: and with him went up all the servants of Pharaoh, the elders of his house, and all the elders of the land of Egypt, 8 and all the house of Joseph, and his brethren, and his father's house: only their little ones, and their flocks, and their herds, they left in the land of Goshen. 9 And there went up with him both chariots and horsemen: and it was a very great company. 11 And when the inhabitants of the land, the Canaanites, saw the mourning in the floor of Atad, they said, This is a grievous mourning to the Egyptians: wherefore the name of it was called Abel-mizraim, which is beyond Jordan.

In Genesis 50: 7-8, 9, 11, Jacob had died and Joseph and his servants traveled back to Goshen to bury his father. The inhabitants of the land made a remark about them being Egyptians. Obviously, the inhabitants couldn't tell the Egyptians from the

Israelites because they looked alike. If the Israelites were of a Caucasian race then how could the inhabitants (Canaanites) of the land confused them with dark skinned Egyptians?

There is much research from Archeological findings; Mummies, Statues and Wall Paintings etc. that one could research to prove that Ancient Egyptians were a dark complexion people. This would make the Hebrews or Israelites dark people if the Canaanites inhabitants could not tell them apart. Also, the Canaanites themselves were a dark race of people from the lineage of HAM.

Example #2 (Old Testament):

Exodus 2:5-10 (KJV)

[5] And the daughter of Pharaoh came down to wash herself at the river; and her maidens walked along by the river's side; and when she saw the ark among the flags, she sent her maid to fetch it. [6] And when she had opened it, she saw the child: and, behold, the babe wept. And she had compassion on him, and said, This is one of the Hebrews' children. [7] Then said his sister to Pharaoh's daughter, Shall I go and call to thee a nurse of the Hebrew women, that she may nurse the child for thee? [8] And Pharaoh's daughter said to her, Go. And the maid went and called the child's mother. [9] And Pharaoh's daughter said unto her, Take this child away, and nurse it for me, and I will give thee thy wages. And the woman took the child, and nursed it. [10] And the child grew, and she brought him unto Pharaoh's daughter, and he became her son. And she called his name Moses: and she said, Because I drew him out of the water.

In Exodus 2: 5-10 Moses was given away by his Hebrew mother, because Hebrew boys were being murdered by Pharaoh. Moses' mother took the child (Moses) along the river brinks where he was found by Pharaoh's maidens and Pharaoh's daughter and eventually, he was raised in the Pharaohs household for about 40 years.

Does this appear to be odd that Moses could be raised in the house of Pharaoh without being recognized he was Hebrew in which Pharaoh was killing at the time? Again, no one could tell the difference between a Hebrew and an Egyptian because of the similarities in appearance. If Moses was Caucasian (white) how could Pharaoh not know this and keep Moses alive? Pharaoh could not tell Moses was not an Egyptian.

Example #3 (Old Testament):

Exodus 4:6-7 (KJV)

[6] And the LORD said furthermore unto him, Put now thine hand into thy bosom. And he put his hand into his bosom: and when he took it out, behold, his hand was leprous as snow. [7] And he said, Put thine hand into thy bosom again. And he put his hand into his bosom again; and plucked it out of his bosom, and, behold, it was turned again as his other flesh.

In Exodus 4:6-7 Moses was a dark-skinned man if his hand turned white with Leprous after pulling it out of his bosom. What color was it before? The scripture says he pulled his hand out of his bosom for the second time and his hand turned back as his other flesh (Dark).

We know that Leprous is a disease that discolors the skin and the scripture says his hand was leprous as snow (White) and then his hand turned back to the color of the rest of his flesh. What color was the rest of his flesh? It had to be dark to see the difference in skin color.

Remember in the movie "The Ten Commandments" (Charleston Heston). This was one miracle that the movie producers skipped over. I wonder why? Because it really would not have been much of a miracle if Moses pulled his hand out of his bosom and it remained white.

Example #4 (Old Testament):

Exodus 2:19 (KJV)

[19] And they said, An Egyptian delivered us out of the hand of the shepherds, and also drew water enough for us, and watered the flock.

In Exodus 2:19 the daughters of Jethro (Priest of Midian) thought that Moses was an Egyptian instead of Hebrew (Israelite). How could the daughters of Jethro confuse Moses for an Egyptian? The Egyptians and Israelites had to have looked alike.

Example #5 (Old Testament):

Genesis 42:5-8 (KJV)

[5] And the sons of Israel came to buy corn among those that came: for the famine was in the land of Canaan.

[6] And Joseph was the governor over the land, and he it was that sold to all the people of the land: and Joseph's brethren came, and bowed down themselves before him with their faces to the earth.

[7] And Joseph saw his brethren, and he knew them, but made himself strange unto them, and spake roughly unto them; and he said unto them, Whence come ye? And they said, From the land of Canaan to buy food.

> [8] And Joseph knew his brethren, but they knew not him.

In Genesis 42: 5-8, Joseph's brothers went to Egypt to buy corn because there was a famine in their land of Canaan at the time. The brothers did not realize Joseph was still alive after selling him into slavery some years prior. When the brothers eventually had interaction with their brother Joseph in Egypt, they did not recognize him. Why?

First, Joseph was second in command in the land of Egypt.

Second, he probably was dressed up in Egyptian garments

Third, Joseph was a teenager when he was sold into slavery by his brothers and during the famine years Joseph was much older and his brothers did not recognize him.

What should immediately be obvious is that if the True Israelites were Caucasian (white). Wouldn't Joseph immediately be recognized by his brothers amongst a dark-skinned people? Maybe, however because Joseph blended in with the Egyptians, there were no distinguished differences in Joseph's appearance from the Egyptians. He looked just like them (Egyptian).

Example #6 (Old Testament):

> **Numbers 12:10 (KJV)**
>
> [10] And the cloud departed from off the tabernacle; and, behold, Miriam became leprous, white as snow: and Aaron looked upon Miriam, and, behold, she was leprous.

Please read the whole chapter of Numbers 12:1-16. It tells the story of Miriam and Aaron (Moses' sister and brother) speaking against Moses for marrying an Ethiopian woman, which by the way was a Hamite from the lineage of Noah's son Ham not Shem.

The Most High God heard them speaking against Moses and it angered him. The Most High God turned Miriam Leprous, white as snow for speaking against Moses because Moses was The Most High God's prophet. So, if Miriam was turned Leprous, white as snow. What color was she before she was turned Leprous? It is very obvious she was a dark person because there would be no need to turn a Caucasian person white if they were white already. This was another example that the true children of Israel were a people of color and still is to this day.

Example #7 (Old Testament):

Job 30:30 (KJV)

[30] My skin is black upon me, and my bones are burned with heat.

During the time of Job's affliction, he cries out "My Skin Is Black Upon Me". Should we assume Job was a black man because of this statement? In conjunction with all the other evidence it is a great assumption Job was a man of color. Why would he make such a statement?

Example #8 (Old Testament):

Song of Solomon 1:5-6 (KJV)

[5] I am black, but comely, O ye daughters of Jerusalem, as the tents of Kedar, as the curtains of Solomon.

[6] Look not upon me, because I am black, because the sun hath looked upon me: my mother's children were angry with me; they made me the keeper of the vineyards; but mine own vineyard have I not kept.

Example #9 (Old Testament):

> **Song of Solomon 5:11 (KJV)**
>
> [11] His head is as the most fine gold, his locks are bushy, and black as a raven.

The female lover in these verses directly says "I AM Black" which means this is someone with a dark complexion working in the sun and became even darker. The male lover is describing as having locks that are bushy. What people on the planet of earth have bushy locks?

Example #10 (Old Testament):

> **Lamentations 4:8 (KJV)**
>
> [8] Their **visage** is blacker than a coal; they are not known in the streets: their skin cleaveth to their bones; it is withered, it is become like a stick.
>
> Note: Visage means a person's face

Example #11 (Old Testament):

> **Lamentations 5:10 (KJV)**
>
> [10] Our skin was black like an oven because of the terrible famine.

In the book of Lamentations presents (5 poems of sorrows) for the fallen city of Jerusalem. In chapter 4:8 and 5:10 it is stated that their skin was black due to the terrible famine.

When Black people are under the circumstances of starvation their skin complexity darkens tremendously. This characteristic of darker skin pigmentation from starvation takes effect on the True Jews. The Jews had to be Black if their skin complexion darkened up from starvation. According to the scripture the Jews had faces blacker than coal as a result of the famine.

Example #12 (Old Testament):

Exodus 11:7 (KJV)

[7] But against any of the children of Israel shall not a dog move his tongue, against man or beast: that ye may know how that the LORD doth put a difference between the Egyptians and Israel.

Exodus 11:7 states that God himself puts a difference between the Egyptians and the Hebrews or Israelites. This verse makes it perfectly clear that Israelites were not originally African people although they looked similar in appearance.

The Israelites were actually a nation of totally different people which have been scattered all over into other nations even until this day. But they are not of the seed of HAM but the seed of Shem, his brother.

THE TRUE COLOR OF ISRAEL
(THE NEW TESTAMENT)

The Old Testament have many scriptures to support that True Israel are people of color. What about the New Testament? We already discovered that Egyptians are a people of color and you'll see this same pattern throughout the New Testament. Let's explore more biblical proof.

Example 1# (New Testament):

Matthew 2:13 (KJV)

[13] And when they were departed, behold, the angel of the Lord appeareth to Joseph in a dream, saying, Arise, and take the young child and his mother, and flee into Egypt, and be thou there until I bring thee word: for Herod will seek the young child to destroy him.

After the Messiah was born, his earthy father Joseph was instructed by an angel to take him to Egypt because Herod wanted to kill him. Why Egypt? It is apparent Egypt was a place to hide the child (The Messiah) because it would be easy for the family to blend in with a people who looked just like them. If they were Caucasian (White) they would have stuck out like a sore thumb to be easily found by Herod.

Example #2 (New Testament):

Acts 21:37-39 (KJV)

[37] And as Paul was to be led into the castle, he said unto the chief captain, May I speak unto thee? Who said, Canst thou speak Greek?

[38] Art not thou that Egyptian, which before these days madest an uproar, and leddest out into the wilderness four thousand men that were murderers?

[39] But Paul said, I am a man which am a Jew of Tarsus, a city in Cilicia, a citizen of no mean city: and, I beseech thee, suffer me to speak unto the people.

Here in Acts 21:37-39 Paul is mistaken for being an Egyptian by the chief captain and Paul corrected him by saying "I AM A MAN WHICH AM A JEW Of TARSUS". Once again, an Israelite is mistaken for an Egyptian and Paul is an Israelite per his own words.

Romans 11:1-2 (KJV)

[1] I say then, Hath God cast away his people? God forbid. For I also am an Israelite, of the seed of Abraham, of the tribe of Benjamin.

[2] God hath not cast away his people which he foreknew. Wot ye not what the scripture saith of Elias? how he maketh intercession to God against Israel saying,

---

Notice in this scripture Paul says that God has not cast away his people. What people? Israelites, which means Paul is honoring the covenant that was made with his fore fathers Abraham, Isaac and Jacob. He is very aware that the Most High God has not done away with his people. This topic will be explored more in detail in upcoming chapters of this book.

Example #3 (New Testament):

Acts 13:1 (KJV)

1 Now there were in the church that was at Antioch certain prophets and teachers; as Barnabas, and Simeon that was called Niger, and Lucius of Cyrene, and Manaen, which had been brought up with Herod the tetrarch, and Saul.

Here you have Simeon (Prophet and Teacher) of the church of Antioch being called ***Niger*** and the word Niger actually means black according to Zondervan Compact Bible Dictionary Pg. 399. He helped Saul and Barnabas in their missionary endeavors.

NIGER DEFINED: (Black)

A surname of Symeon, one of the five "prophets and teachers" of the church at Antioch who were lead of the Lord to send forth Paul and Barnabas on the first missionary journey (Acts 13:1-3)

There is not a whole lot of information concerning this Simeon however the fact he is a missionary and has a Hebrew name could mean he is a Hebrew descendant from one of the tribes of Israel which appears to be a dark-skinned person by the fact he is called ***Niger.***

Throughout history the nation of Israel has always entered and dwelled with the people of Egypt (HAMITES) when in fact the Israelites are (SHEMETIC) and has always been mistaken for Egyptians.

Psalm 105:23 (KJV)

[23] Israel also came into Egypt; and Jacob sojourned in the land of Ham.

WHAT ABOUT THE MESSIAH?

The Messiah is described in the scriptures as being a dark-skinned man. Notice the following scriptures:

Revelation 1:14-15 (KJV)

[14] His head and his hairs were white like wool, as white as snow; and his eyes were as a flame of fire;

[15] And his feet like unto fine brass, as if they burned in a furnace; and his voice as the sound of many waters.

Revelation 2:18 (KJV)

[18] And unto the angel of the church in Thyatira write; These things saith the Son of God, who hath his eyes like unto a flame of fire, and his feet are like fine brass;

In the book of Daniel (Old Testament) The Messiah physical attributes are seen by Daniel in a vision. What he saw describes The Messiah as having hair of his head like pure wool.

Daniel 7:9 (KJV)

[9] I beheld till the thrones were cast down, and the Ancient of days did sit, whose garment was white as snow, and the hair of his head like the pure wool: his throne was like the fiery flame, and his wheels as burning fire.

Note: Ancient of days meaning (The Messiah).

The following definition of the word "Negro" found in the 1957 Webster's dictionary describes exactly how the bible describes The Messiah. This definition is removed in most modern dictionaries today.

Negro:

One of a dark-skinned race having wooly hair, flat nose, thick protruding lips and a prognathous form of skull etc.

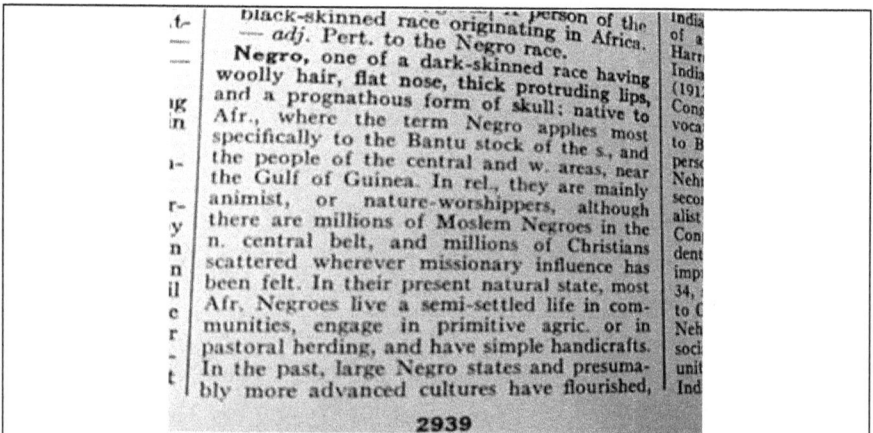

The entry for "Negro" in the 1957 Webster's dictionary published by Educational Book Guild Inc. of New York.

http://myauctionfinds.com/2015/03/02/how-one-webster-dictionary-defined-negroes-in-the-1950s/

This definition of Negro in the **Columbia of Encyclopedia Vol I. Page 1371 Published in 1950** is similar to the definition in the Webster's dictionary (1957).

Negro - Member of any several groups of peoples, characterized physically by a black or dark brown skin, Wooly hair, broad flat nose, prominent eyes with yellowish cornea, thick lips and prognathous jaw.

https://archive.org/stream/columbiaencyclop030445mbp#page/n1383/mode/2up

WHAT ABOUT THE FATHER (THE MOST HIGH)

In the book of revelation, the disciple John had a vision in the spirit and he saw a throne in heaven and the one who sat on it looked like a jasper and sardine stone. Anybody that knows what a jasper and sardine stone look like in color would recognize it to be a reddish brown.

> **Revelation 4:2-3 (KJV)**
>
> [2] And immediately I was in the spirit: and, behold, a throne was set in heaven, and one sat on the throne.
>
> [3] And he that sat was to look upon like a jasper and a sardine stone: and there was a rainbow round about the throne, in sight like unto an emerald.

THE WORLD KNOWS / THE HISTORICAL EVIDENCE

The elite people of the world (scientist, biblical scholars, researchers, authors and leaders of world governments) know who the true Israelites of the world are today. They know they were people of color and choose not to admit this openly. For example, the definition of "HAM" at the beginning of this chapter let us know that Ham was the progenitor of the dark races but not the Negroes. In order for the bible scholars to have put that information in a bible dictionary, they must have done some research to know that there are two different blood lines of people and all the dark races do not stem from the lineage of Ham but another lineage of dark people (The Negros).

There is much evidence that scientist reluctantly reveal concerning the True Color of Israel. In **Science Magazine dated October 31, 1997** an article entitled "Y Chromosome Shows That Adam Was an African" by Ann Gibbons This article reveals scientist discovering a genetic DNA trail leading to the first man on earth (Adam). They had compared mitochondrial DNA variants around the world and traced a common ancestor by sorting out the variants on an ancestral phylogenetic tree. It is suspected the first man Adam was a black man according to their research.

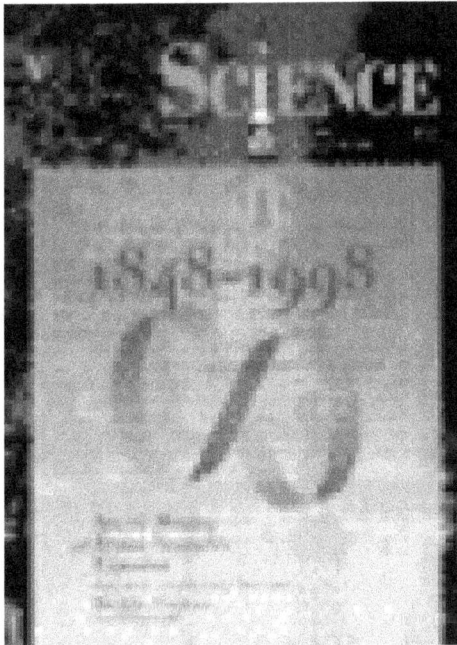

Science 31 Oct 1997:
Vol. 278, Issue 5339, pp. 804-805

In Newsweek Magazine dated January 11, 1988 an article entitled "The Search For Adam and Eve" An article suggesting that Eve lived in sub-Saharan Africa or southern China. But the DNA seemed to form a family tree rooted in Africa. The article quotes that The DNA fell into two general categories, one found in some babies of recent African descent and the second found in everyone else and the other Africans. On the cover of this Newsweek edition, they posted a black couple posing as Adam and Eve.

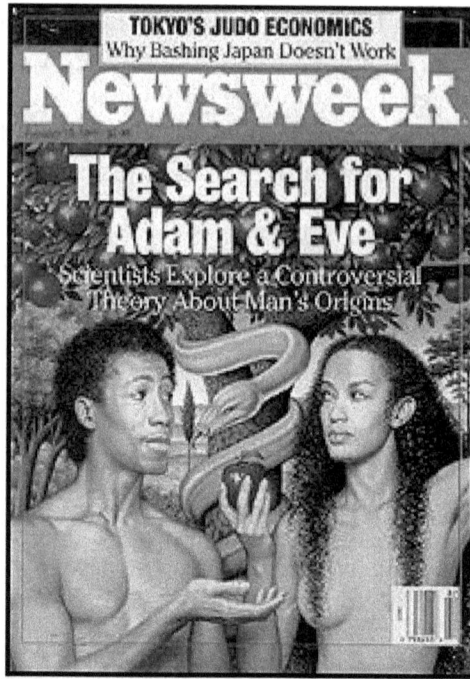

The Search for Adam and Eve
Newsweek 11 Jan 1988:
Source: *Newsweek* 111 (Jan. 11, 1988): 46-52.

The lost book of King Og has surfaced from the Vatican exposing some very interesting claim concerning the color of the ancient Israelites. King Og was a Rephaim, a Biblical race of Giants that Moses had to defeat on their way to possessing the promise land. The book of King Og has been a source of great controversy and hidden within the Secret Vatican Library at the Department of Ancient Documents and Surviving Occult Findings.

The account of King Og of Bashan is located in the book of Numbers 21:21-35, Deuteronomy 2:20-21, 3:11. The point concerning the color of True Israel lies in chapter 7 that begins with taunts from King Og to Israel. The taunt is the children of

Israel being called a corrupt "Blackened Fecal Worm". This is significant since it is an account witness in those days where the Israelites are being compared to ants buried in fecal matter.

The Lost Book of King Og of Bashan brought forth from the Vatican Library talks about his encounter with the Hebrew Israelite's; he verifies that the Hebrew Israelite's were black. He calls them "Blackened Fecal Worms". If they were Caucasian, why would they be called "Blackened Fecal Worms"?

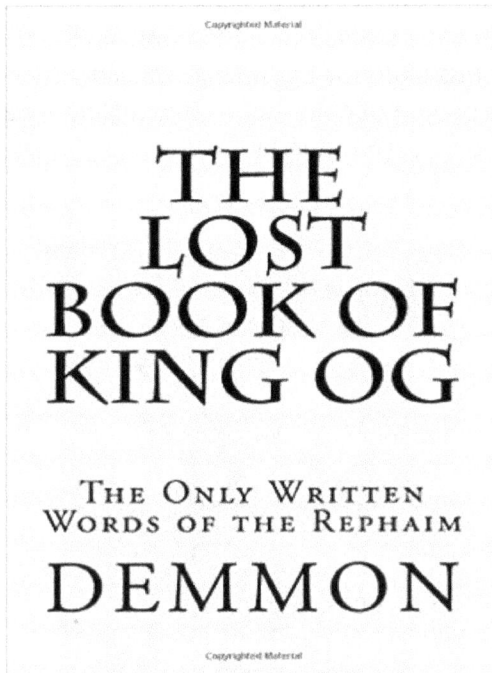

THE
LOST
BOOK OF
KING OG

THE ONLY WRITTEN
WORDS OF THE REPHAIM

DEMMON

Chapter7
The Lost Book of King Og
The Only Written Words of the Rephaim – Copyright 2016 by
DEMMOM
http://thelostbookofkingog.com/

In the magazine National Geographic, published in February of 2008 there is an article entitled "Black Pharaohs" by Robert Draper. In this article Mr. Draper explains the conquerors of Ancient Egypt were black (The Nubians from present day Sudan). He also mentions that all ancient Egyptians were black from King Tut to Cleopatra were black Africans. Although there is plenty of criticism about this article trying to mislead in some sense that there was only a period of time, they were black but the first and third dynasty isn't mentioned. In any case the pictures associated with this article displays the Nubians and Egyptians are black people that were in that region in ancient times. This confirms that if the Egyptians were a black race of people and in the bible the Israelites were mistaken for Egyptians, we can only conclude that they both were people of color but of two different nationalities, bloodlines or lineage. (Exodus 11:7).

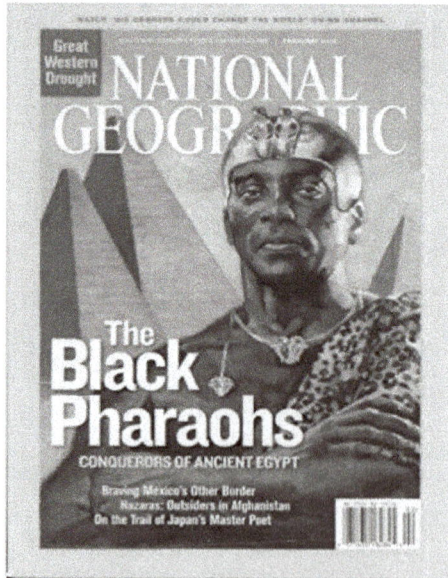

The Black Pharaohs
National Geographic
February 2008, Pages 35 59

Statutes of Nubian kings up to ten feet high were found buried at the Nubian capital of Kerma, in Sudan. Smashed during Egyptian king Psamtek II's incursion south around 593 B.C., they were recently reassembled. **(The Black Pharaohs, National Geographic, February 2008, Pages 35-59).**

At the height of his power, king Taharqa leads
his queens through the crowds during a
festival at the temple complex of Nubia's Jebel
Barkal, its pinnacls gleaming with gold.
Accompanied by a sacred ship bearing an
image of the god Amun, Taharqa is robed in a
priestly leopard skin and crowned with the
double uraeus that declares him Lord of the
two Lands-ruler of both Nubia and Egypt .
**(The Black Pharaohs, National Geographic,
February 2008, Pages 35-59).**

Nubia was a major source of gold for ancient Egypt. At thebes the tomb of King Tutankhmun's viceroy to Nubia – a man named Huy – shows Nubian royalty in procession delivering rings of gold as part of their tribute to their overlord. The skilled goldsmiths of Nubia created masterpieces such as a pendant of the goddess Isis from the tomb of a Nubian king at Nuri. **(The Black Pharaohs, National Geographic, February 2008, Pages 35-59).**

Did the power queen Tiye, king Tut's grandmother, have Nubian ancestry? This bust, made of wood that has darkened with age, has inspired claims that she did. **(The Black Pharaohs, National Geographic, February 2008, Pages 35-59).**

THE BOOKS (THEY KNOW)

There are many other clues and hints in other books to reveal the true color of the TRUE ISRAELITES of the bible.

THE REVELL BIBLE DICTIONARY:

The Revell Bible Dictionary (Deluxe Color Edition) is another book that confirms the Israelites of the bible are people of color. It is demonstrated by the many pictures displayed throughout the book. Please notice the following pictures.

While Hebrews grew full beards, Egyptians preferred to be clean-shaven (See Genesis 41:14. Scene from tomb of Usehat (Egypt, 18th Dynasty): Barber works while others wait their turn.

The Revell Bible Dictionary [Deluxe Color Edition] Page 130

In this picture, please notice that these Hebrews according to the Revell Bible Dictionary are people of color. Could the artist have drawn these figures white or Caucasian? Yes, look at their skirts, they are white. They know…

An Egyptian slave receives a beating, from a tomb drawing in Thebes. Mosaic Law permitted criminals to be given up to forty lashes (Deut 25:3). The Jews gave "forty lashes minus one," to be sure they did not inadvertently break the Law (2 Cor. 11:24).

The Revell Bible Dictionary [Deluxe Color Edition] Page 138

This picture depicts an Egyptian (black) beating an Israelite (black). They know…

> *Egyptian statue of Semitic prisoner, 19th-18th century B.C. Bondage (slavery) was the usual lot of defeated foes.*

The Revell Bible Dictionary [Deluxe Color Edition] Page 164

Here is a picture of a statue with a description stating that this is a Semitic prisoner of Egypt. Semitic means those who fall in the lineage of Noah's son Shem. Notice this statue is a person of color. They Know...

The Revell Bible Dictionary [Deluxe Color Edition] Page 172

This is a picture of Hebrew Israelites making bricks and they are depicted with dark skin. They know...

Brickmaking captives depicted on a wall painting from the tomb of Rekhmira at Thebes (1533-1450 B.C.) Bearded foreigners, under the supervision of an Egyptian (with stick far right), gather water and work mud and straw together into molds. At top left a worker lifts a mold from a sun-dried brick. At far right a worker carries cured bricks to building site. Israelite workers were making bricks in Egypt at the time this was painted.

The Revell Bible Dictionary [Deluxe Color Edition] Page 434

This picture description is stating that these are Semitic (Shem lineage) envoys and notice they are depicted with dark skin and white clothing. They know…

Semetic envoys bring gold and silver gifts to the Egyptian court (1400 B.C.). Ancient peoples presented gifts as tribute to royalty (2 Sam. 8:2), on festive occasions (Ps. 45:12; Esth. 9:19), or as part of a dowry (Gen. 34:12). Jacob sent a massive gift of livestock ahead of him when he went to meet Esau still bore a grudge against him (Gen. 32:13-21).

Assyrian guard escorts two captive Judeans to King Sennacherib. Detail of the Battle of Lachish (701 B.C.) relief at Nineveh. Elite corps of guards figure importantly in several biblical events (see 2 Ki. 11:4-8; 25; Jer. 52; Mt. 27:62–28:14; Lk. 22:4,52; Phil. 1:13).

The Revell Bible Dictionary [Deluxe Color Edition] Page 456

This picture displays two Israelites (Judeans) and one Assyrian guard and notice all three are black. Look at the popcorn hair and beard on all three figures. They know…

GREAT PEOPLE OF THE BIBLE AND HOW THEY LIVED:

When the tomb of Egyptian king Tutankhamen was discovered virtually intact in the 1920's, it yielded a breathtaking collection of art objects from the 14th century B.C – just a few years before the Exodus.

Great People of the Bible and How They Lived, Page 68

This is a picture found in the tomb showing an Egyptian king speaking to his queen and notice ancient Egyptian's picture themselves as a dark race of people. This is why Joseph was able to blend in eventually becoming second in command in Egypt. Remember Joseph was an Israelite not an Egyptian. They know...

HERITAGE CIVILIZATION AND THE JEWS:

The expulsion of the Hyksos may have marked the end of Hebrew power in Egypt and the beginning of the descent into bondage. Here, Semite humbles himself in an Egyptian tomb painting.

Heritage Civilization and the Jews, Page 24

This picture shows a Hebrew Israelite (Semitic) humbling himself before Egyptians. Notice both the Israelite and the Egyptians are the same color. They know…

NEAR EASTERN MYTHOLOGY (MESOPOTAMIA, SYRIA, PALESTINE):

Mural painting from the tomb of Rekhmire (Fifteenth century B.C) near Thebes in Upper Egypt. It depicts displaced persons (khabiru, Egyptian 'apirw, hence Hebrews) as state slaves moulding bricks for public works. It was from this class that Moses led a group out of Egypt, which became 'Israel' after the Covenant experience at the holy mountain in Sanai.

Near Eastern Mythology (Mesopotamia, Syria, Palestine), Page 109. They Know…

THE NAZIS (WORLD WAR II):

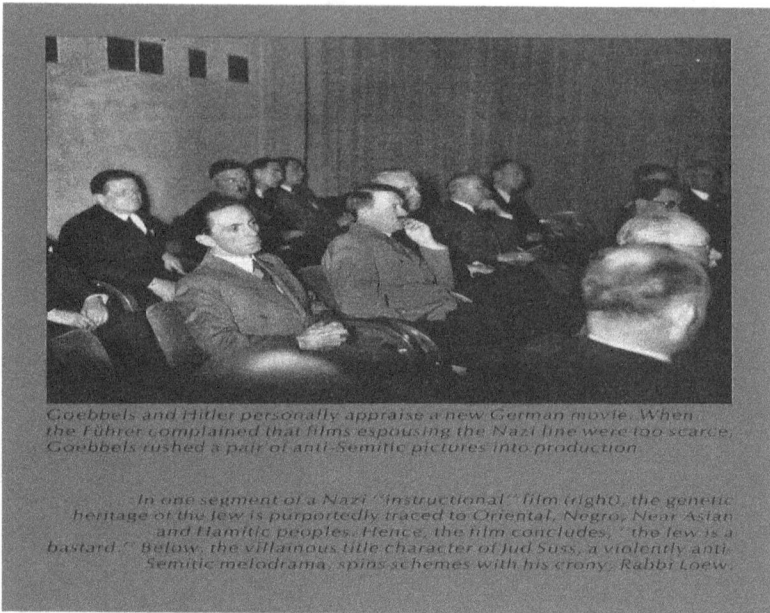

Goebbels and Hitler personally appraise a new German movie. When the Führer complained that films espousing the Nazi line were too scarce, Goebbels rushed a pair of anti-Semitic pictures into production.

In one segment of a Nazi "instructional" film (right), the genetic heritage of the Jew is purportedly traced to Oriental, Negro, Near Asian and Hamitic peoples. Hence, the film concludes, "the Jew is a bastard." Below, the villainous title character of Jud Süss, a violently anti-Semitic melodrama, spins schemes with his crony, Rabbi Loew.

The Nazis: (World War II), Page 132

This picture is taken out of a book called The Nazis (World War II) where Adolf Hitler is showing an instructional film exposing the genetic heritage of the true Jews or Israelites. Hitler understood who the true Jews were and he knew they were people of color and he called the fake Jews Bastards knowing they were imposters. They Know…

In conclusion concerning the true color of the Israelites of the bible cannot be disputed that they were a people of color and cannot be the Jews in the land of Israel today who are white or Caucasian people. This chapter just gives a glimpse of evidence from a biblical and historical perspective that it absolutely cannot be denied that True Israel are black people.

Chapter 3

DID THE MOST HIGH GOD CHOOSE A PEOPLE?

The modern day Christian church teaches that the descendents of the children of Israel doesn't matter anymore today. It's taught that everyone who accepts the Messiah as their Lord and personal Savior becomes a spiritual Israelite and all the promises of The Most High God made with Abraham, Isaac and Jacob now belongs to the Gentile nations or church. According to the scriptures this is not true. In order for one to be an Israelite, one has to born an Israelite because being an Israelite is a nationality or bloodline not a religion. Just as a German person cannot be born a Chinese person, they are two different nationalities.

The bible teaches there was only one nation or nationality of people on the earth that The Most High God has known and those people were and still the nation of Israel. This is stated in Amos 3:1-2, adding that Israel will be punished for their iniquities as well. True Israel is currently in captivity and has served other nations throughout human history. These captivities were due to them not keeping The Most High God Laws, Statutes and Commandments.

Amos 3:1-2 (KJV)

1 Hear this word that the LORD hath spoken against you, O children of Israel, against the whole family which I brought up from the land of Egypt, saying,

2 You only have I known of all the families of the earth: therefore, I will punish you for all your iniquities.

Question: When in history was the Gentile nations punished by God for their iniquities and wrong doings against the true children of Israel? In fact, the scriptures state that Jacob (Israel) alone was shown The Most High God's statutes and judgments. The Most High God has not dealt directly with any other nation in history and his judgments they do not know.

The bible has plenty to say concerning the punishment of the Gentile nations in the prophetic scriptures. But the focus here will be about True Israel.

Psalm 147:19-20 (KJV)

[19] He sheweth his word unto Jacob, his statutes and his judgments unto Israel.

[20] He hath not dealt so with any nation: and as for his judgments, they have not known them. Praise ye the LORD.

Many may say why did The Most High God choose a people? First, The Most High God will never break a promise or oath he has made with the forefathers of the Israelites (Abraham, Isaac and Jacob).

The Most High God wanted to honor his promises made to Abraham, Isaac and Jacob. As stated in Deuteronomy 7:6-8 the Israelites were not chosen because they were a large number of people but simply because The Most High God loved them. He called them a holy people that were special unto him.

Deuteronomy 7:6-8 (KJV)

[6] For thou art an holy people unto the LORD thy God: the LORD thy God hath chosen thee to be a special people unto himself, above all people that are upon the face of the earth.

> [7] The LORD did not set his love upon you, nor choose you, because ye were more in number than any people; for ye were the fewest of all people:
>
> [8] But because the LORD loved you, and because he would keep the oath which he had sworn unto your fathers, hath the LORD brought you out with a mighty hand, and redeemed you out of the house of bondmen, from the hand of Pharaoh king of Egypt.

Question: When did the children of Israel and their descendents become a people not chosen anymore?

The Most High God had a purpose in mind when he chose the Israelite nation. The purpose was for them to become a kingdom of priest and show other nations around the earth how to live righteously by following God's Laws, Statutes and Commandments.

> **Exodus 19:6 (KJV)**
>
> [6] And ye shall be unto me a kingdom of priests, and an holy nation. These are the words which thou shalt speak unto the children of Israel.

In the New Testament apostle Peter also made this same statement reaching out to the scattered Israelites in the other nations.

> **1 Peter 2:9 (KJV)**
>
> [9] But ye are a chosen generation, a royal priesthood, an holy nation, a peculiar people; that ye should shew forth the praises of him who hath called you out of darkness into his marvellous light;

Many people believe I Peter 2:9 is referring to other nations but it's referring to those Israelites or better known as Jewish Christians that were primarily scattered from the Northern Kingdom into those other nations. If we read I Peter 1:1 you'll see he is addressing the strangers that are scattered to foreign lands and we know that the only people scattered from their own land was True Israel.

---

1 Peter 1:1 (KJV)

Peter, an apostle of Jesus Christ, to the strangers scattered throughout Pontus, Galatia, Cappadocia, Asia, and Bithynia

---

Notice the same scripture in other versions of the bible, (New Living Translation) and (The Living Bible) makes this point much clearer as to who these strangers were.

---

1 Peter 1:1 (NLT)

1 This letter is from Peter, an apostle of Jesus Christ.

I am writing to God's **chosen people** who are living as foreigners in the provinces of Pontus, Galatia, Cappadocia, Asia, and Bithynia.

1 Peter 1:1 (TLB)

1 From: Peter, Jesus Christ's missionary.

To: The **Jewish Christians** driven out of **Jerusalem** and scattered throughout Pontus, Galatia, Cappadocia, Asia Minor, and Bithynia.

James 1:1 clarifies who Peter was addressing because Peter and James were both addressing the same people and James addressed them as the twelve tribes scattered.

James 1:1 (KJV)

James, a servant of God and of the Lord Jesus Christ, to the twelve tribes which are scattered abroad, greeting.

Question: Where in scripture other nations became tribes that were scattered?

In Romans 3:1-2 Paul made a statement that being a Jew or Israelite was an advantage. Why would Paul make such a statement if this was not true? Paul knew that being a Jew or Israelite mattered much in every way because the Laws, Statutes and Commandments (Oracles) were given only to the nation of Israel.

Romans 3:1-2 (KJV)

1 What advantage then hath the Jew? or what profit is there of circumcision?

2 Much every way: chiefly, because that unto them were committed the oracles of God.

Question: Why is Paul making a distinction that being a Jew or Israelite is an advantage?

Paul knew the Old Testament because he quoted from it often in his letters. The New Testament reflects the Old Testament and one must know the Old Testament in order to understand the New Testament. When Paul wrote Romans 3:1-2 he knew of Deuteronomy 4:7-8 that Israel was given the Laws of The Most High God.

> **Deuteronomy 4:7-8 (KJV)**
>
> [7] For what nation is there so great, who hath God so nigh unto them, as the LORD our God is in all things that we call upon him for?
>
> [8] And what nation is there so great, that hath statutes and judgments so righteous as all this law, which I set before you this day?

Apostle Paul bluntly said that the Most High God did not cast away his chosen people by saying "God Forbid" which means no. Paul was also an Israelite from the tribe of Benjamin.

> **Romans 11:1-2 (KJV)**
>
> 1 I say then, Hath God cast away his people? God forbid. For I also am an Israelite, of the seed of Abraham, of the tribe of Benjamin.
>
> [2] God hath not cast away his people which he foreknew. Wot ye not what the scripture saith of Elias? how he maketh intercession to God against Israel saying,

Question: Where is the misunderstanding that The Most High God's chosen people do not matter anymore?

All throughout the Old Testament The Most High God repeatedly stated he was the God of the Israelites and they were the chosen seed.

Isaiah 41:8 (KJV)

[8] But thou, Israel, art my servant, Jacob whom I have chosen, the seed of Abraham my friend.

Psalm 135:4 (KJV)

[4] For the LORD hath chosen Jacob unto himself, and Israel for his peculiar treasure.

1 Chronicles 16:13 (KJV)

[13] O ye seed of Israel his servant, ye children of Jacob, his chosen ones.

The Most High God has loved Israel with an everlasting love.

Jeremiah 31:1-3 (KJV)

[1] At the same time, saith the LORD, will I be the God of all the families of Israel, and they shall be my people.

[2] Thus saith the LORD, The people which were left of the sword found grace in the wilderness; even Israel, when I went to cause him to rest.

[3] The LORD hath appeared of old unto me, saying, Yea, I have loved thee with an everlasting love: therefore with lovingkindness have I drawn thee.

True Israel was ordained to be a peculiar people as long as they followed the Laws, Statutes and Commandments of The Most High God.

Deuteronomy 26:18-19 (KJV)

[18] And the LORD hath avouched thee this day to be his peculiar people, as he hath promised thee, and that thou shouldest keep all his commandments;

[19] And to make thee high above all nations which he hath made, in praise, and in name, and in honour; and that thou mayest be an holy people unto the LORD thy God, as he hath spoken.

The prophetic scripture (Isaiah 14:1-2) explains in the later days that The Most High God will choose True Israelites and put them in their own land as promised to Abraham.

This verse goes on to say there will be strangers that will join them (Other people from other nations) and will cleave to them after recognizing they are the True Israelites of the bible. There will be people of the other nations assisting True Israelites to get to their promised land. True Israel will not be oppressed anymore once back in their land. In fact, other nations will be servants and handmaids unto them.

Isaiah 14:1-2 (KJV)

[1] For the LORD will have mercy on Jacob, and will yet choose Israel, and set them in their own land: and the strangers shall be joined with them, and they shall cleave to the house of Jacob.

[2] And the people shall take them, and bring them to their place: and the house of Israel shall possess them in the land of the LORD for servants and handmaids: and they shall take them captives, whose captives they were; and they shall rule over their oppressors.

True Israel has always been The Most High God's elected people.

Isaiah 45:3-4 (KJV)

[3] And I will give thee the treasures of darkness, and hidden riches of secret places, that thou mayest know that I, the LORD, which call thee by thy name, am the God of Israel.

[4] For Jacob my servant's sake, and Israel mine elect, I have even called thee by thy name: I have surnamed thee, though thou hast not known me.

The scriptures repeatedly support the Israelites being God's chosen people. The Israelites were even called the Apple of God's eye. Notice Deuteronomy 32:8, in the King James Version. The phrase "children of Israel" is a possible misinterpretation, but when this verse is compared to other translations the meaning becomes clearer. The end of this verse should state according to other translations of the bible:

The Living Bible Reads "He gave each of them a supervising angel"
Today's English Version Reads: "He assigned each nation a heavenly being"
The New English Bible Reads: "According to the number of the sons of god"
The New American Bible Reads: "After the number of the divine beings"

Deuteronomy 32:8-10 (KJV)

[8] When the Most High divided to the nations their inheritance, when he separated the sons of Adam, he set the bounds of the people according to the number of the **children of Israel.**
(Possible Misinterpreted)

> [9] For the LORD's portion is his people; Jacob is the lot of his inheritance.
>
> [10] He found him in a desert land, and in the waste howling wilderness; he led him about, he instructed him, he kept him as the apple of his eye.

Deuteronomy 32:8-10 means The Most High God divided the human race into nations with separate gods (70) over them (Angels). However, True Israel (Israelites) became his portion or inheritance of the human race and this is why he was and still the God of Israel as stated in the Old and New Testament.

> **Zechariah 2:8 (KJV)**
>
> [8] For thus saith the LORD of hosts; After the glory hath he sent me unto the nations which spoiled you: for he that toucheth you toucheth the apple of his eye.

In the book of Jeremiah chapter 31 verse 35-37 there is a statement undeniably that supports God's chosen people are still God's chosen people. It states that if the moon and stars depart from The Most High God and heaven can be measured then God's chosen people are no more.

However, the moon and stars are still located in the sky and the stars cannot be measured which means God has not done away with his chosen people (True Israel).

> **Jeremiah 31:35-37 (KJV)**
>
> [35] Thus saith the LORD, which giveth the sun for a light by day, and the ordinances of the moon and of the stars for a light by night, which divideth the sea when the waves thereof roar; The LORD of hosts is his name:

> [36] If those ordinances depart from before me, saith the LORD, then the seed of Israel also shall cease from being a nation before me for ever.
>
> [37] Thus saith the LORD; If heaven above can be measured, and the foundations of the earth searched out beneath, I will also cast off all the seed of Israel for all that they have done, saith the LORD

There are many other scriptures in the bible that strongly suggest The Most High God is not done away with his chosen people. Currently the True Israelites of the bible are in a slumber or sleep mode not truly knowing who they are.

However, The Most High God is currently waking up True Israel (Israelites) that are scattered across the four corners of the earth. The Most High God has hid his face from True Israelites due to breaking the covenant of keeping the Laws, Statutes and Commandments of the Most High God. Although the Most High God hid his face from True Israel, he promised he will not make a total end of them but be a little sanctuary while they are still in captivity to this day.

Jeremiah 5:18 (KJV)

> [18] Nevertheless in those days, saith the LORD, I will not make a full end with you.

When we think about how the Most High God has been a little sanctuary to his people. We can list several provisions such as Welfare, Food Stamps, Section 8 and Affirmative Action etc. Without The Most High God making provisions for his chosen people, they would have probably been totally annihilated in places of their captivity by their oppressors a long time ago but yet True Israel still exist.

> **Ezekiel 11:16-17 (KJV)**
>
> [16] Therefore say, Thus saith the Lord GOD; Although I have cast them far off among the heathen, and although I have scattered them among the countries, yet will I be to them as a little sanctuary in the countries where they shall come.

As a matter of fact, in Baruch 2:29-35 (Apocrypha) the scriptures suggest that True Israel will begin to praise and remember the Most High God while they are in the land of their captivity. This is being displayed throughout the world in these last days and True Israel (blacks around the world) are indeed learning who they are and returning to their own God in righteousness.

> **Baruch 2:29-35**
>
> [29] If ye will not hear my voice, surely this very great multitude shall be turned into a small number among the nations, where I will scatter them. [30] For I knew that they would not hear me, because it is a stiffnecked people: but in the land of their captivities they shall remember themselves. [31] And shall know that I am the Lord their God: for I will give them an heart, and ears to hear: [32] **And they shall praise me in the land of their captivity, and think upon my name,** [33] And return from their stiff neck, and from their wicked deeds: for they shall remember the way of their fathers, which sinned before the Lord. [34] And I will bring them again into

> the land which I promised with an oath unto their fathers,
>
> Abraham, Isaac, and Jacob, and they shall be lords of it: and I will
>
> increase them, and they shall not be diminished. [35]And I will make
>
> an everlasting covenant with them to be their God, and they shall
>
> be my people: and I will no more drive my people of Israel out of
>
> the land that I have given them.

After examining this chapter, one must re-think that True Israel is not completely done away with. There are far too many prophetic scriptures that deal directly with God's chosen people and are linked directly to the so-called African Americans or people of color around the world.

Throughout the whole earth in these last days God's True people are waking up at an alarming rate to the reality of who they are. We must take notice that those imposters in Israel today do not fit any of the ensigns or prophecies concerning The Most High God's true inheritance.

Chapter 4

DEUTERONOMY 28

Deuteronomy the 28th chapter lends much information as to who the True Israelites are on the earth today. This chapter remarkably describes the True Israelite's identity without question. True Israel have been under the curses of Deuteronomy 28 and it is very specific concerning those curses in detail.

Deuteronomy 28:46 (KJV)

[46] And they shall be upon thee for a sign and for a wonder, and upon thy seed for ever.

The curses of Deuteronomy 28 only describe one group of people on the earth today and that would be the so-called African Americans and people of color that had been scattered around the four corners of the earth. The fake Jews in Israel today do not come close to fitting the curses of Deuteronomy 28 and therefore could not be the people of the book (Bible).

The theme of Deuteronomy 28 is the blessings and the curses. If we were to read versus 1-14, you'll be introduced to all the blessings that True Israel would have experienced if they chose to follow The Most High God Laws, Statutes and Commandments.

Deuteronomy 28:1 (KJV)

[1] And it shall come to pass, if thou shalt hearken diligently unto the voice of the LORD thy God, to observe and to do all his commandments which I command thee this day, that the LORD thy God will set thee on high above all nations of the earth:

Once again, the scriptures are supporting the fact that True Israel would have been high above all nations of the earth if they had observed and kept all of God's Laws, Statutes and Commandments. However, versus 15-68 describes what their life would be like if they disobeyed the Laws, Statutes and Commandments of God and unfortunately True Israel chose to disobey and now experiences all of the curses promised in Deuteronomy 28.

Deuteronomy 28:15 (KJV)

[15] But it shall come to pass, if thou wilt not hearken unto the voice of the LORD thy God, to observe to do all his commandments and his statutes which I command thee this day; that all these curses shall come upon thee, and overtake thee:

THE BIBLICAL SIGNS OF TRUE ISRAEL

There are many curses presented in Deuteronomy 28 but we will explore only a few in this chapter to establish some understanding as to what happen and to identify the true Israelites of the bible. Although Deuteronomy 28 is the main focus of this chapter other precepts will be used to support this claim that the True children of Israel are / were under these curses today.

THE SIGNS:

1. No Defense / Powerless
2. Oppression / Poverty
3. The Insults
4. The Illnesses
5. Lost Heritage / Culture
6. The Captivity
7. Sons & Daughters Sold
8. Yoke of Iron

The signs of True Israel would be a people that will be exiled from the Promised Land. They will not be able to fight back against their captors or enemies. They will constantly live-in oppression and poverty in the lands they were captive. They will be belittled, insulted and ridiculed by their captors within the lands of their captivity. They will be known as an ill group of people with a higher rate of illness than any other people on the planet. They will lose all knowledge of their past / beliefs and will be ***taken*** as ***slaves*** into many nations.

NO DEFENSE / POWERLESS:

> **Deuteronomy 28:25 (KJV)**
>
> [25] The LORD shall cause thee to be smitten before thine enemies: thou shalt go out one way against them, and flee seven ways before them: and shalt be removed into all the kingdoms of the earth.

During the times of slavery many blacks were lynched, hanging from trees and poles etc. During these hangings the bodies were left there to rot in which fowls of the air would eat the flesh of the carcasses.

If we research the history, the Israelites (blacks) have never been able to defeat their enemies during slavery. There are many stories of the Israelites having their towns destroyed (Rosewood Massacre – 1923) (Black Wall Street - 1921) and being murdered by white killers without punishment. However, the so-called modern day Jewish people in the land of Israel today have successfully defeated their enemies in military battles in 1948, 1956 and 1973. They do not fit the curses.

When reading the last portion of Deuteronomy 28:25 notice it states: "shalt be removed into all the kingdoms of the earth". This means by force, taken or stolen and as for any other ethnic group in the world, who can make that claim? No other people on the planet were taken by force into other nations but the so-called African Americans and other people of color around the world. Other versus that support the No Defense / powerless argument are:

Deuteronomy 28:31 (KJV)

[31] Thine ox shall be slain before thine eyes, and thou shalt not eat thereof: thine ass shall be violently taken away from before thy face, and shall not be restored to thee: thy sheep shall be given unto thine enemies, and thou shalt have none to rescue them.

Leviticus 26:17 (KJV)

[17] And I will set my face against you, and ye shall be slain before your enemies: they that hate you shall reign over you; and ye shall flee when none pursueth you.

Leviticus 26:37 (KJV)

[37] And they shall fall one upon another, as it were before a sword, when none pursueth: and ye shall have no power to stand before your enemies.

OPPRESSION / POVERTY:

Deuteronomy 28:29 (KJV)

[29] And thou shalt grope at noonday, as the blind gropeth in darkness, and thou shalt not prosper in thy ways: and thou shalt be only oppressed and spoiled evermore, and no man shall save thee.

The word grope means to search uncertainty or with difficulty for answers or solutions. True Israel / blacks need to constantly navigate his or her surroundings to survive or try to make ends meet not knowing why the struggle continues.

Deuteronomy 28:33 (KJV)

[33] The fruit of thy land, and all thy labours, shall a nation which thou knowest not eat up; and thou shalt be only oppressed and crushed alway:

True Israel continues to be oppressed by other nations.

Deuteronomy 28:43-44 (KJV)

[43] The stranger that is within thee shall get up above thee very high; and thou shalt come down very low.

[44] He shall lend to thee, and thou shalt not lend to him: he shall be the head, and thou shalt be the tail.

True Israel is at the bottom of society in every nation that they have been scattered. Other nations are very high above True Israel and will remain the tail until The Messiah returns and restore True Israel to their proper place according to the scriptures.

THE INSULTS:

> **Deuteronomy 28:37 (KJV)**
>
> [37] And thou shalt become an astonishment, a proverb, and a byword, among all nations whither the LORD shall lead thee.

Astonishments: Extreme Surprise; Amazement
Proverb: To make a byword of
Byword: Nicknames

When it comes to astonishments, proverbs and bywords, the so called African American community has been overwhelmed by them throughout history. Again, no other people on the planet of Earth have been subjected to such cruelty of name calling by other nations. It appears the black community has been called everything except for their true identity (An Israelite).

Nigger	Coons	Negroes
Black	African American	Colored
Slaves	Boy	Afro American
Niggas	Jigga-Boo	Sambo
Spook	Porch-Monkey	Gorilla Face
Jim Crow	Mr. Tambo	Zip Coon
Blackey	Spade	Snow ball

THIS IS A FACT

OK MY HEBREW BROTHERS AND SISTERS, HERE ARE A COUPLE OF NAMES GIVEN TO US BY THE GENTILE RACE (WHITE PEOPLE) FOR NEARLY 400 YEARS.

1619 - 1834 SLAVES

1834-1892 COONS/COLORED

1892-1934 NIGGERS/NIGGAS

1934-1970 BOY/AFRICANS

1970-1983 AFRO AMERICANS

1983-2002 BLACK AMERICANS

2002-2013 AFRICAN AMERICANS

WHAT WILL THEY THINK OF NEXT ?

BROTHERS AND SISTERS

WE ARE NOTHING MENTIOND OBOVE WE ARE HEBREWS FROM THE LAND OF ISREAL, TRIBE OF JUDAH THE LION.

2013 - 2019 HEBREW ISREALITES FROM ISREAL

The lost sheep sons of Noah, Shem, Abraham, Jacob and so on. Isreal is mentioned in the holy bible over 2,500 times.

YAH   STARTING WITH THE HOLY BILE

OUR HEVENLY FATHER   **PSLAM 83:4**

DO THE RESEARCH FOR YOUR SELF.

Many names the Israelites adopted since being captured in this country and in other parts of the world

THE ILLNESS:

> **Deuteronomy 28:59-61 (KJV)**
>
> [59] Then the LORD will make thy plagues wonderful, and the plagues of thy seed, even great plagues, and of long continuance, and sore sicknesses, and of long continuance.
>
> [60] Moreover he will bring upon thee all the diseases of Egypt, which thou wast afraid of; and they shall cleave unto thee.
>
> [61] Also every sickness, and every plague, which is not written in the book of this law, them will the LORD bring upon thee, until thou be destroyed.

Statistics reveal that the so-called African Americans are leading in all diseases and other health related issues that are deadly. Some of those diseases include Heart Disease, Diabetes, High Blood Pressure, Sickle Cell Anemia, Thyroid Tumors, Lupus and STD's etc.

The Most High God made it very clear if his chosen people would hearken unto his voice and follow his commandments He would not have put any diseases upon them but of course True Israel disobeyed again.

> **Exodus 15:26 (KJV)**
>
> [26] And said, If thou wilt diligently hearken to the voice of the LORD thy God, and wilt do that which is right in his sight, and wilt give ear to his commandments, and keep all his statutes, I will put none of these diseases upon thee, which I have brought upon the Egyptians: for I am the LORD that healeth thee.

Leviticus 26:21 (KJV)

²¹ And if ye walk contrary unto me, and will not hearken unto me; I will bring seven times more plagues upon you according to your sins.

LOST HERITAGE/ CULTURE AND HISTORY:

Deuteronomy 28:36 (KJV)

³⁶ The LORD shall bring thee, and thy king which thou shalt set over thee, unto a nation which neither thou nor thy fathers have known; and there shalt thou serve other gods, wood and stone.

Deuteronomy 28:64 (KJV)

⁶⁴ And the LORD shall scatter thee among all people, from the one end of the earth even unto the other; and there thou shalt serve other gods, which neither thou nor thy fathers have known, even wood and stone.

When True Israel was captured into slavery much of their history, heritage and knowledge of their true God or Elohim were diminished. They were captured and brought into a land they and their forefathers have never known (America and other nations). This took place during the Transatlantic Slave Trade in the 1600's.

Also notice the scripture mentions that True Israel will be scattered among all people across the earth and in those places or nations they will serve other gods of wood and stone. First, the so-called Jewish people in Israel today was never scattered into other nations but willingly traveled into other lands. However, it is a known fact that the so-called African Americans and other people of color were forcibly scattered among other nations around the world.

What is meant by wood and stone? Clearly the scripture states True Israel will serve other gods in the lands of their captivity. It is reasonable to think wood could represent Christianity and the stone can represent Islam. When carefully researched, these two religions could easily fit this prophecy due to them being the most influential religions of True Israel today. Both of these religions have practices and / or beliefs that are quite the opposite from the biblical scriptures.

THE CAPTIVITY:

> **Deuteronomy 28:30 (KJV)**
>
> [30] Thou shalt betroth a wife, and another man shall lie with her: thou shalt build an house, and thou shalt not dwell therein: thou shalt plant a vineyard, and shalt not gather the grapes thereof.

Once True Israel was captive into slavery many events took place that is easily identified with the African Americans and not the so-called Jewish people. During slavery often the black woman was taken and raped by slave masters even during the middle passage when slaves were coming over on the ships. Just as the scripture mentions another man did take the wives and lie with them against their will.

> **Deuteronomy 28:32 (KJV)**
>
> [32] Thy sons and thy daughters shall be given unto another people, and thine eyes shall look, and fail with longing for them all the day long; and there shall be no might in thine hand.

Deuteronomy 28:41 (KJV)

[41] Thou shalt beget sons and daughters, but thou shalt not enjoy them; for they shall go into captivity.

It was a regular practice to sell the children of slaves to other slave masters during the times of slavery. The children were sold and treated like property and this practice continued throughout this period of history. This prophecy definitely fit the so-called African Americans and not the so-called Jewish people. When and where in history were the so-called children of the Jewish people sold on auction blocks?

Deuteronomy 28:48 (KJV)

[48] Therefore shalt thou serve thine enemies which the LORD shall send against thee, in hunger, and in thirst, and in nakedness, and in want of all things: and he shall put a yoke of iron upon thy neck, until he have destroyed thee.

True Israel had to serve their enemies in all the lands they have been scattered and, in those lands, they were and still in want of all things. But the most significant part of the verse is when it states "he shall put a yoke of iron upon thy neck". There were no other people in history with yokes of iron upon their necks except the so called African American people. Again, when in history did the so-called Jewish people have yokes of iron upon their necks? (Not even in the Holocaust).

The yokes of iron were not lifted until 1863 during Abraham's Lincoln's Emancipation Proclamation. By this time True Israel were destroyed by losing their rich heritage or history, not knowing who they were and who their true God was. This process of damaging a nation of people was through horrendous tactics as portrayed in the "Willie Lynch Letter & Making of a Slave".

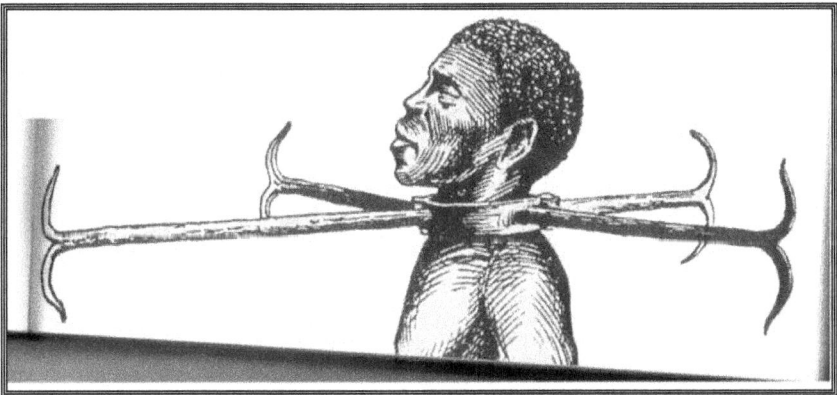

Deuteronomy 28:43-44 (KJV)

[43] The stranger that is within thee shall get up above thee very high; and thou shalt come down very low.

[44] He shall lend to thee, and thou shalt not lend to him: he shall be the head, and thou shalt be the tail.

What strangers are we talking about in this scripture? The stranger is referring to the Europeans or those who captured True Israel into slavery or captivity. No matter where you go in the world, blacks are the minority and suffer on every end of the economic scale etc. The Europeans are the ones that are very high or the head and True Israel is the tail or at least until The Messiah returns to deliver his people and put them where he intended.

Have you ever noticed that other foreigners could come into this country (USA) and start businesses much easier than True Israel? Even the businesses within the black communities are not owned by blacks but by the so called Jewish, Arabs and Asians etc. Why?

The so-called Jewish people are rich owning Financial Services, Real Estate, Television, Film, Video, Technology, Tourism, Hotels, News Papers, Publishing, Food and Retail. This proves that the Jewish people cannot be the people of the book (Bible). True Israel today is the tail according to the scriptures and not the head.

Deuteronomy 28:68 (KJV)

[68] And the LORD shall bring thee into Egypt again with ships, by the way whereof I spake unto thee, Thou shalt see it no more again: and there ye shall be sold unto your enemies for bondmen and bondwomen, and no man shall buy you.

This is the ultimate scripture that cannot be denied of who the real children of Israel are today. It simply states that the "Lord shall bring thee into Egypt again with ships". Who were taken into slavery by way of ships? Could this have been prophecy about the Transatlantic Slave Trade?

When this scripture mentions Egypt, it's not stating a physical Egypt but a spiritual Egypt. The word Egypt in the bible actually means "bondage" (Exodus 13:3, 14 & Exodus 20:2). Certainly, True Israel / blacks were sold by their enemies for bondmen and bondwoman meaning male and female slaves and no one shall buy them meaning save or redeem them from this current captivity. The only one who can save True Israel from this current captivity is The Most High God himself.

This current captivity was told to Abraham in Genesis 15:13. Although, many are of the opinion that this prophecy was meant for when the children of Israel was captured in physical Egypt (Moses Days), however, the children of Israel was not in physical Egypt being afflicted for 400 years. First, they walked into Egypt, not by ships. Secondly, Joseph was 2nd in command under Pharaoh and him and his family was not being afflicted the whole time they were in Egypt. Third, they knew of the land of Egypt due to them traveling back and forth from Canaan, they were not strangers. Finally, all of the curses of Deuteronomy 28 fit True Israel's captivity perfectly. Also read Leviticus chapter 26 for more signs of True Israel descendants today.

Genesis 15:13 (KJV)

[13] And he said unto Abram, Know of a surety that thy seed shall be a stranger in a land that is not theirs, and shall serve them; and they shall afflict them four hundred years;

Although Deuteronomy 28 chapter is usually a main source of information to identify True Israel today, there are many other scriptures that can do the same. The Bible is true Black history and there are no other people on the planet earth that fits all of the prophecies concerning the True descendants of the children of Israel.

The Bible let us know that the True children of Israel will be exiled from the Promised Land and this happened in 70 AD when the children of Israel was fleeing from Roman persecution and slavery as stated in "From Babylon to Timbuktu" page 84 by Rudolph R. Windsor.

True Israel will be unable to fight against their captors or enemies, they will constantly live-in oppression and poverty in their captive lands, and they will be belittled, insulted and ridiculed by their captor's. They will be known as an ill people, will lose all knowledge of their past / culture and will be taken as slaves into many nations.

All of the above has come to past for True Israel; however True Israel will not always be in a state of oppression. There are many more prophecies to come that are directly related towards Israel's restoration. This will be explored more in another chapter of this book.

In conclusion, the main reason why True Israel is in this current situation today is due to the continuous breaking of God's laws, statutes and commandments. The scriptures states that all Israel has transgressed the law and therefore are suffering the curses of Deuteronomy 28. True Israel must return back to following God's laws, statutes and commandments for the ultimate protection just as he promised.

Daniel 9:11 (KJV)

[11] Yea, all Israel have transgressed thy law, even by departing, that they might not obey thy voice; therefore the curse is poured upon us, and the oath that is written in the law of Moses the servant of God, because we have sinned against him.

The Curses	Israelites	Jews	Gentiles	Islam
1. Slavery & Captivity Deuteronomy 28: 41, 49-50, 68	X			
2. Having No Power To Stand Against Thy Enemies Deuteronomy 28: 25, 65	X			
3. Sent Back To Mitzrayim (Egypt) Again by Ships Deuteronomy 28: 68	X			
4. Exiled In The Land of Their Enemies Deuteronomy 28: 25	X			
5. Scattered Among All Nations Deuteronomy 28: 25, 64	X	X	X	X
6. A Very Sick And Diseased Stricken People Deuteronomy 28: 21-22, 25, 27, 59-61	X			
7. At The Bottom Socially With Other Peoples High Above Them Deuteronomy 28: 36, 43	X			
8. Lost The True Knowledge of Who They Are and Will Be Called by Many Scornful Nicknames Other Than Yisrael & Hebrew Deuteronomy 28: 37	X			
9. Packed Into Prisons and Jails Deuteronomy 28: 48	X			
10. A Non- Prosperous People Deuteronomy 28: 17-20, 23-24, 29-31, 33, 38-41, 51	X			
11. An Oppressed People By Their Enemies Deuteronomy 28: 25, 48	X	X		
12. Very Religious and Members of All Religions Deuteronomy 28: 36, 64	X		X	

Chapter 5
THE SCATTERING

True Israel has always been a hard headed or sniff necked people which mean they were always stubborn or hardened and would not listen to the instructions of the Most High God. This stiff neck behavior nearly caused True Israel to be destroyed by the Most High God.

If it were not for Moses pleading with the Most High God, on behalf of the children of Israel, the children of Israel would have been destroyed by the Most High God and He would have chose another people. This rebellious behavior was consistent with True Israel's history and this is the real reason Israel was scattered throughout into all nations.

Exodus 33:5 (KJV)

5 For the LORD had said unto Moses, Say unto the children of Israel, Ye are a stiffnecked people: I will come up into the midst of thee in a moment, and consume thee: therefore now put off thy ornaments from thee, that I may know what to do unto thee.

Deuteronomy 9:13-14 (KJV)

[13] Furthermore the LORD spake unto me, saying, I have seen this people, and, behold, it is a stiffnecked people:

[14] Let me alone, that I may destroy them, and blot out their name from under heaven: and I will make of thee a nation mightier and greater than they.

Exodus 32:9-12 (KJV)

[9] And the LORD said unto Moses, I have seen this people, and, behold, it is a stiffnecked people:

[10] Now therefore let me alone, that my wrath may wax hot against them, and that I may consume them: and I will make of thee a great nation.

[11] And Moses besought the LORD his God, and said, LORD, why doth thy wrath wax hot against thy people, which thou hast brought forth out of the land of Egypt with great power, and with a mighty hand?

[12] Wherefore should the Egyptians speak, and say, For mischief did he bring them out, to slay them in the mountains, and to consume them from the face of the earth? Turn from thy fierce wrath, and repent of this evil against thy people.

Exodus 33:3 (KJV)

[3] Unto a land flowing with milk and honey: for I will not go up in the midst of thee; for thou art a stiffnecked people: lest I consume thee in the way.

There is a popular belief that Israel was scattered because they did not except their "MESSIAH". This belief is far from the truth because when True Israel was scattered, they were scattered as a nation of people including those who accepted the Messiah and those who did not. There are no biblical references or passages to indicate they were scattered due to not accepting the "MESSIAH". But strong evidence from the scriptures indicating their captivity and scattering was because of disobedience to God's laws, statutes and commandments.

Another popular reasoning for the scattering is it is the Whiteman's (Europeans) fault; although what the other nations did and still are doing to True Israel today was horrendous and absolutely in humane in every way possible, it is not the Whiteman's (Europeans) fault.

The nations that took part in the horrific and terrible captivities and scattering of True Israel will be judged on the account of how it was carried out through the lynching's, beatings, murdering and all kinds of brutal treatment towards True Israel throughout history. But ultimately, it was the Most High God 's decision to scatter True Israel into all nations of the world not the Whiteman or any other nation.

Ezekiel 12:15 (KJV)

[15] And they shall know that I am the LORD, when I shall scatter them among the nations, and disperse them in the countries.

Many of the Old Testament prophets (Moses, Jeremiah, Ezekiel etc.) gave plenty of warnings of True Israel's captivity and scattering way before it came to past. These prophets foretold how True Israel will be scattered among the heathens within all nations.

Moses:

Moses mentions in several passages that True Israel will be smitten before their enemies and removed into all kingdoms of the earth. Smitten means to inflict with a heavy blow or be killed. This is certainly historical as to what happened to True Israel without question.

Deuteronomy 28:25 (KJV)

[25] The LORD shall cause thee to be smitten before thine enemies: thou shalt go out one way against them, and flee seven ways before them: and shalt be removed into all the kingdoms of the earth.

Again, Moses stresses the point that the children of Israel must observe and do all these words of the law that are written in the book. This would have kept the children of Israel blessed instead of cursed and there would have been no need for the nation of Israel to be scattered.

It is a terrifying thing to fall into the hands of the angry God of Abraham, Isaac and Jacob. He will not tolerate disobedience.

Deuteronomy 28:58 (KJV)

[58] If thou wilt not observe to do all the words of this law that are written in this book, that thou mayest fear this glorious and fearful name, THE LORD THY GOD;

As Moses continues to warn the children of Israel concerning them being scattered among all nations, the children of Israel chose to disobey and they were eventually scattered.

Deuteronomy 28:64 (KJV)

[64] And the LORD shall scatter thee among all people, from the one end of the earth even unto the other; and there thou shalt serve other gods, which neither thou nor thy fathers have known, even wood and stone.

Leviticus 26:33 (KJV)

[33] And I will scatter you among the heathen, and will draw out a sword after you: and your land shall be desolate, and your cities waste.

Hebrews 10:31 (KJV)

[31] It is a fearful thing to fall into the hands of the living God.

Moses also wrote Psalm 90 and he mentions the Most High's anger can manifest into his wrath.

Psalm 90:11 (KJV)

[11] Who knoweth the power of thine anger? even according to thy fear, so is thy wrath.

Jeremiah:

The prophet Jeremiah was already sanctified and ordained to be a prophet before he was even born. He was to be a prophet unto all Israel and to other nations.

Jeremiah 1:5 (KJV)

5 Before I formed thee in the belly I knew thee; and before thou camest forth out of the womb I sanctified thee, and I ordained thee a prophet unto the nations.

The prophet Jeremiah has a remarkable track record for serving the Most High God. He lived during the time of other prophets such as Zephaniah, Nahum, Habakkuk, Daniel and Ezekiel. He was prophet during the rain of five kings (Josiah, Jehoahaz, Jehoiakim, Johoichin and Zedelkiah). He was a prophet for over forty years.

He also warned the people of Judah that they should obey the words of the Most High God but instead they turned back to their iniquities (sin) of their forefathers and broke the covenant.

Jeremiah 11:10 (KJV)

10 They are turned back to the iniquities of their forefathers, which refused to hear my words; and they went after other gods to serve them: the house of Israel and the house of Judah have broken my covenant which I made with their fathers.

Jeremiah stated that Israel will eventually be scattered among the nations in several of passages or scriptures.

Jeremiah 9:16 (KJV)

[16] I will scatter them also among the heathen, whom neither they nor their fathers have known: and I will send a sword after them, till I have consumed them.

Jeremiah 13:24-25 (KJV)

[24] Therefore will I scatter them as the stubble that passeth away by the wind of the wilderness.

[25] This is thy lot, the portion of thy measures from me, saith the LORD; because thou hast forgotten me, and trusted in falsehood.

Jeremiah 16:13-15 (KJV)

[13] Therefore will I cast you out of this land into a land that ye know not, neither ye nor your fathers; and there shall ye serve other gods day and night; where I will not shew you favour.

[14] Therefore, behold, the days come, saith the LORD, that it shall no more be said, The LORD liveth, that brought up the children of Israel out of the land of Egypt;

[15] But, The LORD liveth, that brought up the children of Israel from the land of the north, and from all the lands whither he had driven them: and I will bring them again into their land that I gave unto their fathers.

David:

King David knew and mentioned the scattering as well. This scattering of Israel was no secret to the nation due to many warnings of God's prophets.

Psalm 106:27 (KJV)

[27] To overthrow their seed also among the nations, and to scatter them in the lands.

Psalm 44:11 (KJV)

[11] Thou hast given us like sheep appointed for meat; and hast scattered us among the heathen.

Ezekiel:

Ezekiel was a prophet who lived during the same time as Jeremiah and both had a lot to say about the scattering. The only difference is that it appears Ezekiel was focusing on the house of Israel and not the southern kingdom of Judah. He only mentions the house of Judah five times (Ezekiel 4:6, 8:17, 25:3, 8, 12).

Ezekiel makes a point to say although the Most High God will scatter the nation of Israel and Judah among the countries; He will be a little sanctuary in the countries where they should be scattered, meaning that He will preserve a remnant of his people even in captivity.

Ezekiel 11:16 (KJV)

¹⁶ Therefore say, Thus saith the Lord GOD; Although I have cast them far off among the heathen, and although I have scattered them among the countries, yet will I be to them as a little sanctuary in the countries where they shall come.

Ezekiel 20:23 (KJV)

²³ I lifted up mine hand unto them also in the wilderness, that I would scatter them among the heathen, and disperse them through the countries;

Ezekiel 22:15 (KJV)

¹⁵ And I will scatter thee among the heathen, and disperse thee in the countries, and will consume thy filthiness out of thee.

Ezekiel 36:19 (KJV)

¹⁹ And I scattered them among the heathen, and they were dispersed through the countries: according to their way and according to their doings I judged them.

OTHER GODS

There are many scriptures of other prophets that mention the scattering of True Israel and how they will be scattered all over the world into heathen nations such as in Leviticus 26:32-37, which is worth mentioning due to its descriptive view of the captivity / scattering.

A review of the scattering scriptures presented in this chapter brings out another point that should be mentioned and that is how much the Most High God hates idolatry, the worshiping of idols or other gods. This was a huge problem with the Israelites and a major cause for the scattering (Deuteronomy 28:64, Jeremiah 13:24-25 and Jeremiah 16:13).

The Israelites constantly went whoring after other gods from other nations. This act was forbidden because it made the God of Abraham, Isaac and Jacob angry and jealous. It was never meant for True Israel to serve any other gods but the true and living God. (The Most High God).

The Most High God was truly broken that his chosen people continued over and over again desiring to serve other gods besides Himself. So, He decided to scatter them and make them serve other gods of wood and of stone etc.

Ezekiel 6:9 (KJV)

⁹ And they that escape of you shall remember me among the nations whither they shall be carried captives, because I am broken with their whorish heart, which hath departed from me, and with their eyes, which go a whoring after their idols: and they shall lothe themselves for the evils which they have committed in all their abominations.

Ezekiel 23:30 (KJV)

[30] I will do these things unto thee, because thou hast gone a whoring after the heathen, and because thou art polluted with their idols.

Hosea 9:1 (KJV)

[1] Rejoice not, O Israel, for joy, as other people: for thou hast gone a whoring from thy God, thou hast loved a reward upon every cornfloor.

1 Chronicles 5:25 (KJV)

[25] And they transgressed against the God of their fathers, and went a whoring after the gods of the people of the land, whom God destroyed before them.

Numbers 15:39-40 (KJV)

[39] And it shall be unto you for a fringe, that ye may look upon it, and remember all the commandments of the LORD, and do them ; and that ye seek not after your own heart and your own eyes, after which ye use to go a whoring:

[40] That ye may remember, and do all my commandments, and be holy unto your God.

Deuteronomy 31:16 (KJV)

16 And the LORD said unto Moses, Behold, thou shalt sleep with thy fathers; and this people will rise up, and go a whoring after the gods of the strangers of the land, whither they go to be among them, and will forsake me, and break my covenant which I have made with them.

Deuteronomy 28:64 (KJV)

64 And the LORD shall scatter thee among all people, from the one end of the earth even unto the other; and there thou shalt serve other gods, which neither thou nor thy fathers have known, even wood and stone.

Question: Is True Israel still worshipping other gods today? Yes, but they are unaware of it due to the changing of names throughout the centuries of certain rituals taught in the lands of their captivity and not knowing who they really are today. This will be addressed in another chapter of this book.

How long will True Israel be scattered into other nations around the world? The Messiah knew that True Israel will be scattered into all nations around the world and stated that Jerusalem will be trodden down of the Gentiles, until the times of the Gentiles be fulfilled.

Luke 21:24 (KJV)

24 And they shall fall by the edge of the sword, and shall be led away captive into all nations: and Jerusalem shall be trodden down of the Gentiles, until the times of the Gentiles be fulfilled.

What we know today is that the land of Israel is occupied by Gentiles and not True Israel and this is reason to believe that those in Israel today, who call themselves Israelis, are not the chosen people of the Most High God but imposters portraying to be True Israel. Again, the bible identifies them as the synagogue of Satan (Revelation 2:9 and 3:9).

Revelation 2:9 (KJV)

[9] I know thy works, and tribulation, and poverty, (but thou art rich) and I know the blasphemy of them which say they are Jews, and are not, but are the synagogue of Satan.

Revelation 3:9 (KJV)

[9] Behold, I will make them of the synagogue of Satan, which say they are Jews, and are not, but do lie; behold, I will make them to come and worship before thy feet, and to know that I have loved thee.

True Israel is still scattered in the four corners of the earth today and will be scattered until The Messiah returns. The Messiah himself will place True Israel back in their own land.

In conclusion the scattering only pertains to the True Israelites of the bible. There are no scripture references that supports that another nation besides True Israel was scattered and /or will be gathered. Neither are there any world history documentation to support Gentile nations had been scattered forcibly in the four corners of the earth. However, there is biblical support to suggest that people from other nations will accompany True Israelites in the last days.

Chapter 6

THE TRANSATLANTIC SLAVE TRADE

One of the most noted and horrific scattering of True Israel was The Transatlantic Slave Trade. This was the ultimate scattering of True Israel because The Most High God stated how he would eventually scatter True Israel into the four corners of the earth by ships. Could Deuteronomy 28:68 have been a prophecy concerning the Transatlantic Slave Trade?

Deuteronomy 28:68 (KJV)

[68] And the LORD shall bring thee into Egypt again with ships, by the way whereof I spake unto thee, Thou shalt see it no more again: and there ye shall be sold unto your enemies for bondmen and bondwomen, and no man shall buy you.

The Transatlantic Slave Trade took place in the 15th to 19th century, mainly by the Portuguese, the British, the French, the Spanish, the Africans and the Dutch Empire. The trade took place on the west coast of Africa through different ports. The slaves were used to manufacture Tobacco, Coffee, Cotton, Sugar, Rice and Mining.

Although the slave trade on some historical documents started in the 1400's. The first slave ship arrived in Jamestown, Virginia in 1619 and many slave ships thereafter delivered more slaves up and down the east coast of the United States and the Caribbean's for approximately 245 years. Throughout the years of slavery nearly 17 million slaves were captured from the West Coast of Africa and treated harshly in the new land (America) etc.

The last account of the southern kingdom of the Israelites (Judah, Benjamin and Levi) is when they fled into the mountains to the west of Israel, which was Africa. The Israelites has a long history of fleeing to the west, especially to Egypt. (Genesis 46:7, 12:10; Jeremiah 42:14-16; 43:7; Matthew 2:13). These trips to Africa were usually because of Famine, Military Threats and Safety. It was always towards the Hamites (Descendents of Noah's son Ham), the people that the Israelites resemble in skin color and physical appearance.

This was the beginning of the migration of the Israelites into deep Africa. The Israelites made their way across Africa to the west coast and began setting up their kingdoms and or place of dwelling.

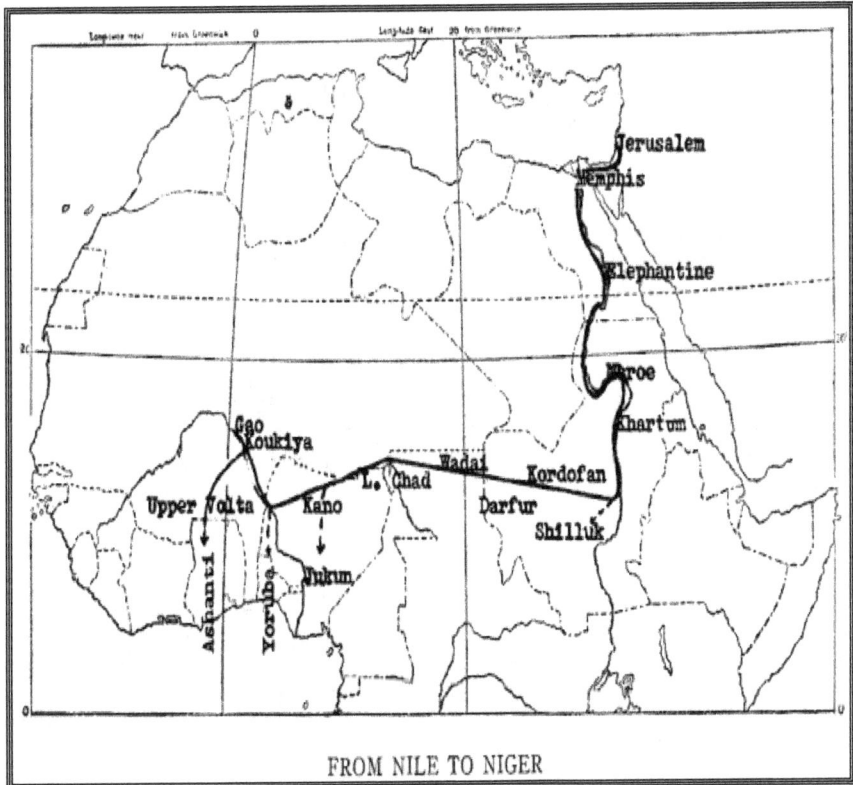

FROM NILE TO NIGER

Hebrewisms of West Africa (written by Joseph Williams in 1930). a map outlining Israelite migration from from Jerusalem to Memphis in Egypt to Elephantine through Darfur to Lake Chad and into Nigeria on the West Coast of Africa

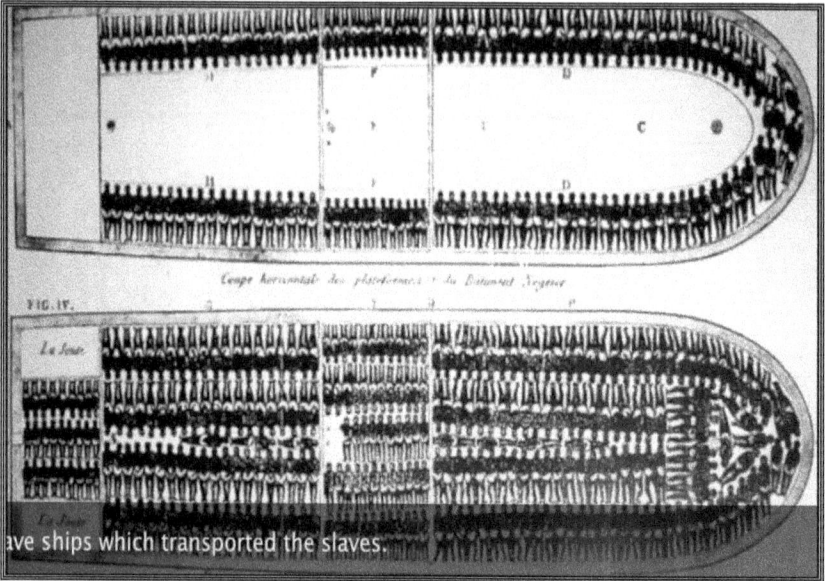

The Middle Massage Slave Trade Ship Layout

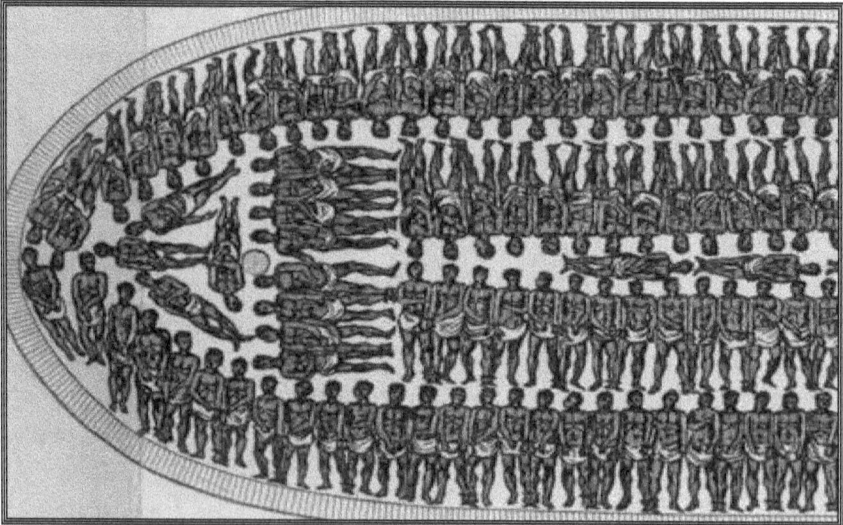

(A closer look at the packing of Israelites on the slave ships)

In the following 1747 year maps of Africa you'll see there was an area of Africa called Negroland and in that area you'll see some of the tribe names of the Israelites who settled in that area. One name noted is the Kingdom of Juda also noted as FIDA, Whydah, Hueda, Ouidah and Whidah. Notice other areas such as the Desert of Seth which was the son of Adam (First Man) located on the map.

Many of the tribes on the West Coast of Africa were descendants of the Israelites, probably dwelling there for more than 1500 years before the Transatlantic Slave Trade.

1747 Map of West Africa
Notice Juda, Whidah, Desert of Seth on this map etc.

1747 Map of West Africa
Notice Shankala, wandering tribes and Jews exiled on this map
etc.

1747 Map of West Africa
Notice Tribe of Juda and other names of the 12 tribe of Israel
on this map

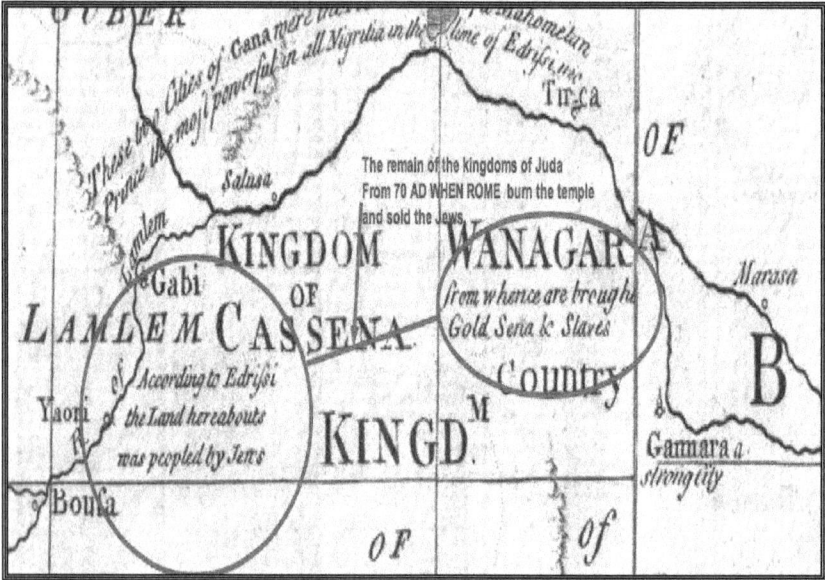

1747 Map of West Africa
Notice it states these were the remains of the tribe of Juda in this area of Africa

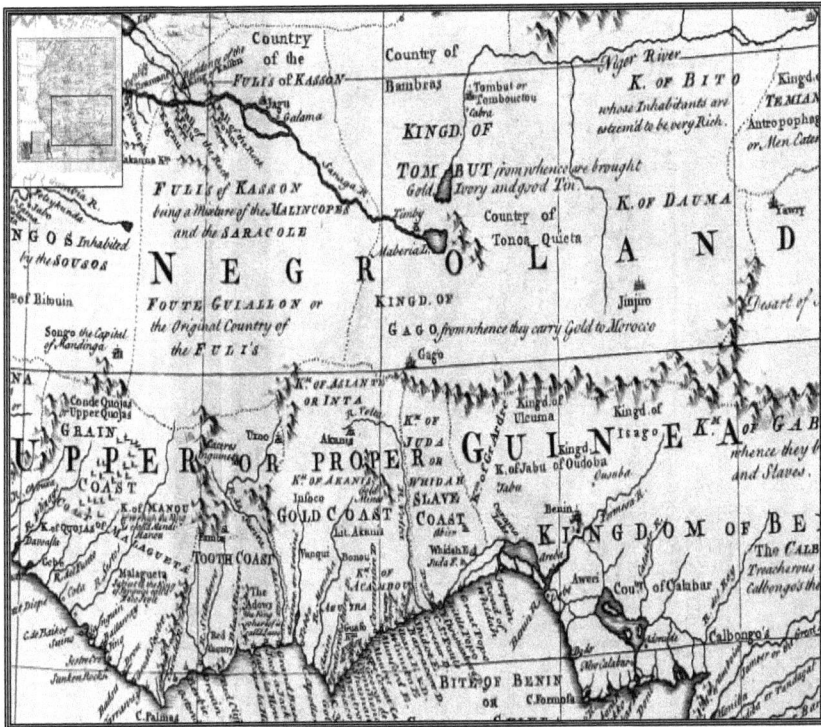

1747 Map of West Africa
Notice the west coast of Africa was called Negro Land with
Hebrew / Israelite inhabitants

1747 Map of West Africa
**Notice Juda and Whidah Tribes in Africa. (These were Jews in
this land not Africans)**

1747 Map of West Africa
Notice Semeon, Juda, Jerusalem etc. (All Jews in the land of Africa)

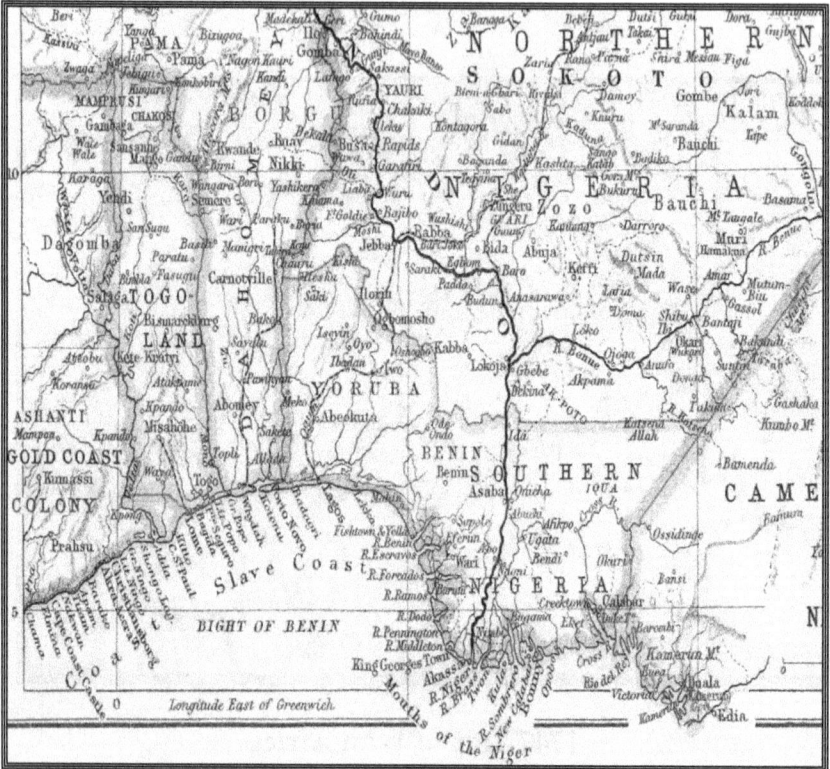

1914 Map of West Africa (8)

Notice: On this map you have Yoruba and Ashanti tribes on the west coast of Africa. These tribes are noted to be dwelling in the areas of the Hebrews migration and more likely Hebrews not African.

The following African Tribes are noted as being possible descendants of the original Israelites:

1. Balanta	2. *Ibo*	3. GA
4. Fanti	5. Sefti	6. *Fulani*
7. Krio	8. Mende	9. Mandingo
10. *Yoruba*	11. *Ashanti*	12. Lunda
13. Angola	14. Tekrur	15. * Songhui*
16. Mali	17. Mossi	18. Segu
19. Nupe	20. Dyula	21. Oyo
22. *Dahomey*	23. Benin	24. Luango
25. Konco	26. Bakongos	27. Mbundu
28. Hausas	29. Wolofs	30. Malinkes
31. Sekes	32. Bantu	33. Falaha

* Scholars believe to be the descendants of the Israelites by their Hebrew practices and / or traditions.

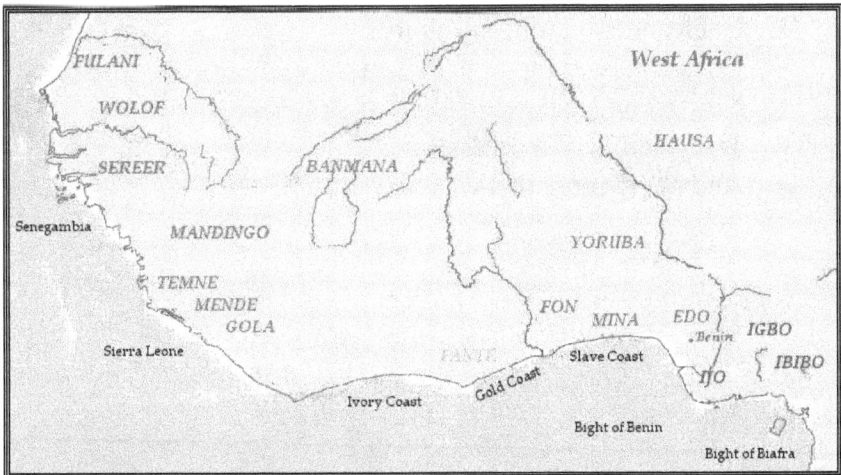

Tribe locations in West Africa

EMPIRE	YEARS
Mali Empire	1230-1600's
Ghana Empire	790-1076
Songhai Empire	1400-1500's
Ashanti Empire	1701-1896
Kingdom of Dahomey	1600-1894

Tribes of West Africa & Dates

These tribes are known to hold on to some Hebraic rituals that could only originate from the original Hebrews / Israelites. Some of their customs noted were:

- Circumcision
- The division of their tribes into twelve, blood sprinkling upon their altars and door posts
- Marrying of their brother's wife after death
- Separation and purification after child birth.
- Uncleanness during childbirth
- Uncleanness during menstruation
- New moon Celebrations
- The wearing of a breastplate
- And many more that was noted

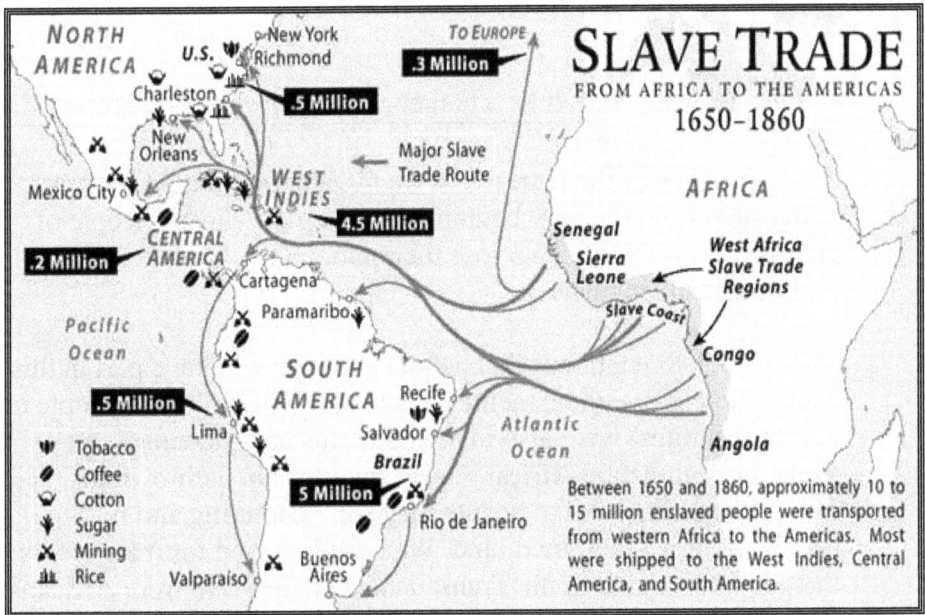

SLAVE TRADE
FROM AFRICA TO THE AMERICAS
1650–1860

NORTH AMERICA — New York, Richmond, Charleston, New Orleans, Mexico City

.3 Million (TO EUROPE)
.5 Million
4.5 Million
.2 Million
.5 Million
5 Million

Major Slave Trade Route

WEST INDIES
CENTRAL AMERICA — Cartagena, Paramaribo
SOUTH AMERICA — Lima, Recife, Salvador, Brazil, Rio de Janeiro, Buenos Aires, Valparaiso

Pacific Ocean
Atlantic Ocean

AFRICA — Senegal, Sierra Leone, Slave Coast, Congo, Angola

West Africa Slave Trade Regions

Tobacco
Coffee
Cotton
Sugar
Mining
Rice

Between 1650 and 1860, approximately 10 to 15 million enslaved people were transported from western Africa to the Americas. Most were shipped to the West Indies, Central America, and South America.

Principal Trade Slave Routes of the Israelites

The Israelites has a long history of captivities dating back to the days of Moses. First, to the Assyrians, Second to the Babylonians, third to the Persians/Medes, fourth to the Greeks and fifth to the Romans. Would it be strange to say that the so-called African Americans and those of the Islands of the Sea etc. would be descendants of the original Israelites that were taken during the Transatlantic Slave Trade?

One must keep in mind that the Israelites are the only nation of people in the entire world by history and biblically that have been captured into slavery in the masses.

As a matter of fact, the Israelites were in slavery so much that the prophet Jeremiah had to ask in (Jeremiah 2:14)

Jeremiah 2:14

[14] *Is* Israel a servant? *is* he a homeborn *slave?*why is he spoiled?

The captivities of the Israelites were not an afterthought but a crafty plan from the very beginning to keep the chosen people of God down by having them lose their nationality, heritage, traditions and language etc.

Psalm 83:1-8 mentions what people and land will have part in this counsel to enslave the Israelites / Hebrews. The authentic people of Africa (Hamites) were also involved in this crafty counsel. Remember authentic Africans sold Israelites not their own people. The Africans knew what people they were capturing and it certainly wasn't their own kind. We have believed for many years that the People sold in the Transatlantic Trade Slave were Africans (Hamites).

Why would the Africans be selling their own people or relatives? No, the people sold were Israelites, descendants of Abraham. Isn't it funny that these details are not explained within our school textbooks or taught in the churches of today?

In the book "The Nazis World War II" by Robert Edwin Herzstein, Adolf Hitler made reference that he knew who the real Hebrew Israelites are and he knew the Jews in Israel today are imposters.

In this book it stated:

In one segment of a Nazi 'instructional" film, the genetic heritage of the Jew is purportedly traced to Oriental, Negro, near Asian and Hamitic peoples, Hence, the film concludes, "the Jew is a bastard".

Although Hitler thought the original Jews were Hamitic not Semitic, he still knew the Jews who called themselves Jews were not the original Jews. Gamal Abdel president of Egypt 1956 – 1970 also knew this fact.

WAR for Israel

When he was asked about peace in the middle east....The late president of Egypt, Gamal Abdel Nasser, stated.... *"The Jews will never be able to live here in peace, because they left here **black** but came back **white**.*

EGYPT'S PREMIER NASSER

Gamal Abdel Statement (Knew the real Jews)
Gamal Abdel (President of Egypt 1956 – 1970) knew the original Jews were Black

Psalm 83:1-8 (KJV)

1 Keep not thou silence, O God: hold not thy peace, and be not still, O God.

2 For, lo, thine enemies make a tumult: and they that hate thee have lifted up the head.

3 They have taken crafty counsel against thy people, and consulted against thy hidden ones.

4 They have said, Come, and let us cut them off from being a nation; that the name of Israel may be no more in remembrance.

5 For they have consulted together with one consent: they are confederate against thee:

6 The tabernacles of Edom, and the Ishmaelites; of Moab, and the Hagarenes;

7 Gebal, and Ammon, and Amalek; the Philistines with the inhabitants of Tyre;

8 Assur also is joined with them: they have holpen the children of Lot. Selah.

The Most High God allowed these captivities to take place as a punishment for not following his Laws, Statutes and Commandments. He allowed the Israelites to be captured and take on the culture and ways of their enemies since they did not want to serve Him by following his rules. The Israelites eventually was scattered throughout the four corners of the earth and till this day the real descendants of True Israel are still scattered.

Jeremiah 17:4

[4] And thou, even thyself, shalt discontinue from thine heritage that I gave thee; and I will cause thee to serve thine enemies in the land which thou knowest not: for ye have kindled a fire in mine anger, which shall burn for ever.

Jeremiah 33:24

[24] Considerest thou not what this people have spoken, saying, The two families which the LORD hath chosen, he hath even cast them off? thus they have despised my people, that they should be no more a nation before them.

Ezekiel 22:14-15

[14] Can thine heart endure, or can thine hands be strong, in the days that I shall deal with thee? I the LORD have spoken it, and will do it. [15] And I will scatter thee among the heathen, and disperse thee in the countries, and will consume thy filthiness out of thee.

Deuteronomy 32:26

[26] I said, I would scatter them into corners, I would make the remembrance of them to cease from among men:

Amos 9:9 (KJV)

[9] For, lo, I will command, and I will sift the house of Israel among all nations, like as corn is sifted in a sieve, yet shall not the least grain fall upon the earth.

Luke 21:24

[24] And they shall fall by the edge of the sword, and shall be led away captive into all nations: and Jerusalem shall be trodden down of the Gentiles, until the times of the Gentiles be fulfilled.

James 1:1

[1] James, a servant of God and of the Lord Jesus Christ, to the twelve tribes which are scattered abroad, greeting.

After all the crafty counsel against the Israelites till this day, it appears the plan worked due to the fact that not many so-called African Americans etc. know who they really are as a nation of people.

The Most High God chose the Israelites to be a special people unto himself and with that came a responsibility, even the punishments were all meant for the Israelites because no other nation had the privilege to deal with the Most High God directly. The other nations did not know him at all. The Israelites were supposed to be that light unto all nations and they failed miserably.

The following scriptures make reference that the Most High God chose the people of Israel unto his own, he separated them from other people, he dealt with no other nation of people in punishment or judgments and because of the Israelites he made the world.

Deuteronomy 7:6

[6] For thou art an holy people unto the LORD thy God: the LORD thy God hath chosen thee to be a special people unto himself, above all people that are upon the face of the earth.

Leviticus 20:24-26

[24] But I have said unto you, Ye shall inherit their land, and I will give it unto you to possess it, a land that floweth with milk and honey: I am the LORD your God, which have separated you from other people. [25] Ye shall therefore put difference between clean beasts and unclean, and between unclean fowls and clean: and ye shall not make your souls abominable by beast, or by fowl, or by any manner of living thing that creepeth on the ground, which I have separated from you as unclean. [26] And ye shall be holy unto me: for I the LORD am holy, and have severed you from other people, that ye should be mine.

---

1 Chronicles 17:21-22

[21] And what one nation in the earth is like thy people Israel, whom God went to redeem to be his own people, to make thee a name of greatness and terribleness, by driving out nations from before thy people, whom thou hast redeemed out of Egypt? [22] For thy people Israel didst thou make thine own people for ever; and thou, LORD, becamest their God.

Amos 3:1-2 (KJV)

1 Hear this word that the LORD hath spoken against you, O children of Israel, against the whole family which I brought up from the land of Egypt, saying,

[2] You only have I known of all the families of the earth: therefore I will punish you for all your iniquities.

Psalm 147:19-20 (KJV)

[19] He sheweth his word unto Jacob, his statutes and his judgments unto Israel.

[20] He hath not dealt so with any nation: and as for his judgments, they have not known them. Praise ye the LORD.

II Esdras 7:10-11

10. And I said, It is so, Lord. Then said he unto me, Even so also is Israel's portion 11. Because for their sakes I made the world: and when Adam transgressed my statutes, then was decreed that now is done.

The descendants of the Israelites / Hebrews did not disappear from the face of the earth. They continue to exist awaiting their fate by the Most High God when prophecy is revealed. Most of the Israelites today do not even know who they are just as the Most High stated in the scriptures. God meant for the Israelites to be captured into many slaveries that they would forget their heritage and nation.

Many saw the miniseries "ROOTS" that displayed how this heritage was stripped from the Israelites. This was accomplished by oppressing them physically, mentally and psychologically to full supremacy to slave owners. Please read ***"The Willie Lynch Letter & The Making of A Slave"*** it will spell out how this process was accomplished during the days of slavery. I must warn you if listening or reading this letter it could bring some very uneasy feelings due to the inhumane treatment of the Israelites during slavery in America and everywhere else the scattering took place.

Chapter 7

THE GATHERING

It had been said that True Israel was gathered in 1948. Is this true or false? Did True Israel get gathered by "The Messiah" or the United Nations or UN? There are many discrepancies concerning the true gathering of the true DNA Israelites of the bible. Remember, True Israel is a nation of people not a religion such as those in Judaism.

The Most High God is very clear and specific in the scriptures concerning the gathering of the true Israelites of the bible. Just as the bible references' the **scattering** of True Israel, it also references the **gathering** of True Israel. Many books of the bible, Old and New Testament mentions the gathering of True Israel without any question to who will be gathered.

The gathering of True Israel is an event that has not taken place as of yet. Here is why the Israeli's or fake Jews that are occupying the land of Israel today are imposters and could not be the True Israelites of the bible.

First, let's lay down some ground work concerning the fake Jews who are in the land today. Most people believe they are the true Jews or Israelites for the following reasons:

1. Because they say they are…without any proof.
2. Because they supposedly follow the Torah, religion or laws of the Most High God
3. Because they supposedly fulfilled the prophecy of being gathered back into the land of Israel in 1948.

Notice the Jews call themselves "Jewish". When the suffix "ish" is used, it usually means (having the characteristic of), not necessarily meaning the real thing. For example, the word "bluish" (A color similar to the color blue but not actually blue). Why don't they call themselves "Israelites"? or the Tribe of Judah? Just because the Jewish people imitate the true Israelites does not make them the nationality of the true people of the book (bible).

In spite of all the evidence that is presented in the bible and world history, it's hard for people to believe that the so-called Jewish people in the land of Israel today are not the true Israelites of the bible. There are several books written by the so-called Jewish people today that debunk their own lineage to being true Israelites of the bible. The books are:

I. "The Invention of the Jewish People" by Shlomo Sand
II. "The Thirteenth Tribe" by Arthur Koestler

Truth be told the Ashkenazi Jews are Khazars descendants from Europe, who has no claims to the land of Israel.

Now, let's debunk some reasons why the people in the land of Israel today could not possibly be the true Israelites of the bible. The prophecies do not fit this group of people and therefore could not be the real people of the scriptures concerning the gathering.

Deuteronomy 30:1-6 addresses specifically the people of Israel concerning their restoration. The key phrases are: "gather thee from all the nations, whither the Lord thy God has scattered thee", "will bring thee into the land which thy fathers possessed". When were the Jewish people (Europeans) in history, forcibly scattered throughout all nations? Since they were not scattered, how can they be the people gathered in the scriptures?

Deuteronomy 30:1-6 (KJV)

1 And it shall come to pass, when all these things are come upon thee, the blessing and the curse, which I have set before thee, and thou shalt call them to mind among all the nations, whither the LORD thy God hath driven thee,

2 And shalt return unto the LORD thy God, and shalt obey his voice according to all that I command thee this day, thou and thy children, with all thine heart, and with all thy soul;

3 That then the LORD thy God will turn thy captivity, and have compassion upon thee, and will return and gather thee from all the nations, whither the LORD thy God hath scattered thee.

4 If any of thine be driven out unto the outmost parts of heaven, from thence will the LORD thy God gather thee, and from thence will he fetch thee:

5 And the LORD thy God will bring thee into the land which thy fathers possessed, and thou shalt possess it; and he will do thee good, and multiply thee above thy fathers.

6 And the LORD thy God will circumcise thine heart, and the heart of thy seed, to love the LORD thy God with all thine heart, and with all thy soul, that thou mayest live.

We now know that the land promised to True Israel would be the land that their fathers possessed. What land did their fathers possessed? Israel. Right before "The Messiah" ascended into the heavens after his crucifixion the disciples asked him a question.

The question was "Lord, wilt thou at this time restore again the kingdom to Israel?"

Acts 1:6 (KJV)

⁶ When they therefore were come together, they asked of him, saying, Lord, wilt thou at this time restore again the kingdom to Israel?

The disciples knew of the prophecies of Israel's restoration; however, the time of restoration was not near at that time according to The Messiah's reply:

Acts 1:7 (KJV)

⁷ And he said unto them, It is not for you to know the times or the seasons, which the Father hath put in his own power.

One of the scriptures used to falsely prove the Jewish people are the people of the book (bible) is Isaiah 66:8-11. This scripture mentions a nation being born in a day and most people believe that this scripture validates or confirms the 1948 gathering of the Jewish people in the land of Israel. However, this decision was mandated by the United Nations not by the Most High God. If we read Isaiah 66:15-16 you'll see there was more to the prophecy. It states there would be flames of fire that will accompany the return of The Most High God (The Messiah). Did this happen yet? Absolutely not!

Isaiah 66:8-11 (KJV)

[8] Who hath heard such a thing? who hath seen such things? Shall the earth be made to bring forth in one day? or shall a nation be born at once? for as soon as Zion travailed, she brought forth her children.

[9] Shall I bring to the birth, and not cause to bring forth? saith the LORD: shall I cause to bring forth, and shut the womb? saith thy God.

[10] Rejoice ye with Jerusalem, and be glad with her, all ye that love her: rejoice for joy with her, all ye that mourn for her:

[11] That ye may suck, and be satisfied with the breasts of her consolations; that ye may milk out, and be delighted with the abundance of her glory.

Isaiah 66:15-16 (KJV)

[15] For, behold, the LORD will come with fire, and with his chariots like a whirlwind, to render his anger with fury, and his rebuke with flames of fire.

[16] For by fire and by his sword will the LORD plead with all flesh: and the slain of the LORD shall be many.

THE DEBUNK

According to the Christian belief system, theologians and some bible scholars believe the May 14, 1948 gathering constitutes the official gathering of True Israel into the land of Israel; however, there is a problem with that theory. If we read Ezekiel 37:1-10, 11-22 there is some points to be made that would debunk that True Israel is not in their land today.

Ezekiel 37:1-10 gives an explanation of True Israel's future restoration that has not been fulfilled as of yet. This point is supported by verses 11-22, stating how this will happen and what this will look like when it happens.

When "True Israel" is gathered it will be the whole house of Israel which includes both Northern and Southern Kingdom, which will be the nation being born in one day (V. 11). This is supported by verses 16-19, stating that Israel and Judah will be one stick, meaning one nation. They will no longer be two nations and living among the heathens (V. 21). Finally, True Israel will be ruled by one king for them all. Is Israel today being ruled by a king? The answer is no.

Let's examine if Israel today fit this description. **One**, they call themselves Jews. Where is Reuben, Asher, Issachar, Levi and the other tribes of Israel? They are not in the land today. This is also supported by Isaiah 11:13, Hosea 1:11 and John 10:14-16. **Two**, why aren't they ruled by a king according to the scriptures?

Ezekiel 37:1-10 (KJV)

1 The hand of the LORD was upon me, and carried me out in the spirit of the LORD, and set me down in the midst of the valley which was full of bones,

² And caused me to pass by them round about: and, behold, there were very many in the open valley; and, lo, they were very dry.

³ And he said unto me, Son of man, can these bones live? And I answered, O Lord GOD, thou knowest.

⁴ Again he said unto me, Prophesy upon these bones, and say unto them, O ye dry bones, hear the word of the LORD.

⁵ Thus saith the Lord GOD unto these bones; Behold, I will cause breath to enter into you, and ye shall live:

⁶ And I will lay sinews upon you, and will bring up flesh upon you, and cover you with skin, and put breath in you, and ye shall live; and ye shall know that I am the LORD.

⁷ So I prophesied as I was commanded: and as I prophesied, there was a noise, and behold a shaking, and the bones came together, bone to his bone.

⁸ And when I beheld, lo, the sinews and the flesh came up upon them, and the skin covered them above: but there was no breath in them.

⁹ Then said he unto me, Prophesy unto the wind, prophesy, son of man, and say to the wind, Thus saith the Lord GOD; Come from the four winds, O breath, and breathe upon these slain, that they may live.

¹⁰ So I prophesied as he commanded me, and the breath came into them, and they lived, and stood up upon their feet, an exceeding great army.

Ezekiel 37:11-22 (KJV)

[11] Then he said unto me, Son of man, these bones are the whole house of Israel: behold, they say, Our bones are dried, and our hope is lost: we are cut off for our parts.

[12] Therefore prophesy and say unto them, Thus saith the Lord GOD; Behold, O my people, I will open your graves, and cause you to come up out of your graves, and bring you into the land of Israel.

[13] And ye shall know that I am the LORD, when I have opened your graves, O my people, and brought you up out of your graves,

[14] And shall put my spirit in you, and ye shall live, and I shall place you in your own land: then shall ye know that I the LORD have spoken it, and performed it, saith the LORD.

[15] The word of the LORD came again unto me, saying,

[16] Moreover, thou son of man, take thee one stick, and write upon it, For Judah, and for the children of Israel his companions: then take another stick, and write upon it, For Joseph, the stick of Ephraim and for all the house of Israel his companions:

[17] And join them one to another into one stick; and they shall become one in thine hand.

[18] And when the children of thy people shall speak unto thee, saying, Wilt thou not shew us what thou meanest by these?

[19] Say unto them, Thus saith the Lord GOD; Behold, I will take the stick of Joseph, which is in the hand of Ephraim, and the tribes of Israel his fellows, and will put them with him, even with the stick of Judah, and make them one stick, and they shall be one in mine hand.

> ²⁰ And the sticks whereon thou writest shall be in thine hand before their eyes.
>
> ²¹ And say unto them, Thus saith the Lord GOD; Behold, I will take the children of Israel from among the heathen, whither they be gone, and will gather them on every side, and bring them into their own land:
>
> ²² And I will make them one nation in the land upon the mountains of Israel; and one king shall be king to them all: and they shall be no more two nations, neither shall they be divided into two kingdoms any more at all.

The bible states when True Israel is gathered it will be done with the Most High God's mighty hand, stretched out arm and with fury poured out. When did this happen with Israel to date?

> **Ezekiel 20:33-34 (KJV)**
>
> ³³ As I live, saith the Lord GOD, surely with a mighty hand, and with a stretched out arm, and with fury poured out, will I rule over you:
>
> ³⁴ And I will bring you out from the people, and will gather you out of the countries wherein ye are scattered, with a mighty hand, and with a stretched out arm, and with fury poured out.

The true Israelites of the bible will need to go through the wilderness again (The 2nd Exodus) just like their fathers during the time of Moses. There the Most High God will plead with them face to face and pass them under the rod and bring them back into the bond of the covenant. The covenants were only made with True Israel and not with any other nation. This did not happen to the so-called Jewish people in the land today? If so, then when? This is an event that did not happen yet.

> **Ezekiel 20:35-39 (KJV)**
>
> 35 And I will bring you into the wilderness of the people, and there will I plead with you face to face.
>
> 36 Like as I pleaded with your fathers in the wilderness of the land of Egypt, so will I plead with you, saith the Lord GOD.
>
> 37 And I will cause you to pass under the rod, and I will bring you into the bond of the covenant:
>
> 38 And I will purge out from among you the rebels, and them that transgress against me: I will bring them forth out of the country where they sojourn, and they shall not enter into the land of Israel: and ye shall know that I am the LORD.
>
> 39 As for you, O house of Israel, thus saith the Lord GOD; Go ye, serve ye every one his idols, and hereafter also, if ye will not hearken unto me: but pollute ye my holy name no more with your gifts, and with your idols.

THE FUTURE EXODUS

The bible mentions a future exodus or gathering that will supersede the exodus that happened during the time of the Egyptian captivity. This gathering or exodus will be so great, it will make the exodus from the time of Moses look like nothing simply because True Israel will be gathered from the four corners of the earth and not just from one location as in Egypt. Again, this is not an event that has happened yet.

Jeremiah 16:14-15 (KJV)

[14] Therefore, behold, the days come, saith the LORD, that it shall no more be said, The LORD liveth, that brought up the children of Israel out of the land of Egypt;

[15] But, The LORD liveth, that brought up the children of Israel from the land of the north, and from all the lands whither he had driven them: and I will bring them again into their land that I gave unto their fathers.

TRUE ISRAEL IN THE LAND

Once True Israel is in the land that is promised to them by the Most High God, which by the way is a covenant made only with the True Israelite nation, not Gentile nations; the picture simply does not fit the characteristics of the land today. The scripture describes, when True Israel is in the land, the wolf and the lamb will lie together peaceably, leopards will lie down with children peaceably and the lion will eat straw like an ox. We know this is not happening in the land of Israel today or anywhere on earth since the Garden of Eden. The question remains: Is True Israel in the land today?

Isaiah 11:6-12 (KJV)

[6] The wolf also shall dwell with the lamb, and the leopard shall lie down with the kid; and the calf and the young lion and the fatling together; and a little child shall lead them.

^{7} And the cow and the bear shall feed; their young ones shall lie down together: and the lion shall eat straw like the ox.

^{8} And the sucking child shall play on the hole of the asp, and the weaned child shall put his hand on the cockatrice' den.

^{9} They shall not hurt nor destroy in all my holy mountain: for the earth shall be full of the knowledge of the LORD, as the waters cover the sea.

^{10} And in that day there shall be a root of Jesse, which shall stand for an ensign of the people; to it shall the Gentiles seek: and his rest shall be glorious.

^{11} And it shall come to pass in that day, that the Lord shall set his hand again the second time to recover the remnant of his people, which shall be left, from Assyria, and from Egypt, and from Pathros, and from Cush, and from Elam, and from Shinar, and from Hamath, and from the islands of the sea.

^{12} And he shall set up an ensign for the nations, and shall assemble the outcasts of Israel, and gather together the dispersed of Judah from the four corners of the earth.

Isaiah 65:25 (KJV)

^{25} The wolf and the lamb shall feed together, and the lion shall eat straw like the bullock: and dust shall be the serpent's meat. They shall not hurt nor destroy in all my holy mountain, saith the LORD.

Hosea 2:18 (KJV)

[18] And in that day will I make a covenant for them with the beasts of the field and with the fowls of heaven, and with the creeping things of the ground: and I will break the bow and the sword and the battle out of the earth, and will make them to lie down safely.

When True Israel is in the land, the land will produce as if it was like the Garden of Eden. Today this land is not producing what the Most High God said that it would, because all of True Israel is not in the land today.

Ezekiel 36:35 (KJV)

[35] And they shall say, This land that was desolate is become like the garden of Eden; and the waste and desolate and ruined cities are become fenced, and are inhabited.

Another trait to know if True Israel is in the land today is by the governing of the land. The land will be governed by the Laws, Statutes and Commandments of the Most High God. These laws are the same laws that the Christian institutions of today say are done away or don't matter anymore. Clearly the same laws of the scriptures will be followed in the land of Israel at the Messiah's return and when True Israel is in the land. No one will be in the Kingdom without following these laws period.

There is no way possible the so-called Jewish people in the land today are following the laws of the scriptures which make it impossible for them to be the people of the bible. Currently you have war after war in this region of the world and if True Israel was in the land today there should be no more war in that land, only peace. Today, that region of the world is war city and that debunks these people in the land are God's chosen people.

THE GATHERING

Although there are many more scriptures that can be used to debunk the 1948 gathering of the Isracli's state today, these are sufficient. Now, we will explore more of the gathering of True Israel and what this will look like with more biblical support that True Israel is not in their land today. They have not been gathered as of yet.

In several books of the bible this gathering is mentioned several times that it could hardly be missed. Let's explore some of these passages from the different books of the bible that mentions the gathering.

The book of Isaiah...

In the book of Isaiah it mentions a day of completion, meaning a remnant of True Israel will be gathered and return back to the land of Israel. Isaiah 10:20-23 mentions how large True Israel has become by comparing it to the sand of the sea but only a remnant will return. Please also read (Romans 9:27).

Isaiah 10:20-23 (KJV)

20 And it shall come to pass in that day, that the remnant of Israel, and such as are escaped of the house of Jacob, shall no more again stay upon him that smote them; but shall stay upon the LORD, the Holy One of Israel, in truth.

21 The remnant shall return, even the remnant of Jacob, unto the mighty God.

22 For though thy people Israel be as the sand of the sea, yet a remnant of them shall return: the consumption decreed shall overflow with righteousness.

23 For the Lord GOD of hosts shall make consumption, even determined, in the midst of all the land.

Isaiah 11:9-13 is more specific in terms of where True Israel will be gathered from. It is clear that True Israel will be gathered from the four corners of the earth. The verse even mentions it would be the second time he would gather True Israel. The first time was from the land of Egypt in the days of Moses.

True Israel has been scattered all over the world throughout its existence (Transatlantic Slave Trade) and today they are in Assyria, Egypt, Pathros, Cush, Elam, Shinar, Hamath, the United States and from the island of the sea. This could not apply to the converts (Fake Jews) in the land of Israel today because they were never scattered all over the world by force. True Israel have not been gathered as of yet.

This scripture also expounds on the fact that Judah (Southern Kingdom) and Ephraim (Northern Kingdom) will not envy each other during this time and become one stick or one nation as mentioned earlier in this chapter. Are all the tribes of Israel in the land today? No, the scripture says "IN THAT DAY". This would be the same day wolves will lie with the lamb and leopards will lie with children. We have not seen this take place on the planet anywhere as of this day.

Isaiah 11:9-13 (KJV)

[9] They shall not hurt nor destroy in all my holy mountain: for the earth shall be full of the knowledge of the LORD, as the waters cover the sea.

[10] And in that day there shall be a root of Jesse, which shall stand for an ensign of the people; to it shall the Gentiles seek: and his rest shall be glorious.

[11] And it shall come to pass in that day, that the Lord shall set his hand again the second time to recover the remnant of his people, which shall be left, from Assyria, and from Egypt, and from Pathros, and from Cush, and from Elam, and from Shinar, and from Hamath, and from the islands of the sea.

[12] And he shall set up an ensign for the nations, and shall assemble the outcasts of Israel, and gather together the dispersed of Judah from the four corners of the earth.

[13] The envy also of Ephraim shall depart, and the adversaries of Judah shall be cut off: Ephraim shall not envy Judah, and Judah shall not vex Ephraim.

The book of Psalm…

Whenever the scripture mentions the gathering of True Israel, it is always referencing being gathered from the heathen nations back into Jerusalem. This is no difference in the book of Psalms. Psalms 102, a prayer of the afflicted is noted declaring the name of The Most High God when the people are gathered together in Jerusalem.

Psalms 106:47 records this same gathering from the heathen nations concerning the children of Israel. This is a consistent theme throughout the bible. Why? Because the Most High God will always remember his promise he gave to Abraham as stated in Psalm 105:42-43. We know this because the Most High God is addressing Abraham's seed, his chosen people (V6). This is confirmed in verses 8-19. However, the condition is obedience (following his laws, statutes and commandments) is the key.

Psalms 107:2-3 also mentions the gathering from the hands and lands of True Israel's enemies. This gathering is from the East, West, North and South of the land of Israel (Jerusalem). In every instance of the gathering of True Israel it is always from the four corners of the earth. This cannot be by chance that the Most High God is making it clear that True Israel is a nation in exile and will always have the right to the land of Israel by the promise of the Most High God Himself.

Psalm 102:21-22 (KJV)

[21] To declare the name of the LORD in Zion, and his praise in Jerusalem;

[22] When the people are gathered together, and the kingdoms, to serve the LORD.

Psalm 106:47 (KJV)

47 Save us, O LORD our God, and gather us from among the heathen, to give thanks unto thy holy name, and to triumph in thy praise.

Psalm 105:42-43 (KJV)

42 For he remembered his holy promise, and Abraham his servant.

43 And he brought forth his people with joy, and his chosen with gladness:

Psalm 105:6 (KJV)

6 O ye seed of Abraham his servant, ye children of Jacob his chosen.

Psalm 105:8-19 (KJV)

8 He hath remembered his covenant for ever, the word which he commanded to a thousand generations.

9 Which covenant he made with Abraham, and his oath unto Isaac;

10 And confirmed the same unto Jacob for a law, and to Israel for an everlasting covenant:

11 Saying, Unto thee will I give the land of Canaan, the lot of your inheritance:

¹² When they were but a few men in number; yea, very few, and strangers in it.

¹³ When they went from one nation to another, from one kingdom to another people;

¹⁴ He suffered no man to do them wrong: yea, he reproved kings for their sakes;

¹⁵ Saying, Touch not mine anointed, and do my prophets no harm.

¹⁶ Moreover he called for a famine upon the land: he brake the whole staff of bread.

¹⁷ He sent a man before them, even Joseph, who was sold for a servant:

¹⁸ Whose feet they hurt with fetters: he was laid in iron:

¹⁹ Until the time that his word came: the word of the LORD tried him.

The book of Jeremiah...

The book of Jeremiah is full of scriptures noting the future gathering of True Israel. Jeremiah frequently makes mention of the separation of Israel and Judah (Northern and Southern Kingdom). He realizes these two entities will become one in the future again. He states that Israel was more treacherous than Judah, but that they both angered the Most High God by offering incense unto Baal.

Jeremiah 3:11 (KJV)

[11] And the LORD said unto me, The backsliding Israel hath justified herself more than treacherous Judah.

Jeremiah 11:17 (KJV)

[17] For the LORD of hosts, that planted thee, hath pronounced evil against thee, for the evil of the house of Israel and of the house of Judah, which they have done against themselves to provoke me to anger in offering incense unto Baal.

Although The Most High God became angry with both Israel and Judah for their transgressions, he also said he would gather them both back into their own land that he gave their fathers. This will only happen **in those days**, meaning in the future. Israel and Judah have not become one in their own land as of yet.

Jeremiah 30:3 (KJV)

[3] For, lo, the days come, saith the LORD, that I will bring again the captivity of my people Israel and Judah, saith the LORD: and I will cause them to return to the land that I gave to their fathers, and they shall possess it.

Jeremiah 50:4 (KJV)

[4] In those days, and in that time, saith the LORD, the children of Israel shall come, they and the children of Judah together, going and weeping: they shall go, and seek the LORD their God

> **Jeremiah 23:3 (KJV)**
>
> [3] And I will gather the remnant of my flock out of all countries whither I have driven them, and will bring them again to their folds; and they shall be fruitful and increase.

The scriptures states he will bring them (Israel & Judah) from the North Country and from the coast of the earth. The only people scattered to be gathered is the true nation of Israel (both sticks).

> **Jeremiah 31:8-11 (KJV)**
>
> [8] Behold, I will bring them from the north country, and gather them from the coasts of the earth, and with them the blind and the lame, the woman with child and her that travaileth with child together: a great company shall return thither.
>
> [9] They shall come with weeping, and with supplications will I lead them: I will cause them to walk by the rivers of waters in a straight way, wherein they shall not stumble: for I am a father to Israel, and Ephraim is my firstborn.
>
> [10] Hear the word of the LORD, O ye nations, and declare it in the isles afar off, and say, He that scattered Israel will gather him, and keep him, as a shepherd doth his flock.
>
> [11] For the LORD hath redeemed Jacob, and ransomed him from the hand of him that was stronger than he.

The Most High God is adamant about his plans to restore the nation of Israel back into their land. He expresses that he will do this from his whole heart and soul. He will bring Israel back into his habitation in the future without question.

Jeremiah 32:41 (KJV)

⁴¹ Yea, I will rejoice over them to do them good, and I will plant them in this land assuredly with my whole heart and with my whole soul.

In today's biblical teachings, it is taught Israel doesn't matter anymore, but not according to Jeremiah 31:35-37. Israel will only cease if the ordinances of the sun, moon and stars stop giving light and the heavens, earth beneath can be measured and searched. We know today that the sun, moon and stars are still giving light, so True Israel did not cease as a nation but only scattered and punished due to their transgressions (breaking the laws of God) (Daniel 9:11).

Jeremiah 31:35-37 (KJV)

³⁵ Thus saith the LORD, which giveth the sun for a light by day, and the ordinances of the moon and of the stars for a light by night, which divideth the sea when the waves thereof roar; The LORD of hosts is his name:

³⁶ If those ordinances depart from before me, saith the LORD, then the seed of Israel also shall cease from being a nation before me for ever.

³⁷ Thus saith the LORD; If heaven above can be measured, and the foundations of the earth searched out beneath, I will also cast off all the seed of Israel for all that they have done, saith the LORD.

True Israel will be gathered from all nations of the earth according to Jeremiah. The covenant made with Israel fathers still stand and that promise will be kept no matter what. When the God of Abraham, Isaac and Jacob states that he will make a new covenant with Israel and Jacob he means it. He stated it in the Old Testament and the New Testament.

Jeremiah 31:31-32 (KJV)

[31] Behold, the days come, saith the LORD, that I will make a new covenant with the house of Israel, and with the house of Judah:

[32] Not according to the covenant that I made with their fathers in the day that I took them by the hand to bring them out of the land of Egypt; which my covenant they brake, although I was an husband unto them, saith the LORD:

Hebrews 8:8 (KJV)

[8] For finding fault with them, he saith, Behold, the days come, saith the Lord, when I will make a new covenant with the house of Israel and with the house of Judah

---

Jeremiah 50:4-5 (KJV)

[4] In those days, and in that time, saith the LORD, the children of Israel shall come, they and the children of Judah together, going and weeping: they shall go, and seek the LORD their God.

[5] They shall ask the way to Zion with their faces thitherward, saying, Come, and let us join ourselves to the LORD in a perpetual covenant that shall not be forgotten.

When True Israel is gathered, they will always have a king over them, in other words True Israel will always be a monarchy, not as it is today. Again, True Israel have not been gathered as of yet because they are still scattered in the four corners of the earth.

Jeremiah 33:17 (KJV)

[17] For thus saith the LORD; David shall never want a man to sit upon the throne of the house of Israel;

The book of Ezekiel...

In the book of Ezekiel there are some important points concerning the gathering of True Israel. Ezekiel makes a clear distinction who will be gathered and it only pertains to True Israel not other nations.

Ezekiel 11:17 (KJV)

[17] Therefore say, Thus saith the Lord GOD; I will even gather you from the people, and assemble you out of the countries where ye have been scattered, and I will give you the land of Israel.

There is always a controversy as to whether The Most High God separates nations or peoples. The doctrine of inclusiveness does not appear to be a biblical belief system. However, Ezekiel makes it very clear that True Israel is the target in the gathering and not other nations. He clearly writes about the separation of True Israel and the heathen nations.

Ezekiel 39:21-29 (KJV)

[21] And I will set my glory among the heathen, and all the heathen shall see my judgment that I have executed, and my hand that I have laid upon them.

[22] So the house of Israel shall know that I am the LORD their God from that day and forward.

[23] And the heathen shall know that the house of Israel went into captivity for their iniquity: because they trespassed against me, therefore hid I my face from them, and gave them into the hand of their enemies: so fell they all by the sword.

[24] According to their uncleanness and according to their transgressions have I done unto them, and hid my face from them.

[25] Therefore thus saith the Lord GOD; Now will I bring again the captivity of Jacob, and have mercy upon the whole house of Israel, and will be jealous for my holy name;

[26] After that they have borne their shame, and all their trespasses whereby they have trespassed against me, when they dwelt safely in their land, and none made them afraid.

[27] When I have brought them again from the people, and gathered them out of their enemies' lands, and am sanctified in them in the sight of many nations;

[28] Then shall they know that I am the LORD their God, which caused them to be led into captivity among the heathen: but I have gathered them unto their own land, and have left none of them any more there.

[29] Neither will I hide my face any more from them: for I have poured out my spirit upon the house of Israel, saith the Lord GOD.

In the places where True Israel have been scattered was never meant to be a permanent home. The Most High God's covenant promise must be fulfilled to the true nation of Israel or he would not have told the truth. The Most High God is not a liar and everything he promises must come to past. This is true concerning his gathering of True Israel as well.

Ezekiel 20:34-42 expresses the same sentiments just as the prophet Jeremiah did about The Most High God's gathering of True Israel from all of the countries in which they were scattered. The passage goes on to say that he will bring them into the wilderness and plead with them face to face just as he did when they were leaving Egypt. Yes, this will happen again. This is why it's important for True Israel to know their history because history always repeats itself. There is nothing new under the sun.

Ezekiel 16:60 (KJV)

[60] Nevertheless I will remember my covenant with thee in the days of thy youth, and I will establish unto thee an everlasting covenant.

Ezekiel 20:34-42 (KJV)

[34] And I will bring you out from the people, and will gather you out of the countries wherein ye are scattered, with a mighty hand, and with a stretched out arm, and with fury poured out.

[35] And I will bring you into the wilderness of the people, and there will I plead with you face to face.

[36] Like as I pleaded with your fathers in the wilderness of the land of Egypt, so will I plead with you, saith the Lord GOD.

[37] And I will cause you to pass under the rod, and I will bring you into the bond of the covenant:

[38] And I will purge out from among you the rebels, and them that transgress against me: I will bring them forth out of the country

where they sojourn, and they shall not enter into the land of Israel: and ye shall know that I am the LORD.

³⁹ As for you, O house of Israel, thus saith the Lord GOD; Go ye, serve ye every one his idols, and hereafter also, if ye will not hearken unto me: but pollute ye my holy name no more with your gifts, and with your idols.

⁴⁰ For in mine holy mountain, in the mountain of the height of Israel, saith the Lord GOD, there shall all the house of Israel, all of them in the land, serve me: there will I accept them, and there will I require your offerings, and the firstfruits of your oblations, with all your holy things.

⁴¹ I will accept you with your sweet savour, when I bring you out from the people, and gather you out of the countries wherein ye have been scattered; and I will be sanctified in you before the heathen.

⁴² And ye shall know that I am the LORD, when I shall bring you into the land of Israel, into the country for the which I lifted up mine hand to give it to your fathers.

Ecclesiastes 1:9 (KJV)

⁹ The thing that hath been, it is that which shall be; and that which is done is that which shall be done: and there is no new thing under the sun.

THE OTHER BOOKS ON THE GATHERING

The bible is full of information concerning the gathering of True Israel and due to the length of this subject matter a graph is created for a quick reference to support that True Israel is the nation The Most High God will gather because it's the only nation on earth that has been forcibly scattered.

The Scripture	Note
Daniel 7: 13-14	The gathered will be the kingdom of Israel and will be separate from all nations with other nations serving Israel.
Daniel 12:1	The Archangel Michael is standing and leading True Israel to deliverance. No other nation is being lead in this way.
Malachi 3:6	Here, The Most High God remembers the sons of Jacob, which is True Israel.
Malachi 3:17-18	In the last days The Most High God states True Israel shall be his and spare them that serve him.
Zechariah 2:12	The Most High God will inherit and choose Judah (True Israel) in the holy land of Jerusalem again.

Zechariah 8:7-8	The Most High God will save his chosen people (Israel) from the countries in where they were scattered (from the east and west of countries). He will deliver and bring them back to their own land of Jerusalem. This is not referring to other nations, only True Israel.
Zechariah 8:13	The gathering will include both Judah (southern kingdom) and Israel (northern kingdom).
Zechariah 10:6	The Most High God will have mercy upon True Israel and place them back into their own land as if he had never cast them off.
Haggai 2:5	Haggai confirms the anointed people are those who came out of Egypt to receive the covenant and therefore are those that has the promise of being gathered back to their own land which are Israelites.
Zephaniah 3:17-20	Zephaniah states The Most High God will gather his people again just as he did when his chosen people came out of Egypt. Zephaniah states The Most High will undo his affliction on True Israel and save them by gathering them from places he had scattered them. He will turn back True Israel's captivity right before their very eyes.

Habakkuk 3:13,18	Habakkuk uses the word "salvation" and God's anointed when speaking of True Israel. **Salvation** basic meaning is "deliverance". In this context, meaning deliverance from an enemy(s) as in (II Samuel 3:18, Psalm 44:7 and Luke 1:68-71). The Most High God will gather True Israel from their enemies which are other nations they have been scattered.
Nahum 2:2	The term "turned away" in this scripture can be translated "gathered or restore". Here, The Most High God is restoring Israel from the plunderers of Nineveh. In other words, The Most High God always defends and aids his chosen people when the time comes.
Micah 2:12	Micah plainly states The Most High God will gather the remnant of True Israel (The Israelites).
Amos 9:11-15	Amos makes it clear that after the judgment and destruction of the land of Edom that True Israel will take over and rebuild the waste cities. This land was promised to Abraham anyway. True Israel will be planted in their land and never be pulled out again in the future.

Joel 3:1-2	Joel makes a point to state in those days (future), The Most High God will gather (True Israel) from their captivity. But he will also gather other nations and plead with them on behalf of True Israel, just as he did with Pharaoh in the days of Moses. The Most High God's heritage and land (Jerusalem) is still unchanged in the future prophesies.
Joel 3:16-17	Joel states The Most High God will be the hope of his people and their strength. This is future because the heavens and earth has not been shaken yet.
Hosea 1:10-11	Hosea is claiming the children of Israel will be numerous and will yet be The Most High God's people and shall be called the sons of the living God. Verse 11 states True Israel will be gathered together. This is all future events. Paul in the book of Romans 9:25-27 quoted from Hosea 1:10. He was addressing and talking about Israelites.
Hosea 8:10, 14:5	Hosea mentions that The Most High God will be as the dew unto True Israel and will gather them from where they are today which is all over the world.

The New Testament On The Gathering

The Scripture	Note
Matthew 1:21	True Israel is always a focus in the scriptures and in the new Testament there is no difference. This scripture directly states why Messiah needed to come. It states the Messiah shall save **his people**. Who are The Most High God's people? Israelites.
Matthew 2:6	This scripture makes known the fact that a governor will come out of Juda and rule the people of Israel. In the scripture it says **my people.** Who are the people? Israelites.
Matthew 23:37	Here is the Messiah feeling sorry for Jerusalem (his people) who did not accept him. In spite of the rejection of his people he still had the desire to gather them (True Israel). The Messiah is speaking of a gathering like a hen gathers her chicks. Please read, Psalm 91:4, Psalm 17:8, Psalm 57:1, Psalm 36:7, Psalm 61:4, Psalm 63:7. Even the missing book from the Apocrypha uses the analogy the hen gathering her chickens (II Esdras 1:30). True Israel will be under the shadow of The Most High God's wings.

The Scripture	Note
Matthew 24:29-31	Here is the Messiah warning when he will return to gather his elect from the four winds of the earth, from one end of heaven to the other. Remember, the only people who were scattered to the four winds or the corners of the earth were the Israelites (True Israel) by force. Please read Isaiah 27:12-13, Zechariah 2:6, Deuteronomy 28:64, Mark 13:27, Isaiah 11:12, Deuteronomy 32:26, Ezekiel 20:23 and Deuteronomy 30:4
John 11:50-52	The traditional belief of these verses is that this gathering would be for Gentiles and True Israel, however these verses states that the Messiah would die for that nation. What nation? Judah and those that were scattered abroad was the house of Israel (Northern Kingdom), which were scattered at that time.
Acts 1:6-7	The disciples ask The Messiah a question. "Wilt thou at this time restore again the Kingdom to Israel?" The Messiah answered and said "It is not for you to know the times or the season". In other words it will happen in the future. The key word in this verse is "RESTORE" which means True Israel will need to be gathered back into their land in

	the coming future. There is no mention of any other nation in these passages.
II Thessalonians 2:1-17	Paul mentions the gathering here that pertains to the **"brethren"** (kinsmen of the womb) being gathered by The Messiah. This in context is speaking of the second coming of The Messiah. Please read the whole chapter.

In conclusion True Israel is the people who were scattered by The Most High God and the people that he will gather upon the coming of The Messiah. Surely, other nations have their prophetic journey in all of this but True Israel is the focus of this book. We must understand the only people on the planet of earth that was scattered are the same people that will be gathered back into their own land. They are the so called Negroes or African Americans which are truly the Israelites of the bible.

True Israel has been cut off as a nation (Psalm 83), but is waking up by the thousands during these last days. True Israel will always be a separate entity on the planet because the scriptures say so not this author.

In our religious institutions or churches, the topic of the gathering of True Israel is rarely taught. We have been conditioned to believe the narrative that has been fed to us for generations without researching, studying or questioning those who suppose to lead us into righteousness but instead lead us into unrighteousness (sin). Instead, we have become accustomed to believing in the lie and therefore are sent a strong delusion when we do. We must believe the truth (II Thessalonians 2:10-12).

The gathering of True Israel is a fact of the bible and the focus is on Israel not the other nations for the following reasons.

1. No other nation in the world have been forcibly scattered per world history or in the bible. The only nation that went into captivity as the bible describes are the so-called African Americans who truly are the biblical Israelites.

2. The scriptures support The Most High God will have mercy on True Israel (Jacob) and set them in their own land and the other nations or strangers will cleave unto True Israel and be servants and handmaids (Isaiah 14:1-7).

3. The scripture supports the Gentile nations will recognize the seed of True Israel and see that they are blessed (Isaiah 61:9).

4. The promise land and / or the gates of heaven has always been divided among the twelve tribes of Israel only not other nations. **(Joshua 13:8 – 17:18)** (Ezekiel 48:31) (Revelations 21:21).

5. The gathering and the kingdom have much in common. The people have the same nationality.

6. All the prophetic scriptures dealing with the gathering pertains to True Israel (Israelites), not other nations.

Chapter 8
THE TERM "ISRAEL"

The term **"Israel"** appears in the New Testament bible 75 times (KJV) and all 75 times it points towards the natural descendants of Abraham, Isaac and Jacob or the land of Israel. This term is never remotely speaking of another people besides the natural Israelites. The popular teaching in today's religious circles is that the church replaced the chosen people of Israel. This is called "Replacement Theology" and as you can see from the chart in this chapter the term "Israel" means "Israel" not the church. Those who believe in "Replacement Theology" believe the church has taken the place of the "True Israelites" of the bible. The two entities are never mistaken for each other in the scriptures.

The Phrase "Spiritual Israel" is another popular phrase to support that anyone who accepts the Messiah as their Lord and personal savior becomes a "Spiritual Israelite". There is not one scripture denoting one can become a "Spiritual Israelite" other than those who derive from the bloodline of Abraham, Isaac and Jacob. The phrase 'Spiritual Israel" does not even appear in the bible anywhere. The Most High God deals with natural ethnicity and nations not spiritual ones.

There are a few phrases in the bible that requires more attention or explanation concerning Israel and the church. Although Israel is part of the body of the Messiah, Israel is still a separate entity with all the promises of the Most High God belonging to Israel not the church. Phrases like **"Israel of God"** in the book Galatians can be confusing to those who believe this phrase was speaking of the church. But more explanation will be given later.

The Term "Israel" (The People)	
1. Matthew 2:6 – My People Israel	36. Acts 7:37 – Children of Israel
2. Matthew 10:6 – House of Israel	37. Acts 7:42 – House of Israel
3. Matthew 15:24 – House of Israel	38. Acts 9:15 – Children of Israel
4. Matthew 15:31 – God of Israel	39. Acts 10:36 – Children of Israel
5. Matthew 19:28 – 12 Tribes of Israel	40. Acts 13:16 – Men of Israel
6. Matthew 27:9 – Children of Israel	41. Acts 13:17 – People of Israel
7. Matthew 27:42 – King of Israel	42. Acts 13:23 – Raised unto Israel
8. Mark 12:29 – Hear O' Israel	43. Acts 13:24 – People of Israel
9. Mark 15:32 – King of Israel	44. Acts 21:28 – Men of Israel
10. Luke 1:16 – Children of Israel	45. Acts 28:20 – Hope of Israel
11. Luke 1:54 – His Servant Israel	46. Romans 9:6 – Not All Israel
12. Luke 1:68 – God of Israel	47. Romans 9:6 – Which are of Israel
13. Luke 1:80 – Shewing unto Israel	48. Romans 9:27 – Concerning Israel
14. Luke 2:25 – Consolation of Israel	49. Romans 9:27 – Children of Israel
15. Luke 2:32 – Thy people Israel	50. Romans 9:31 – But Israel
16. Luke 2:34 – Many of Israel	51. Romans 10:1 – God for Israel
17. Luke 4:27 – Lepers in Israel	52. Romans 10:19 – Did not Israel
18. Luke 7:9 – Not one in Israel (Faith)	53. Romans 10:21 – But to Israel
19. Luke 23:30 – 12 Tribes of Israel	54. Romans 11:2 – God against Israel
20. Luke 24:21 – Redeemed Israel	55. Romans 11:7 – Israel hath not obtained
21. John 1:31 – Manifest to Israel	56. Romans 11:25 – Happened to Israel
22. John 1:49 – King of Israel	57. Romans 11:26 – So all Israel
23. John 3:10 – Master of Israel	58. I Corinthians 10:18 – Behold Israel

24. John 12:13 – King of Israel	59. II Corinthians 3:7 – Children of Israel
25. Acts 1:6 – Kingdom of Israel	60. II Corinthians 3:13 – Children of Israel
26. Acts 2:22 – Men of Israel	61. Galatians 6:16 – Israel of God
27. Acts 2:36 – House of Israel	62. Ephesians 2:12 – Common Israel
28. Acts 3:12 – Men of Israel	63. Philippians 3:5 – Stock of Israel
29. Acts 4:8 – Elders of Israel	64. Hebrews 8:8 – House of Israel
30. Acts 4:10 – People of Israel	65. Hebrews 8:10 – House of Israel
31. Acts 4:27 – People of Israel	66. Hebrews 11:22 – Children of Israel
32. Acts 5:21 – Children of Israel	67. Revelation 2:14 – Children of Israel
33. Acts 5:31 – Repentance to Israel	68. Revelation 7:4 – Children of Israel
34. Acts 5:35 – Men of Israel	69. Revelation 21:12 – Children of Israel
35. Acts 7:23 – Children of Israel	

The Term "Israel" (The Land)

1. Matthew 2:20 – Land of Israel	4. Matthew 9:33 – Land of Israel
2. Matthew 2:21 – Land of Israel	5. Matthew 10:23 – Cities of Israel
3. Matthew 8:10 – Not In Israel / People	6. Luke 4:25 – Were in Israel

The Term "Israelite (s)" (The People)

1. Romans 9:4 – Who are Israelites	2. II Corinthians 11:22 – Are they Israelites
3. John 1:47 – An Israelite indeed	4. Roman 11:1 – For I also Am an Israelite

The term "Israel" is defined by the Strong's Concordance #2474 as Israel of Hebrew origin, the adopted name of Jacob, including his descendants. Other sources that define the term "Israel" is:

NAS Exhaustive Concordance:
- The name of Jewish people and their land

Thayer's Greek Lexicon:
- A name given to the patriarch Jacob (Genesis 35:10)
- The family or descendants of Israel, the race of Israel (Genesis 32:28)
- Israelites by natural birth (I Corinthians 10:18)

The term "Israelite" is defined by the Strong's Concordance #2475 as Israelite, descendant of Israel. Again, this term Israel and or Israelite is not connected to any other body of people or the church but only to the descendants of Abraham, Isaac and Jacob (True Israel).

The bible appears to break up man into three categories: Israelites (Jews), Greeks (Gentiles) and The Church).

---

1 Corinthians 10:31-33 (KJV)

[31] Whether therefore ye eat, or drink, or whatsoever ye do, do all to the glory of God.

[32] Give none offence, neither to the Jews, nor to the Gentiles, nor to the church of God:

[33] Even as I please all men in all things, not seeking mine own profit, but the profit of many, that they may be saved.

Before Abraham, The Most High God dealt with man as a whole, however after Abraham was chosen by The Most High God the game had changed. A promise to a particular people was developing. A people that will be a blessing to all nations and these people were the Hebrews (specifically, Hebrew Israelites, once Isaac and Jacob were approached by the Most High God).

Genesis 12:1-3 (KJV)

12 Now the LORD had said unto Abram, Get thee out of thy country, and from thy kindred, and from thy father's house, unto a land that I will shew thee:

^{2} And I will make of thee a great nation, and I will bless thee, and make thy name great; and thou shalt be a blessing:

^{3} And I will bless them that bless thee, and curse him that curseth thee: and in thee shall all families of the earth be blessed.

Genesis 14:13 (KJV)

^{13} And there came one that had escaped, and told Abram the Hebrew; for he dwelt in the plain of Mamre the Amorite, brother of Eshcol, and brother of Aner: and these were confederate with Abram.

Genesis 17:5 (KJV)

^{5} Neither shall thy name any more be called Abram, but thy name shall be Abraham; for a father of many nations have I made thee.

At this point the second entity of The Most High God was being introduced (The chosen people). This entity was known to be the Israelites of today. The entity of Gentiles and the Israelites continued until Paul introduced the church which is the third entity. These three entities still exist today and each entity has its own function.

The term "Israel" is a technical term and is always used in the scriptures for the physical descendants of Jacob (Israel). Sometimes "Israel" could mean both the northern tribe and the southern tribe after the nation was split into two kingdoms or the entire nation.

Just a note to say the third entity (The Church) was a secret until Paul. The prophets never spoke about it. The twelve disciples never knew of it until Paul revealed it and The Messiah never taught it. The body of the Messiah or Christ was not mentioned in any letters until Paul. This was after The Messiah had ascended into the heavens. (Ephesians 2:11-22; 3:3-9, Colossians 1:26-27, Romans 16:25-27).

Chapter 9
GALATIANS 6:16

The scripture Galatians 6:16 have caused a bit of controversy as to its meaning when it states the phrase "Israel of God". Some believe it's speaking of the church and some believe it's speaking of natural Israel, Israelites or God's chosen people within the church. Let's examine this scripture and get to the bottom of the issue. It reads:

"And as many as walk according to this rule, peace be on them, and mercy, and upon the **Israel of God.** "(Galatians 6:16) **(King James Version).**

Why would the word "Israel" mean anything different in this scripture other than ethic or natural Israel as it does in all the other 74 places it appears in the New Testament? Now, all of a sudden in this scripture it means the modern church. Paul, the writer of Galatians was very consistent in his writings. He knew the Old Testament; he was an Israelite himself (Romans 11:1) and he never confused the church with ethic Israel within the church.

Clearly Galatians 6:16 is addressing two groups of people by the word "THEM" and "ISRAEL OF GOD". Who is "THEM and who is the "ISRAEL OF GOD"?
The conjunction "and" in this verse in the English language means "Together with or along with, as well as, added to etc.".

According to Strong's #G2532 the word "AND" in the Greek language translate back to the word "Kai" which means and, also, even, both, then, so, & likewise.

καί kaí, kahee; apparently, a primary particle, having a copulative and sometimes also a cumulative force; and, also, even, so then, too, etc.; often used in connection (or composition) with other particles or small words:—and, also, both, but, even, for, if, or, so, that, then, therefore, when, yet. (Strong's Definition: G2532, Pg. 1637).

The dispensational view on this matter makes perfect sense that the word "THEM" is referring to Gentile believers and the phrase "ISRAEL OF GOD" is referring to the remnant of ethic Israel believers. Paul has always singled out believing Israelites or True Israel in his writings. Please see chart (Paul Recognizing Israel as a Separate Entity).

If Galatians 6:16 is read in context, one could proclaim the term 'Israel of God" is about physical Israel not the church. Read the previous verse (Galatians 6:15), it becomes apparently clear these are two groups which became the new creature (The church). The circumcision is the Jews (Israelites) and the uncircumcision is the Gentiles which equals the church.

Galatians 6:15 (KJV)

[15] For in Christ Jesus neither circumcision availeth any thing, nor uncircumcision, but a new creature.

Paul Recognizing Israel As A Separate Entity

Romans 2:28-29	[28] For he is not a Jew, which is one outwardly; neither is that circumcision, which is outward in the flesh: [29] But he is a Jew, which is one inwardly; and circumcision is that of the heart, in the spirit, and not in the letter; whose praise is not of men, but of God.
Romans 9:6	[6] Not as though the word of God hath taken none effect. For they are not all Israel, which are of Israel:
Romans 11:1	[1] I say then, Hath God cast away his people? God forbid. For I also am an Israelite, of the seed of Abraham, of the tribe of Benjamin.
Romans 11:5	[5] Even so then at this present time also there is a remnant according to the election of grace.
I Corinthians 10:18	[18] Behold Israel after the flesh: are not they which eat of the sacrifices partakers of the altar?
Galatians 2:7-8	[7] But contrariwise, when they saw that the gospel of the uncircumcision was committed unto me, as the gospel of the

	circumcision was unto Peter;
	[8] (For he that wrought effectually in Peter to the apostleship of the circumcision, the same was mighty in me toward the Gentiles:)
Galatians 6:15	[15] For in Christ Jesus neither circumcision availeth any thing, nor uncircumcision, but a new creature.

Special Note: Romans 9:6 is pointing towards two type of Israelites or Jews (believing and unbelieving). If one read from Romans 9:4 -6 you'll notice Paul is addressing Israelites not another nation.

The Most High God will always have a remnant of his chosen people according to the election of grace (Romans 11:5). So, it is not farfetched to think that Galatians 6:16 makes a distinction between two groups of people (Gentiles and Israel), both part of the church, but separate.

Please review Galatians 6:16 chart and notice many bible versions of this verse uses the conjunction "AND & EVEN". The most popular use is "AND" which is the continuative viewpoint. The rarest is the use of the word "EVEN" which is the Appositional viewpoint. The "AND" viewpoint denotes there are two groups and the "EVEN viewpoint supports both groups are one in the same. The rarest viewpoint should not be used when the continuative viewpoint makes sense.

Notice the **New American Standard Bible** version of Galatians 6:16. It uses the preposition "UPON" twice, noting and separating two groups of people (Gentiles and Israelites).

Galatians 6:16

King James Version	[16] And as many as walk according to this rule, peace be on them, and mercy, **and** upon the Israel of God.
New American Standard Bible	[16] And those who will walk by this rule, peace and mercy *be* **upon them**, **and upon** the Israel of God.
New King James Version	And as many as walk according to the rule, peace and mercy be upon them, **and** upon the Israel of God.
The New English Bible	Whoever they are who take this principle for their guide, peace and mercy be upon them, **and** upon the Israel of God!
New Century Version	Peace and mercy to those who follow this rule **and** to all of God's people.
The New American Bible	Peace and mercy be to all who follow this rule **and** to the Israel of God.
**Good News Bible	As for those who follow this rule in their lives, may peace and mercy be with them – with them **and** with all of God's people!
Life Application Bible	As for those who will follow this rule – peace be upon them, and mercy,

	and upon the Israel of God.
The Scriptures	And as many as walk according to this rule, peace and compassion be upon them, **and** upon the Yisrael of Elohim.
Today's English Version	As for those who follow this rule in their lives, may peace and mercy be with them – with **and** with all of God's people.
Amplified Bible	[16] Peace and mercy be upon all who walk by this rule [who discipline themselves and regulate their lives by this principle], **even** upon the [true] Israel of God (Jewish believers).
Amplified Bible, Classic Edition	[16] Peace and mercy be upon all who walk by this rule [who discipline themselves and regulate their lives by this principle], **even** upon the [true] Israel of God!
New International Version	[16] Peace and mercy to all who follow this rule **even** to the Israel of God.

In every instance or occurrence of the term "Israel" in the Old and New Testament refers to the physical offspring of Jacob. No instance exist in which "Israel" means the Church or Gentile. In every case the term "Israel" refers to believing or unbelieving physical Israelite's period.

Chapter 10
PAUL AND ISRAEL

How did Paul use the term "Israel" and how did he relate this term in his writings? Every writer of the bible addressed the term in the same manner without exception. Paul really focused on Israel in the book of Romans, chapter 9-11. He addressed Israel's past in chapter 9, Israel's present in chapter 10 and Israel's future in chapter 11.

Paul never taught that "Israel" was Gentile or the Church. Paul never suggest that the Church was "Israel" but he did teach that both would form the body of the Messiah which was a secret until Paul writings (Ephesians 2:11-22; 3:3-9, Colossians 1:26-27, Romans 16:25-27).

Paul consistently admits that all the blessings and promises belong to the Israelites. These promises include the adoption, the glory, all the covenants, the giving of the law and the temple service. The only promise given to other nations was the general Abrahamic covenant in (Genesis 12:2-3), stating that "In thee shall all the families of the earth be blessed", other than that all other blessings and promises were to be through the nation of Israel (Remember, in John 4:22, he said (SALVATION IS OF THE JEWS).

Romans 9:1-5 (KJV)

1 I say the truth in Christ, I lie not, my conscience also bearing me witness in the Holy Ghost,

2 That I have great heaviness and continual sorrow in my heart.

3 For I could wish that myself were accursed from Christ for my brethren, my kinsmen according to the flesh:

4 Who are Israelites; to whom pertaineth the adoption, and the glory, and the covenants, and the giving of the law, and the service of God, and the promises;

5 Whose are the fathers, and of whom as concerning the flesh Christ came, who is over all, God blessed for ever. Amen.

Genesis 12:2-3 (KJV)

2 And I will make of thee a great nation, and I will bless thee, and make thy name great; and thou shalt be a blessing:

3 And I will bless them that bless thee, and curse him that curseth thee: and in thee shall all families of the earth be blessed.

Isaiah 42:1 (KJV)

1 Behold my servant, whom I uphold; mine elect, in whom my soul delighteth; I have put my spirit upon him: he shall bring forth judgment to the Gentiles.

This prophetic statement in Zechariah 8:23 clearly reveal that other nations will realize the God of Abraham, Isaac and Jacob are with the True Israelites of the bible. This is supported with every other writer of the scriptures.

Zechariah 8:23 (KJV)

23 Thus saith the LORD of hosts; In those days it shall come to pass, that ten men shall take hold out of all languages of the nations, even shall take hold of the skirt of him that is a Jew, saying, We will go with you: for we have heard that God is with you.

Paul taught that True Israel will receive mercy in the last days and will be grafted back into the Olive tree. This process is a natural transition for True Israel than for other nations to be grafted into the Olive tree as stated in Romans chapter 11.

Paul often quoted the Old Testament scriptures and he knew that Israel was special and still mattered. He knew The Most High God will turn back to Israel and face his chosen people again. Hosea 1:9-10 reveals this future revelation.

Hosea 1:9-10 (KJV)

9 Then said God, Call his name Loammi: for ye are not my people, and I will not be your God.

10 Yet the number of the children of Israel shall be as the sand of the sea, which cannot be measured nor numbered; and it shall come to pass, that in the place where it was said unto them, Ye are not my people, there it shall be said unto them, Ye are the sons of the living God.

Paul flat out said in Romans 11:1-2 that Israel is not cast away, so do we think Paul did not know how to use the term "Israel" and what it meant? Surely, he could not have meant it to mean Gentile or the Church but he was simply using it to describe ethic Israel because he was an Israelite himself and knew what that meant.

Romans 11:1-2 (KJV)

1 I say then, Hath God cast away his people? God forbid. For I also am an Israelite, of the seed of Abraham, of the tribe of Benjamin.

2 God hath not cast away his people which he foreknew. Wot ye not what the scripture saith of Elias? how he maketh intercession to God against Israel saying,

---

Scriptures Paul most likely knew from the Old Testament: (I Samuel 12:22 and Psalm 94:14).

---

1 Samuel 12:22 (KJV)

22 For the LORD will not forsake his people for his great name's sake: because it hath pleased the LORD to make you his people.

Psalm 94:14 (KJV)

14 For the LORD will not cast off his people, neither will he forsake his inheritance.

Paul made it very clear that there will always be a remnant of True Israel. For example, he cited the Old Testament again, when Elijah thought he was the only believer during his time and he needed to be reminded by the Most High God he is not the only man of Israel that did not bow down to Baal. The Most High God let him know he had 7,000 men that did not bow down to Baal during that time.

I Kings 19:18 (KJV)

[18] Yet I have left me seven thousand in Israel, all the knees which have not bowed unto Baal, and every mouth which hath not kissed him.

Romans 11:4 (KJV)

[4] But what saith the answer of God unto him? I have reserved to myself seven thousand men, who have not bowed the knee to the image of Baal.

Matthew agrees with Paul that the remnant who finds the truth will be small. The narrow way leads to everlasting life and the broad way leads to destruction.

Matthew 7:13-14 (KJV)

[13] Enter ye in at the strait gate: for wide is the gate, and broad is the way, that leadeth to destruction, and many there be which go in thereat:

[14] Because strait is the gate, and narrow is the way, which leadeth unto life, and few there be that find it.

Paul continued to express his views from the Old Testament and other New Testament writers by stating that True Israel will be blinded, hardened and be in their stupor or slumber for a time. The Most High God is able to put one in a deep sleep when they refuse to accept the truth of the scriptures. This condition of True Israel continues until this day; however, we are now beginning to see True Israel awaken all over the four corners of the earth, due to The Most High God's will for such a time as this.

Romans 11:7-8 (KJV)

[7] What then? Israel hath not obtained that which he seeketh for; but the election hath obtained it, and the rest were blinded.

[8] (According as it is written, God hath given them the spirit of slumber, eyes that they should not see, and ears that they should not hear;) unto this day.

Isaiah 29:10 (KJV)

[10] For the LORD hath poured out upon you the spirit of deep sleep, and hath closed your eyes: the prophets and your rulers, the seers hath he covered.

John 12:40 (KJV)

[40] He hath blinded their eyes, and hardened their heart; that they should not see with their eyes, nor understand with their heart, and be converted, and I should heal them.

PAUL FOLLOWED THE LAW	
Abraham = Genesis 26:5 = Kept the laws	Paul = Acts 17:2, 18:4 = Kept the Sabbath
Paul = Acts 24:14 = Believed the Law (Torah)	Paul = Acts 20:6, 20:16 = Kept Feast Days
Paul = I Corinthians 5:7-8 = Keep the Feast	Paul = Romans 3:31 = Established the law
Paul = Acts 21:24 = Taught the Law (Torah)	Paul = Acts 28:23 = Taught the Law (Torah)
Paul = Romans 7:25 = Taught the Law (Torah)	Paul = Romans 7:22 = delighted in the law

Chapter 11

REPLACEMENT THEOLOGY

Replacement Theology is a term used to say that the Christian Church took the place of ethic / national Israel. It claims that all the promises given to Abraham have been transferred to the Christian Church.

Replacement Theology adds that the modern-day Israelites are no longer The Most High God's chosen people and God's covenants with them have been cancelled. According to Replacement Theology Theory, today's descendants of the biblical Israelites (Jews) no longer have a unique part to play in God's plans.

As read in previous chapters of this book this theory does not prove to be biblical (read Romans chapter 9-11). It is consistent throughout the whole bible that the restoration of the Israelites (Israel) is promised and will take place in the future. To argue that The Most High God replaced Israel with the Christian Church is to ignore all the biblical evidence presented.

There are many reasons that Replacement Theology has become a strong belief system. One is how the scriptures concerning the prophecies of Israel are interpreted.

1. **Allegorical:** This means that those who believe in replacement theology tend to interpret scriptures as symbols, folk tales and fables. In other words, scriptures are used as metaphors, figurative, symbolic and emblematic ways instead of literal.

2. **"Spiritualized" or being over spiritual:** This means that those who believe in Replacement Theology have a tendency to over spiritualize the scriptures. Meaning, scriptural interpretation that exceeds its intended meaning or event or action compensated with implications that The Most High God had orchestrated it. Over-spiritualizing can create religious or spiritual fanatics; religious hypocrites; or spiritually confused people. Trying to find everything spiritual and nothing natural will create a false sense of biblical interpretation. We must have a spiritual and natural sense of the scriptures to rightly divide it and give real meaning to it.

Debunking Replacement Theology is no difficult task but we first must keep in mind that we are dealing with nations not individuals. It is clear from Luke 21:24 that the times of the Gentiles have not yet been fulfilled. These would be those from other nations, other than the nation of Israel. It is apparent that The Most High God is selecting people from each nation to fulfill his plan.

Surely as The Most High God is dealing with individuals from each nation he is also dealing with individuals from the nation of True Israel. However, it does not exclude how The Most High God deal with nations and this is what Replacement Theology has done by replacing the nation of Israel with Gentile nations or the church. This theory does not add up with the scriptures.

Luke 21:24 (KJV)

24 And they shall fall by the edge of the sword, and shall be led away captive into all nations: and Jerusalem shall be trodden down of the Gentiles, until the times of the Gentiles be fulfilled.

Let's remember that other people from other nations are being grafted into a good Olive Tree (True Israel), not the other way around. The Gentiles are considered to be the Wild Olive Tree that can be more easily broken off than the true and natural branches of the tree.

Romans 11:17 (KJV)

17 And if some of the branches be broken off, and thou, being a wild olive tree, wert grafted in among them, and with them partakest of the root and fatness of the olive tree;

Romans 11:21-23 (KJV)

21 For if God spared not the natural branches, take heed lest he also spare not thee.

22 Behold therefore the goodness and severity of God: on them which fell, severity; but toward thee, goodness, if thou continue in his goodness: otherwise thou also shalt be cut off.

23 And they also, if they abide not still in unbelief, shall be grafted in: for God is able to graft them in again.

Here are several reasons why replacement theology cannot be correct.

I. Future Restoration

In the Old Testament there are many scriptures that mention Israel's restoration. These promises are only given to True Israel not other nations. The land is certainly one of the promises that will be given to True Israel not the church.

Deuteronomy 30:3 (KJV)

[3] That then the LORD thy God will turn thy captivity, and have compassion upon thee, and will return and gather thee from all the nations, whither the LORD thy God hath scattered thee.

Deuteronomy 30:5 (KJV)

[5] And the LORD thy God will bring thee into the land which thy fathers possessed, and thou shalt possess it; and he will do thee good, and multiply thee above thy fathers.

Here in Ezekiel 39:27-29 the promise is for True Israel to be gathered from their enemies or heathen lands and be brought back to their own land. Since he is the God of Israel, he said he will no longer hide his face from them. This is a promise given to no other nation but True Israel.

Ezekiel 39:27-29 (KJV)

^{27} When I have brought them again from the people, and gathered them out of their enemies' lands, and am sanctified in them in the sight of many nations;

^{28} Then shall they know that I am the LORD their God, which caused them to be led into captivity among the heathen: but I have gathered them unto their own land, and have left none of them any more there.

^{29} Neither will I hide my face any more from them: for I have poured out my spirit upon the house of Israel, saith the Lord GOD.

The book of Amos makes it very clear that True Israel will be back in their land as well.

Amos 9:14-15 (KJV)

^{14} And I will bring again the captivity of my people of Israel, and they shall build the waste cities, and inhabit them; and they shall plant vineyards, and drink the wine thereof; they shall also make gardens, and eat the fruit of them.

^{15} And I will plant them upon their land, and they shall no more be pulled up out of their land which I have given them, saith the LORD thy God.

Here are more mentionable scriptures that will give more insight into True Israel's restoration please read:

Zephaniah 3:14-20	Zechariah 13:9	Zechariah 14:3, 11
Romans 11 (All of it)	Romans 1:16	Roman 11:1, 28

II. Covenants Are Eternal

There were always a bonding covenant between The Most High God and the children of Israel. These covenants were always bonding with the shedding of blood. All of the covenant promises will be for the nation of Israel. As stated in Romans chapter 9:4, the adoption, the glory, and the covenants belong to True Israel. There is no mention of the church or Gentiles in this verse. It specifically makes it clear (WHO ARE ISRAELITES). God's promises are irrevocable and will not be snatched from one people to another people. The Most High God do not operate that way.

Romans 9:4 (KJV)

[4] Who are Israelites; to whom pertaineth the adoption, and the glory, and the covenants, and the giving of the law, and the service of God, and the promises;

Every nation has a part to play in The Most High God's plans for the world, but the future ruling nation will be Israel.

The Most High God will never forget or break a promise, meaning he will never lie or go back on his word. It will not come back void. All promises of the Most High God must be fulfilled.

Isaiah 55:11 (KJV)

[11] So shall my word be that goeth forth out of my mouth: it shall not return unto me void, but it shall accomplish that which I please, and it shall prosper in the thing whereto I sent it

---

Hebrews 6:18 (KJV)

[18] That by two immutable things, in which it was impossible for God to lie, we might have a strong consolation, who have fled for refuge to lay hold upon the hope set before us:

One of the covenant promises was to Abraham concerning the land for future generations of True Israel. This land will be an everlasting possession for True Israel only. No other nation has this promise for the land of Israel but Israel.

This is why there is so much turmoil in the land of Israel today. The true people of God are not in the land and until True Israel is back in the land the turmoil will continue.

The people in that region of the world are fighting for a land that is not theirs, it was promised to True Israel.

Genesis 17:7-10 (KJV)

[7] And I will establish my covenant between me and thee and thy seed after thee in their generations for an everlasting covenant, to be a God unto thee, and to thy seed after thee.

[8] And I will give unto thee, and to thy seed after thee, the land wherein thou art a stranger, all the land of Canaan, for an everlasting possession; and I will be their God.

[9] And God said unto Abraham, Thou shalt keep my covenant therefore, thou, and thy seed after thee in their generations.

[10] This is my covenant, which ye shall keep, between me and you and thy seed after thee, Every man child among you shall be circumcised.

The land was always a covenant to the descendents of True Israel which included Isaac and Jacob, the chosen line of Abraham. Still no church or Gentile nations included in this promise.

Psalm 105:8-11 (KJV)

[8] He hath remembered his covenant for ever, the word which he commanded to a thousand generations.

[9] Which covenant he made with Abraham, and his oath unto Isaac;

[10] And confirmed the same unto Jacob for a law, and to Israel for an everlasting covenant:

[11] Saying, Unto thee will I give the land of Canaan, the lot of your inheritance:

---

1 Chronicles 16:15-18 (KJV)

[15] Be ye mindful always of his covenant; the word which he commanded to a thousand generations;

[16] Even of the covenant which he made with Abraham, and of his oath unto Isaac;

[17] And hath confirmed the same to Jacob for a law, and to Israel for an everlasting covenant,

[18] Saying, Unto thee will I give the land of Canaan, the lot of your inheritance;

Galatians 3:15-17 (KJV)

[15] Brethren, I speak after the manner of men; Though it be but a man's covenant, yet if it be confirmed, no man disannulleth, or addeth thereto.

[16] Now to Abraham and his seed were the promises made. He saith not, And to seeds, as of many; but as of one, And to thy seed, which is Christ.

[17] And this I say, that the covenant, that was confirmed before of God in Christ, the law, which was four hundred and thirty years after, cannot disannul, that it should make the promise of none effect.

True Israel will not be forgotten…so all of the promised covenants will be fulfilled.

Jeremiah 31:35-37 (KJV)

[35] Thus saith the LORD, which giveth the sun for a light by day, and the ordinances of the moon and of the stars for a light by night, which divideth the sea when the waves thereof roar; The LORD of hosts is his name:

[36] If those ordinances depart from before me, saith the LORD, then the seed of Israel also shall cease from being a nation before me for ever.

[37] Thus saith the LORD; If heaven above can be measured, and the foundations of the earth searched out beneath, I will also cast off all the seed of Israel for all that they have done, saith the LORD.

III. New Testament Confirms The Old Testament

In the New Testament the story does not change concerning the promises to the True Nation of Israel. The New Testament writers reaffirm the promises and restoration of Israel is still intact. Right before the Messiah was to ascend into the heavens after his resurrection the disciples asked him a question. The question was "Lord, wilt thou at this time restore again the kingdom to Israel"?

Why ask this question if they did not understand that the nation of Israel will be the future ruling kingdom? How did they know this? Remember, they had access to the Old Testament and knew of the prophecies. The New Testament had not been written as of yet because they were the New Testament writers. The only conclusion is they knew the Old Testament scriptures.

Acts 1:6-7 (KJV)

[6] When they therefore were come together, they asked of him, saying, Lord, wilt thou at this time restore again the kingdom to Israel?

[7] And he said unto them, It is not for you to know the times or the seasons, which the Father hath put in his own power.

The New Testament goes on to confirm the Old Testament in Luke 21:24, predicting that True Israel will be trodden down of the Gentiles until the times of the Gentiles be fulfilled. We can recognize at this point in history that the Gentile nations are still in control all over the world and True Israel is still being trampled upon.

This can be confirmed again by Romans 11:25 that True Israel is blinded in part today until the fullness of the Gentile nations is come in. If True Israel did not matter then we must ask the question. Why the distinction between the Israelite nation and the

Gentile nations? This could not be possible if Replacement Theology is correct.

Romans 11:25 (KJV)

[25] For I would not, brethren, that ye should be ignorant of this mystery, lest ye should be wise in your own conceits; that blindness in part is happened to Israel, until the fulness of the Gentiles be come in.

The Messiah himself taught his disciples that they will be the ones who will judge the twelve tribes of Israel in the future. We know the disciples are all Israelites and judgment is to the Israelite or Jew first (Romans 2:9). There is no mention of Gentile nations judging anybody, they are all Israelites.

Matthew 19:28 (KJV)

[28] And Jesus said unto them, Verily I say unto you, That ye which have followed me, in the regeneration when the Son of man shall sit in the throne of his glory, ye also shall sit upon twelve thrones, judging the twelve tribes of Israel.

Luke 22:30 (KJV)

[30] That ye may eat and drink at my table in my kingdom, and sit on thrones judging the twelve tribes of Israel.

We can move far into the future or prophetic scriptures and see that there are twelve gates into the city. On all twelve gates are the names of the twelve tribes of the children of True Israel. Where are the names of the Gentiles nations? We know all the twelve tribes of Israel are from the Israelite nation only and no Gentile nation will have access unless they come through an Israelite (John 4:22).

Revelation 21:12 (KJV)

[12] And had a wall great and high, and had twelve gates, and at the gates twelve angels, and names written thereon, which are the names of the twelve tribes of the children of Israel:

John 4:22 (KJV)

[22] Ye worship ye know not what: we know what we worship: for salvation is of the Jews.

Ezekiel 48:31-34 (KJV)

[31] And the gates of the city shall be after the names of the tribes of Israel: three gates northward; one gate of Reuben, one gate of Judah, one gate of Levi.

[32] And at the east side four thousand and five hundred: and three gates; and one gate of Joseph, one gate of Benjamin, one gate of Dan.

[33] And at the south side four thousand and five hundred measures: and three gates; one gate of Simeon, one gate of Issachar, one gate of Zebulun.

[34] At the west side four thousand and five hundred, with their three gates; one gate of Gad, one gate of Asher, one gate of Naphtali.

The Messiah has prophesied to his people in Jerusalem that they will be desolate because they stoned the prophets and did not believe in him after all he had done for them. He stated they will not see him until they say "blessed is he that cometh in the name of the Lord". This promise was toward the Israelites not other nations. Replacement Theology again falls short.

> **Matthew 23:37-39 (KJV)**
>
> [37] O Jerusalem, Jerusalem, thou that killest the prophets, and stonest them which are sent unto thee, how often would I have gathered thy children together, even as a hen gathereth her chickens under her wings, and ye would not!
>
> [38] Behold, your house is left unto you desolate.
>
> [39] For I say unto you, Ye shall not see me henceforth, till ye shall say, Blessed is he that cometh in the name of the Lord.

It is believed that Paul, the writer of the book Romans did not believe in the laws of God or denounced them because of a few misinterpreted scriptures. Paul have always supported the laws of God and quoted from the Old Testament frequently and justifying True Israel's future is no different. When Paul wrote Romans 11:26-27, he stated 'all Israel shall be saved". Why didn't he include the Gentiles in this statement? Because he was holding on to the covenant promised to True Israel in the Old Testament, quoting from Isaiah 59 and 27 (please read).

There is not one quote in the entire bible concerning all Gentiles shall be saved. Now, will there be Gentiles saved, of course but Paul was focusing on the covenant made to True Israel (The chosen people). The Most High God made no such promise of total salvation to any other nation on earth. This is yet another example that the Israelites or Jews have not been replaced by the church. Also read Luke 13:34-35.

Romans 11:26-27 (KJV)

^{26} And so all Israel shall be saved: as it is written, There shall come out of Sion the Deliverer, and shall turn away ungodliness from Jacob:

^{27} For this is my covenant unto them, when I shall take away their sins.

Compare Isaiah 59:20-21 and Psalm 14:7. You'll see when Paul says "as it is written" in Romans 11:26-27, he was referring that it was written in the Old Testament.

Isaiah 59:20-21 (KJV)

^{20} And the Redeemer shall come to Zion, and unto them that turn from transgression in Jacob, saith the LORD.

^{21} As for me, this is my covenant with them, saith the LORD; My spirit that is upon thee, and my words which I have put in thy mouth, shall not depart out of thy mouth, nor out of the mouth of thy seed, nor out of the mouth of thy seed's seed, saith the LORD, from henceforth and for ever.

Psalm 14:7 (KJV)

^{7} Oh that the salvation of Israel were come out of Zion! when the LORD bringeth back the captivity of his people, Jacob shall rejoice, and Israel shall be glad.

Jeremiah 31:33 supports Romans 11:27 please compare. The covenant was made with the nation of Israel not Gentiles or the Church.

> **Jeremiah 31:33 (KJV)**
>
> [33] But this shall be the covenant that I will make with the house of Israel; After those days, saith the LORD, I will put my law in their inward parts, and write it in their hearts; and will be their God, and they shall be my people.

As this chapter concludes with much biblical support that Replacement Theology is a false doctrine and the bible simply does not support it. On an individual level one can be gathered by their faith and should follow the laws, statutes and commandments of God but on a national level all promises belongs to the Israelites according to the scriptures. Replacement Theology does not hold up when compared to the scriptures.

Chapter 12
THE LAW

The biblical Laws, Statutes and Commandments of the Most High God is a topic that must be discussed due to it being the main and only reason True Israel went into so many captivities throughout history. The question remains: Is the law done away? This topic is probably debated everyday by many with different conclusions as a result. This chapter will explore the truth of this matter by using scriptures in context and omitting any philosophy, emotions and / or personal opinions.

In Christianity it's taught that the laws of God are done away because The Messiah nailed them to the cross and said it is finished. What law was nailed to the cross? What about grace? It is generally taught we no longer need to follow the Laws, Statutes and Commandments of The Most High God. Is this True? As this relates to True Israel, one question needs to be asked. Why did True Israel go into captivity again after the Messiah died on the cross? What happen to the grace? Below are the major captivities of True Israel that are documented in scriptures and in world history.

The Major Captivities of True Israel

1. **The Assyrians Captivity:** Northern Kingdom, (II Kings 15:29, 17:1-23, 18:11-12, I Chronicles 5:26).

2. **The Babylonian Captivity:** Southern Kingdom, (I Chronicles 9:1, II Kings 24:14-16, 24:20, 25:11, II Chronicles 36:20, Jeremiah 52:28-30, 25:12).

3. **The Persian / Medes Captivity:** II Chronicles 36:22-23, Ezra 1:1-11, 9:9).

4. **The Greek Captivity:** (I Maccabees 8:18)

5. **The Romans Captivity:** This captivity led the Israelites fleeing into Africa (Luke 21:20-24).

6. **The Transatlantic Slave Trade:** This took place during the 15th to 19th century.

The Messiah was crucified under the Roman Empire's reign or rule. This means that True Israel went back into captivity over 1,500 years later even after the Messiah's death. Keep in mind all of Israel went into slavery, not just those who believed in the Messiah. So, there was something else that provoked The Most High God to allow his people to be enslaved by other nations again. Could it be that True Israel continued to break The Most High God Laws, Statutes and Commandments? Is the law done away? Let's began on this journey of truth.

WHAT IS SIN?

In order to know if God's Laws, Statutes and Commandments are done away with, we must know what sin is. In the religion of Christianity most are unaware what sin really is because it's not taught or emphasized to mean anything in the modern-day Christian churches of today. Most Christians believe sin is a feeling, smoking cigarettes, drinking alcohol, wearing makeup, going to the club, dancing to music other than gospel music etc. however; the bible gives a plain and straight forward definition to what sin really is.

---

1 John 3:4 (KJV)

[4] Whosoever committeth sin transgresseth also the law: for sin is the transgression of the law.

Notice sin is defined as breaking the law of the Most High God. This should rule out our own feelings to what sin really is. Question: if there's no law, how could there be any sin? For by the law is the knowledge of sin. In other words, no one can sin if there are no laws.

The following two scriptures (Romans 3:20 & Romans 2:13) appears to contradict themselves but if read in its context the meaning is clear. Romans 3:20 is making the point that a person that is going through the motion of keeping the law (Pharisees) without ever changing on the inside have no benefit in keeping the law. They have no connection with the Father in heaven. Keeping the law alone cannot save you according to Revelation 14:12 it's going to take faith in /of the Messiah and following the commandments of the Most High God.

Romans 2:13 is stressing those who keep the laws of God and have faith in and of the Messiah will benefit because of the obedience to God's Laws, Statutes and Commandments and having the faith in the Messiah. In other words, you'll need both to be seen as an over comer and one who have demonstrated patience to be received by the Most High God.

Romans 3:20 (KJV)

20 Therefore by the deeds of the law there shall no flesh be justified in his sight: for by the law is the knowledge of sin.

Romans 2:13 (KJV)

13 (For not the hearers of the law are just before God, but the doers of the law shall be justified.

Sin is not imputed, meaning you cannot be charged, faulted or guilty of any crime if there is no law.

Romans 5:13 (KJV)

13 (For until the law sin was in the world: but sin is not imputed when there is no law.

The question is asked is the law sin? Paul responds, God Forbids; meaning no, he only known sin due to there being a law(s).

Romans 7:7 (KJV)

7 What shall we say then? Is the law sin? God forbid. Nay, I had not known sin, but by the law: for I had not known lust, except the law had said, Thou shalt not covet.

Where there is no law, there cannot be any transgressions or sin. As noted in Romans 7:7 it says, "thou shalt not covet". Isn't that one of the Ten Commandments? (Exodus 20:17 & Deuteronomy 5:21).

> **Romans 4:15 (KJV)**
>
> [15] Because the law worketh wrath: for where no law is, there is no transgression.

When faced with the reality of what sin is, there could be no way possible the laws are done away with today. True Israel has been suffering from the curses of Deuteronomy 28 for this very reason of breaking God's Laws, Statutes and Commandments consistently throughout history and this continues to this day.
The questions remain: Why did True Israel go back into captivity after the Messiah's death? What was finished on the cross? Should grace have been sufficient?

It cannot be believed that The Most High God would want any people to practice lawlessness because it's unbecoming of his character and breaking his laws will not be tolerated. It is always judgment on those who choose to break God's laws. As a result of breaking God's laws True Israel suffered and continues to suffer captivity. Lucifer being kicked out of heaven and the flooding of the world was all due to breaking God's Laws, Statutes and Commandments. SIN is the culprit.

WHAT IS RIGHTEOUSNESS?

When the bible teaches on righteousness and unrighteousness its teaching on what The Most High approves and what The Most High does not approve. The bible is very clear on what righteousness is and what unrighteousness is.

Unrighteousness is one who chooses not to follow The Most High's Laws, Statutes and Commandments. Again, sin is involved in all unrighteousness.

---

1 John 5:17 (KJV)

[17] All unrighteousness is sin: and there is a sin not unto death.

One who is walking in RIGHTEOUSNESS would be considered one who follows all of God's Laws, Statutes and Commandments (Obedience). The bible is also clear as to what righteousness mean.

Deuteronomy 6:25 (KJV)

[25] And it shall be our righteousness, if we observe to do all these **commandments** before the LORD our God, as he hath commanded us.

Isaiah 51:7 (KJV)

[7] Hearken unto me, ye that know **righteousness, the people in whose heart is my law;** fear ye not the reproach of men, neither be ye afraid of their revilings.

Psalm 119:172 (KJV)
[172] My tongue shall speak of thy word: for all thy **commandments are righteousness**.

Luke 1:6 (KJV)
[6] And they were both **righteous before God, walking in all the commandments** and ordinances of the Lord blameless.

WHAT ABOUT GRACE?

This chapter is dealing with the subject of the law; however, some dialogue needs to be presented concerning GRACE. What is grace? Most think that grace took the place of the law, however the bible teaches something totally different. First, let's define what grace means.

Grace is defined as God's unmerited favor. That is, grace is The Most High God doing good for us when we don't deserve it. Grace provides good will, loving kindness and mercy. In True Israel's case it provided redemption and an opportunity to reconnect with the Father in heaven. Grace did not give a license to continue in sin. The Messiah is only going to die once for our sins and now the blood is on us. It is stated in the scriptures that he died for the sins of the past (Old Testament) not our future sins.

Romans 3:25 (KJV)

25 Whom God hath set forth to be a propitiation through faith in his blood, to declare his righteousness for the remission of sins that are past, through the forbearance of God;

In other words, no one can use **grace** to justify breaking God's Laws, Statutes and Commandments. Paul said it perfectly in Romans 6:1-2.

Romans 6:1-2 (KJV)

1 What shall we say then? Shall we continue in sin, that grace may abound?

2 God forbid. How shall we, that are dead to sin, live any longer therein?

Paul said God forbid, meaning no. We also cannot use **faith** to establish breaking God's Laws, statutes and Commandments.

Romans 3:31 (KJV)

[31] Do we then make void the law through faith? God forbid: yea, we establish the law

---

Paul said God forbid, meaning no. He said they established the law and the word established means to institute (AS LAW) permanently by enactment or agreement, to make firm or stable, to bring into existence, to introduce and cause to grow and multiply.

The Most High God Laws, Statutes and Commandments will stand forever because it is perfect and there's no way The Most High God could have done away with perfection.

Psalm 19:7 (KJV)

[7] The law of the LORD is perfect, converting the soul: the testimony of the LORD is sure, making wise the simple.

When it comes to grace most Christians would go to Romans 6:14 where it says that "sin shall not have dominion over you, for you are not under the law but under grace". But Christians seem to forget the next verse (15), which says "God forbid, meaning no, we do not continue in sin because of grace". The law still remains with the grace.

Romans 6:14-15 (KJV)
[14] For sin shall not have dominion over you: for ye are not under the law, but under grace.

[15] What then? shall we sin, because we are not under the law, but under grace? God forbid.

WHAT ABOUT THE MESSIAH AND THE LAW?

The Messiah made it very clear that the law is not done away with. If he had not followed the law himself, he would have died in vain and his death would not have meant anything. The very fact that he followed the law made him sinless which means he never transgressed or broken one law. If he had broken the law he would have been blemished and could not have died for Israel's sins and eventually others.

The Messiah himself said he did not come to destroy the law or the prophets but to fulfill. In Christianity it's taught the word fulfill means finished or completed. This is not true because the word fulfill in Greek is the word Pleroo #4137 and this word means to verify, fill to the full, perfect, uphold and to bring to realization. In other words, The Messiah came to magnify the law and be the perfect example in keeping the law. Also notice he mentions he did not come to destroy the prophets either, meaning whatever the prophets prophesied from the Old Testament will continue to take place because they must come to pass.

The Messiah did not and would not stop those prophesies from coming to pass. He said until heaven and earth pass away not one jot or tittle shall pass away from the law until all be fulfilled. Is heaven and earth still standing? Yes, then the law still stands as well.

When reading the Old Testament, you'll realize there are many prophecies that directly affect True Israel and they must come forth in the future. So, why would the Messiah come and do away with all the prophecies and Laws?

The Messiah goes on to say those who break the commandments and teaches others to do so would be the least in the kingdom of heaven (damnation) and those who do them and teach them would be great in the kingdom of heaven.

Matthew 5:17-22 (KJV)

[17] Think not that I am come to destroy the law, or the prophets: I am not come to destroy, but to fulfil.

[18] For verily I say unto you, Till heaven and earth pass, one jot or one tittle shall in no wise pass from the law, till all be fulfilled.

[19] Whosoever therefore shall break one of these least commandments, and shall teach men so, he shall be called the least in the kingdom of heaven: but whosoever shall do and teach them, the same shall be called great in the kingdom of heaven.

[20] For I say unto you, That except your righteousness shall exceed the righteousness of the scribes and Pharisees, ye shall in no case enter into the kingdom of heaven.

[21] Ye have heard that it was said of them of old time, Thou shalt not kill; and whosoever shall kill shall be in danger of the judgment:

[22] But I say unto you, That whosoever is angry with his brother without a cause shall be in danger of the judgment: and whosoever shall say to his brother, Raca, shall be in danger of the council: but whosoever shall say, Thou fool, shall be in danger of hell fire.

After reading The Messiah's words concerning how he feels about the law, certainly he did not support breaking the law but keeping them. Let's see what else The Messiah said about the commandments.

In Matthew 19:16-17 a question is being asked of The Messiah and the question is: "What good thing shall I do, that I may have eternal life"? The Messiah answers and says "but if thou wilt enter into life, keep the commandments". Here you have The Messiah himself saying keep the Commandments and if you keep them you will have eternal life. It seems very clear he is supporting the Laws, Statutes and Commandments of the Old Testament (Torah) and that one's life depends on it.

Matthew 19:16-17 (KJV)

[16] And, behold, one came and said unto him, Good Master, what good thing shall I do, that I may have eternal life?

[17] And he said unto him, Why callest thou me good? there is none good but one, that is, God: but if thou wilt enter into life, keep the commandments.

The Messiah actually mentions a few Commandments in Mark 10:18-19. The Commandments mentioned are:
1. Do Not Commit Adultery
2. Do Not Kill
3. Do Not Steal
4. Do Not Bear False Witness
5. Defraud Not
6. Honour Thy Father and Mother

All of these Commandments are from the Old Testament (Exodus 20:1-17 & Deuteronomy 5:4-21). If the Law was done away with why would The Messiah himself encourage keeping them?

Mark 10:18-19 (KJV)

[18] And Jesus said unto him, Why callest thou me good? there is none good but one, that is, God.

[19] Thou knowest the commandments, Do not commit adultery, Do not kill, Do not steal, Do not bear false witness, Defraud not, Honour thy father and mother.

Luke 18:20 (KJV)

²⁰ Thou knowest the commandments, Do not commit adultery, Do not kill, Do not steal, Do not bear false witness, Honour thy father and thy mother.

If the Messiah was to ask anyone today "How do I know you love me"? What possible answer can one give? The only answer could be (according to scripture) is "because I keep your commandments", notice the scripture does not say anything about grace being a factor to loving him.

John 14:15 (KJV)

¹⁵ If ye love me, keep my commandments

John 14:21 (KJV)

²¹ He that hath my commandments, and keepeth them, he it is that loveth me: and he that loveth me shall be loved of my Father, and I will love him, and will manifest myself to him.

John 15:10 (KJV)

¹⁰ If ye keep my commandments, ye shall abide in my love; even as I have kept my Father's commandments, and abide in his love.

The Messiah makes an interesting statement in Matthew 7:21-23. He says "Not everyone that says unto me Lord, Lord shall enter into the kingdom of heaven", Why? He's even speaking of those that were casting out demons and doing other wonderful works in his name. He said he would tell them "Depart from me, ye that work iniquity".

Matthew 7:21-23 (KJV)

[21] Not every one that saith unto me, Lord, Lord, shall enter into the kingdom of heaven; but he that doeth the will of my Father which is in heaven.

[22] Many will say to me in that day, Lord, Lord, have we not prophesied in thy name? and in thy name have cast out devils? and in thy name done many wonderful works?

[23] And then will I profess unto them, I never knew you: depart from me, ye that work iniquity.

First, we know the word iniquity means Sin, lawlessness, wrong, corruption and wickedness. This claim that The Messiah will turn those away that work iniquity is significant in supporting that it doesn't matter what kind of miracles and wonderful works one can perform but following the Laws, Statutes and Commandments supersedes it all.

If we say we know Him and do not keep the Commandments, the scripture says we are a liar and the truth is not in us. This explains The Messiah turning away those who work iniquity even after casting out demons etc.

1 John 2:3-4 (KJV)

³ And hereby we do know that we know him, if we keep his commandments.

⁴ He that saith, I know him, and keepeth not his commandments, is a liar, and the truth is not in him.

The Messiah certainly did not denounce the law but encouraged, taught and supported it wholeheartedly. He knew he had to do the will of his Father who taught him in heaven. He knew why he came and what his task would be and it certainly was not to destroy the Laws, Statutes and Commandments.

John 8:28 (KJV)

²⁸ Then said Jesus unto them, When ye have lifted up the Son of man, then shall ye know that I am he, and that I do nothing of myself; but as my Father hath taught me, I speak these things.

John 5:30 (KJV)

³⁰ I can of mine own self do nothing: as I hear, I judge: and my judgment is just; because I seek not mine own will, but the will of the Father which hath sent me

John 6:38 (KJV)

³⁸ For I came down from heaven, not to do mine own will, but the will of him that sent me.

Those who follow authentic Christianity are charged to follow in the footsteps of The Messiah. The Messiah never taught the Laws, Statutes and Commandments are done away with but magnified it. One must ask the question, if those in the religion of Christianity are not following Messiah and The Most High God then who are they following? We cannot serve two masters.

Matthew 6:24 (KJV)

[24] No man can serve two masters: for either he will hate the one, and love the other; or else he will hold to the one, and despise the other. Ye cannot serve God and mammon.

In conclusion: If Christianity is charged to follow after the Messiah of the bible. Why then are the Laws, Statutes and Commandments of the Most High God taught they are done away with? It is completely clear the Messiah followed the Laws of The Most High God and He expects us to do the same. We must take up his ways and not develop our own traditions that go against the father's will.

---

1 Peter 2:21-22 (KJV)

[21] For even hereunto were ye called: because Christ also suffered for us, leaving us an example, that ye should follow his steps:

[22] Who did no sin, neither was guile found in his mouth:

The Most High God's Laws, Statutes and Commandments are identical to his character. Please see the following chart.

THE MESSIAH FOLLOWED THE LAW

The Messiah = Luke 4:16 = Kept the Sabbath	The Messiah =Matthew 26:18 = Kept Passover
The Messiah = Matthew 5:19 = Taught Law	

GOD'S LAW AND CHARACTER COMPARED

Romans 16: 26 (God is Eternal) Psalms 111:7-8 (The law is Eternal)	Luke 18:19 (God is Good) Romans 7:12 (The law is Good)
John 4:24 (God is Spiritual) Romans 7:14 (The law is Spiritual)	Deuteronomy 32:4 (God is Just) Romans 7:12 (The law is Just)
Psalm 145:17 (God is Righteous) Psalm 119:172 (The Law is Righteous)	I John 3:3 (God is Pure) Psalm 19:8 (The law is Pure)
Matthew 5:48 (God is Perfect) Psalm 19:7 (The law is Perfect)	I John 4:8 (God is Love) Romans 13: 10 (The law is Love)
I John 1:5 (God is Light) Proverbs 6:23 (The law is Light)	Psalms 48:1 (God is Great) Hosea 8:12 (The law is Great)
Deuteronomy 32:4 (God is Truth) Psalm 119:142 (The law is Truth)	Isaiah 5:16 (God is Holy) Romans 7:12 (The law is Holy)

Question: If the Most High God character lines up with his laws, statutes and commandments; why would he do away with them?

THE LAW THAT IS DONE AWAY

Many believe the law is done away with due to Colossians 2:14, believing the laws of the Most High were nailed to the cross. The question would be what law was nailed to the cross? Certainly, if all the laws were nailed to the cross it would make no sense for the Messiah, Paul and the prophets to continue supporting them if in fact they were done away.

Clearly, the disciples and other biblical patriarchs were keeping the law after the Messiah's death. Again, the question would be what law is done away? If we go back to Colossians 2:14 and read it from the beginning the picture becomes clear.

Colossians 2:14 (KJV)

[14] Blotting out the handwriting of ordinances that was against us, which was contrary to us, and took it out of the way, nailing it to his cross;

The verse starts out by saying "Blotting out the handwriting of the ordinances that was against us". What ordinances or law was blotted out that was against Israel?

What people don't realize is that the laws were broken up into sections. Depending on how one looks at the laws of the Most High, they could be broken down into categories such as this:

1. Moral Law (The Commandments)
2. Dietary Law (What's Lawful to Eat and not Eat)
3. Civil Law (How We Should Conduct Business)
4. Judgment Laws (Cut off and killed)
5. Sacrificial Law (Animal Sacrifices)

We know thus far the Moral Laws still apply today because of scriptures like:

1. **Psalm 19:7** = The law of the Lord is perfect. (Why would the Most High do away with perfection?)

2. **Psalm 119:172** = All of the commandments are righteous. (Why would the Most High get rid of Righteousness?)

3. **Psalm 119:142** = The law is the truth. (Why would the Most High get rid of truth?)

4. **Romans 7:12** = The law is holy. (Why would the Most High get rid of holiness?)

5. **Romans 7:14** = The law is spiritual. (Why would the Most High get rid of a good spiritual component?)

The Moral Law was spoken and written by the Most High himself

1. **Deuteronomy 4:12-13** = The Most High wrote the law on two tablets

2. **Deuteronomy 4:22-23** = The Most High made the covenant (law).

3. **Exodus Chapter 20** = The commandments written by the Most High himself

4. **Deuteronomy 5:22** = The Most High wrote laws on two tablets

5. **Exodus 31:18** = The Most High wrote laws on two tablets with his finger

The Moral Law is eternal and requires obedience forever

1. Romans 3:31 = The law supersedes faith because the law was already established

2. Matthew 5:17 = The Messiah did not come to destroy the law or the prophesies to come but to fulfill them

3. Revelation 22:14 = Blessed are those who keeps the commandments

4. Revelation 14:12 = All those who will overcome in the future was keeping the commandments

There was a law that was blotted out, called a curse and completely abolished today according to the scriptures. The **sacrificial law** is that only law that is completely done away with today. This was the law that was added due to transgressing or breaking of all the other laws the Most High God told the nation of Israel to follow. This law was set in place so that True Israel (Israelites) could live and not die by shedding the blood of animals to atone for their sins.

Galatians 3:19-24 (KJV)

[19] Wherefore then serveth the law? It was added because of transgressions, till the seed should come to whom the promise was made; and it was ordained by angels in the hand of a mediator.

[20] Now a mediator is not a mediator of one, but God is one.

[21] Is the law then against the promises of God? God forbid: for if there had been a law given which could have given life, verily righteousness should have been by the law.

[22] But the scripture hath concluded all under sin, that the promise by faith of Jesus Christ might be given to them that believe.

23 But before faith came, we were kept under the law, shut up unto the faith which should afterwards be revealed.

24 Wherefore the law was our schoolmaster to bring us unto Christ, that we might be justified by faith.

The law that was added is located in Leviticus 4:1-8

Leviticus 4:1-8 (KJV)

1 And the LORD spake unto Moses, saying,

2 Speak unto the children of Israel, saying, If a soul shall sin through ignorance against any of the commandments of the LORD concerning things which ought not to be done, and shall do against any of them:

3 If the priest that is anointed do sin according to the sin of the people; then let him bring for his sin, which he hath sinned, a young bullock without blemish unto the LORD for a sin offering.

4 And he shall bring the bullock unto the door of the tabernacle of the congregation before the LORD; and shall lay his hand upon the bullock's head, and kill the bullock before the LORD.

5 And the priest that is anointed shall take of the bullock's blood, and bring it to the tabernacle of the congregation:

6 And the priest shall dip his finger in the blood, and sprinkle of the blood seven times before the LORD, before the vail of the sanctuary.

7 And the priest shall put some of the blood upon the horns of the altar of sweet incense before the LORD, which is in the tabernacle of the congregation; and shall pour all the blood of the bullock at

the bottom of the altar of the burnt offering, which is at the door of the tabernacle of the congregation.

[8] And he shall take off from it all the fat of the bullock for the sin offering; the fat that covereth the inwards, and all the fat that is upon the inwards,

The sacrificial law of killing animals for one's sins was not perfect and was only a shadow of things to come for the real and ultimate sacrifice.

Hebrews 9:9 (KJV)

[9] Which was a figure for the time then present, in which were offered both gifts and sacrifices, that could not make him that did the service perfect, as pertaining to the conscience;

Hebrews 7:19 (KJV)

[19] For the law made nothing perfect, but the bringing in of a better hope did; by the which we draw nigh unto God.

It was predicted when the animal sacrifices would end in the book of Daniel.

Daniel 9:26-27 (KJV)

[26] And after threescore and two weeks shall Messiah be cut off, but not for himself: and the people of the prince that shall come shall destroy the city and the sanctuary; and the end thereof shall be with a flood, and unto the end of the war desolations are determined.

> [27] And he shall confirm the covenant with many for one week: and in the midst of the week he shall cause the sacrifice and the oblation to cease, and for the overspreading of abominations he shall make it desolate, even until the consummation, and that determined shall be poured upon the desolate.

Once the Messiah came and shed his blood for the atonement of sins the sacrificial law was abolished. The veil of the temple was no longer needed because The Messiah became and was the veil (his flesh).

Hebrews 10:20 (KJV)

> [20] By a new and living way, which he hath consecrated for us, through the veil, that is to say, his flesh;

In other words, the Levitical priesthood ended and therefore no more blood of animals was needed. However, now the blood is on each person today if they continue to sin because the wages of sin is still death.

Romans 6:23 (KJV)

> [23] For the wages of sin is death; but the gift of God is eternal life through Jesus Christ our Lord.

The sacrificial law was a law The Most High God never wanted to institute. All he wanted was for the people (Israel) to follow the laws, statutes and commandments that already existed without having to have another law (Sacrificial). Animals were killed and sacrificed so we as people (True Israel) did not have to die.

Psalm 40:6-8 (KJV)

[6] Sacrifice and offering thou didst not desire; mine ears hast thou opened: burnt offering and sin offering hast thou not required.

[7] Then said I, Lo, I come: in the volume of the book it is written of me,

[8] I delight to do thy will, O my God: yea, thy law is within my heart.

Jeremiah 7:21-24 (KJV)

[21] Thus saith the LORD of hosts, the God of Israel; Put your burnt offerings unto your sacrifices, and eat flesh.

[22] For I spake not unto your fathers, nor commanded them in the day that I brought them out of the land of Egypt, concerning burnt offerings or sacrifices:

[23] But this thing commanded I them, saying, Obey my voice, and I will be your God, and ye shall be my people: and walk ye in all the ways that I have commanded you, that it may be well unto you.

[24] But they hearkened not, nor inclined their ear, but walked in the counsels and in the imagination of their evil heart, and went backward, and not forward.

We know without blood there is no remission of sins so animal sacrifices were necessary before The Messiah sacrificed himself.

Hebrews 9:22 (KJV)

[22] And almost all things are by the law purged with blood; and without shedding of blood is no remission.

Ephesians 5:2 (KJV)

[2] And walk in love, as Christ also hath loved us, and hath given himself for us an offering and a sacrifice to God for a sweetsmelling savour.

Understanding what law was done away will help in understanding other scriptures pertaining to the law (especially in Paul epistles). For example: Galatians 3:10

Galatians 3:10 (KJV)

[10] For as many as are of the works of the **law** are under the curse: for it is written, Cursed is every one that continueth not in all things which are written in the book of the **law** to do them.

Notice in Galatians 3:10 the law is mentioned twice. The first law says we are under a curse if we do the works of the law. The second law says we are cursed if we don't do the works of the law. Now, this could be confusing if one is unlearned in the scriptures just as Peter said in II Peter 3:16 about his brother Paul.

The first law mentioned in this scripture is pertaining to the sacrificial law that is done away and one is cursed if we continue with this law. However, the second law mentioned in this scripture is referring to the moral and the other laws which are still relevant today.

If we don't rightly divide the word of truth then this scripture would make no sense and it would appear as if this scripture is contradicting itself. Please read Galatians 3:21, another scripture with the word law mentioned three times but all of these laws are referring to the commandments we should follow. How do we know? It opens by saying "Is the law then against the promises of God?" the answer is God Forbid which means no. So, we know this is not referring to the sacrificial law but the moral and other laws. The same is for the second and third law mentioned in this scripture because it refers to righteousness being by the law in which we know following the law of The Most High God is what makes us walk in righteousness.

Galatians 3:21 (KJV)

²¹ Is the **law** then against the promises of God? God forbid: for if there had been a **law** given which could have given life, verily righteousness should have been by the **law.**

Deuteronomy 6:25 (KJV)

²⁵ And it shall be our righteousness, if we observe to do all these commandments before the LORD our God, as he hath commanded us.

Luke 1:6 is an example of one (Elizabeth) walking in the commandments making her righteous.

Luke 1:6 (KJV)

⁶ And they were both righteous before God, walking in all the commandments and ordinances of the Lord blameless.

Psalm 119:172 spells out all the commandments or law are righteous.

Psalm 119:172 (KJV)

[172] My tongue shall speak of thy word: for all thy commandments are righteousness

The Most High laws are perfect and he would never do away with them. Why would he do away with perfection?

Psalm 19:7 (KJV)

[7] The law of the LORD is perfect, converting the soul: the testimony of the LORD is sure, making wise the simple.

So, if doing the law is righteousness then one can only come to one conclusion that the laws of the Most High is still binding today and the only law that is done away is the sacrificial law. Hebrews 10:1-10 should sum up what law is done away.

Hebrews 10:1-10 (KJV)

1 For the law having a shadow of good things to come, and not the very image of the things, can never with those sacrifices which they offered year by year continually make the comers thereunto perfect.

[2] For then would they not have ceased to be offered? because that the worshippers once purged should have had no more conscience of sins.

[3] But in those sacrifices there is a remembrance again made of sins every year.

[4] For it is not possible that the blood of bulls and of goats should take away sins.

⁵ Wherefore when he cometh into the world, he saith, Sacrifice and offering thou wouldest not, but a body hast thou prepared me:

⁶ In burnt offerings and sacrifices for sin thou hast had no pleasure.

⁷ Then said I, Lo, I come (in the volume of the book it is written of me,) to do thy will, O God.

⁸ Above when he said, Sacrifice and offering and burnt offerings and offering for sin thou wouldest not, neither hadst pleasure therein; which are offered by the law;

⁹ Then said he, Lo, I come to do thy will, O God. He taketh away the first, that he may establish the second.

¹⁰ By the which will we are sanctified through the offering of the body of Jesus Christ once for all.

Chapter 13

CHRISTIANITY

The majority of True Israel today is part of the religion of Christianity and Islam. This is very concerning for many reasons due to some of the popular teachings of Christianity that does not line up with the biblical scriptures. True Israel was charged with keeping the Laws, Statutes and Commandments as a perpetual covenant and Christianity has taught True Israel to consistently break them.

Deuteronomy 4:40 (KJV)

[40] Thou shalt keep therefore his statutes, and his commandments, which I command thee this day, that it may go well with thee, and with thy children after thee, and that thou mayest prolong thy days upon the earth, which the LORD thy God giveth thee, for ever.

Nearly all the doctrines of Christianity are unbiblical and pagan for many reasons and not all stemming from the religion itself. When reading the bible from Genesis to Revelation you'll find a major theme which is following the Laws, Statutes and Commandments of the Most High God. Many Christians primarily follow whatever the Pastors say instead of searching the word of God for themselves to see whether those things are so.

Acts 17:11 (KJV)

[11] These were more noble than those in Thessalonica, in that they received the word with all readiness of mind, and searched the scriptures daily, whether those things were so.

In other words, most Christians are comfortable following man doctrines and his traditions instead of following the God of Abraham, Isaac and Jacob of the bible.

Acts 5:29 (KJV)

[29] Then Peter and the other apostles answered and said, We ought to obey God rather than men.

Many choose to ignore sound scriptures and use the scriptures to say what they need them to say. The modern-day Christian churches either spiritualize or explain scriptures away and rely completely on feelings instead of reading the facts of the scriptures.

Many of the doctrines of Christianity stems mostly from the Roman Catholic Church who is the mother church of all other Christian churches around the world. The Roman Catholic Church did not do the God of Abraham, Isaac and Jacob any favors due to the created doctrines against the Most High God. There is a prophetic scripture in the book of Daniel that gives an indication that there will be an organization that will change times and laws of the Most High God and the Roman Catholic Church has done so and admitted it.

Daniel 7:25 (KJV)

25 And he shall speak great words against the most High, and shall wear out the saints of the most High, and think to change times and laws: and they shall be given into his hand until a time and times and the dividing of time.

During these last days it is very important to know who we are following or serving. Joshua said "but as for me and my house, we will serve the Lord".

Joshua 24:15 (KJV)

15 And if it seem evil unto you to serve the LORD, choose you this day whom ye will serve; whether the gods which your fathers served that were on the other side of the flood, or the gods of the Amorites, in whose land ye dwell: but as for me and my house, we will serve the LORD.

We must realize that Satan is on the move deceiving the whole world and seeking whom he may devour.

Revelation 12:9 (KJV)

9 And the great dragon was cast out, that old serpent, called the Devil, and Satan, which deceiveth the whole world: he was cast out into the earth, and his angels were cast out with him.

1 Peter 5:8 (KJV)

8 Be sober, be vigilant; because your adversary the devil, as a roaring lion, walketh about, seeking whom he may devour:

What is the deception? What has Satan done? How do we recognize the truth? The bible answers everything we need to know and if we are rightly dividing the word of truth the story becomes very clear as to the root of evil that hovers over Christianity today.

---

2 Timothy 2:15 (KJV)

[15] Study to shew thyself approved unto God, a workman that needeth not to be ashamed, rightly dividing the word of truth.

Modern day Christianity has taken on many different phases since its inception. Even Paul claims that he saw the workings of evil already setting in during his day and time.

---

2 Thessalonians 2:5-7 (KJV)

[5] Remember ye not, that, when I was yet with you, I told you these things?

[6] And now ye know what withholdeth that he might be revealed in his time.

[7] For the mystery of iniquity doth already work: only he who now letteth will let, until he be taken out of the way.

Some of the warnings and true doctrines of the bible is very clear but modern-day Christianity does not take heed to those warnings for some of the following reasons:

1. Misinterpreting the writings of Paul Epistles / letters

2. Spiritualizes everything away

3. Ignore plain and clear scriptures

4. Totally dependent on false prophets (modern day pastors)

5. Totally relying on feelings or emotions instead of scriptures

6. Taking many scriptures out of context

7. Following Traditions of man / Paganism

8. Simply do not care to research the issues

You'll also hear things from professing Christians like "God knows my heart…I feel the Holy Spirit telling me I should do this…I believe God…I listen to my pastor because he's my spiritual covering". All this is usually said without one scripture in context to support the basis of their statement and when shown the truth from the scriptures it's usually ignored or pushed away. Why? There appears to be more comfort in believing a lie instead of truth.

The bible confirms and predicts that there will be a time of great deception. These times will consist of false doctrines preached by false prophets. Most people will turn away from truth and turn to fables because that's what they want to hear.

---

2 Timothy 4:2-4 (KJV)

[2] Preach the word; be instant in season, out of season; reprove, rebuke, exhort with all long suffering and doctrine.

[3] For the time will come when they will not endure sound doctrine; but after their own lusts shall they heap to themselves teachers, having itching ears;

[4] And they shall turn away their ears from the truth, and shall be turned unto fables.

The Messiah confirms that wide is the gate and broad is the way that leads to destruction; however, narrow is the way that leads to life and few will find it. In other words many will not believe, except or embrace the truth of the scriptures but rather ignore the warnings concerning the false prophets in sheep clothing in these last days.

Christianity being one of the largest religions in the world certainly does not constitute a narrow path and must be analyzed to see how much truth actually exists.

Matthew 7:13-15 (KJV)

[13] Enter ye in at the strait gate: for wide is the gate, and broad is the way, that leadeth to destruction, and many there be which go in thereat:

[14] Because strait is the gate, and narrow is the way, which leadeth unto life, and few there be that find it.

[15] Beware of false prophets, which come to you in sheep's clothing, but inwardly they are ravening wolves.

ANOTHER JESUS (MESSIAH)

Paul mentions a time when there will be another Messiah being preached that they (disciples) did not preach. Who could this other Messiah be? Is it the one being preached in the churches today? Paul adds of another spirit and gospel that will also be received instead of the real authentic Messiah, spirit and gospel.

---

2 Corinthians 11:4 (KJV)

[4] For if he that cometh preacheth another Jesus, whom we have not preached, or if ye receive another spirit, which ye have not received, or another gospel, which ye have not accepted, ye might well bear with him.

The Messiah continues to warn us of a false messiah and false prophets in the last days. The deception will be so great that the very elect can and will be fooled. The importance of understanding the truth of God's word is crucial. It's a matter of life and death and should be taken very seriously.

Matthew 24:24 (KJV)

[24] For there shall arise false Christs, and false prophets, and shall shew great signs and wonders; insomuch that, if it were possible, they shall deceive the very elect

---

 True Israel has fallen prey to many of the doctrines of Christianity due to the conditioning during the times of their slavery. When True Israel was captured from the west coast of Africa, they were not Christians. As a matter of fact, they were captured by the

Africans, sold to Europeans who were Christians that were supported and funded by the fake Jews.

Christianity was forced upon True Israel during the days of slavery and was told they were Gentiles when in fact they were the true descendants from the Israelite nation.

Many of the slaves that came over on the slave ships still had the name of their God in their names which is YAH (www.slavevoyages.com). If you read Psalm 68:4, the only scripture that states God's true proper name in the King James Version. God's proper name was removed out of the bible by the church and replaced with title names such as Lord, God and Jehovah etc.

The letter J was added to the English alphabet about 300-400 years ago in the 17th century, so the Y in Yah was changed to a J (JAH). However, in the King James Version 1611 edition it is spelled with an I (IAH). Even the name JESUS was spelled with an I (IESUS) in the 1611 King James Version of the bible.

Psalm 68:4 (KJV)

[4] Sing unto God, sing praises to his name: extol him that rideth upon the heavens by his name JAH, and rejoice before him.

Although Christianity had its beginnings in AD 30, those who followed or believed the scriptures maintained the truth while suffering persecution for their belief. Approximately around 325 AD, Constantine made the church become a legal religion and compromise began to enter due to Constantine's core pagan beliefs. This was a major pivotal point in Christianity and it only gotten worse since that time. True Christianity eventually became unrecognizable when compared to the scriptures of the bible.

By 590 AD the Roman Catholic Church developed after Constantine Pope Gregory and the doctrines of Christianity became more corrupt with all kinds of unbiblical doctrines and / or belief system. By this time another Jesus was created, a Jesus that took on a different belief, a different look and a different chosen people (The fake Jews).

The effects of the modern-day Christian belief system raised havoc on True Israel because it took them farther away from the truth, farther away from true doctrines and most of all farther away from the true God of the scriptures. This other Jesus is still alive today and continues to mislead the people.

Chapter 14

THE CHURCH IN THE GOSPELS

The word "CHURCH" in the gospels (Matthew, Mark, Luke & John) only appears 3 times and that's only in the book of Matthew.

Matthew 16:18 (KJV)

[18] And I say also unto thee, That thou art Peter, and upon this rock I will build my **church**; and the gates of hell shall not prevail against it.

Matthew 18:17 (KJV)

[17] And if he shall neglect to hear them, tell it unto the **church**: but if he neglect to hear the **church**, let him be unto thee as an heathen man and a publican.

What does the word "CHURCH" mean? Is this the same "CHURCH" Paul speaking of? Let's examine: First, the Greek word for "CHURCH" is "ekklesia" according to Strong's Concordance #1577. It basically means an assembly of people or called out.

Although the word "CHURCH" can mean "ASSEMBLY" but not all assemblies mean a "CHURCH". For example: In Acts 19:32, the word assembly is the word "ekklesia" in which this word is translated "CHURCH", however in this context the word

"ASSEMBLY" actually means a mob or a crowd. In Acts 19:39, the word "ASSEMBLY" means the court. So, the word "ekklesia" in these examples was used for a "mob," "a court," and a crowd". However, the basic meaning of the word "ekklesia" is an "assembly" and its particular meaning is determined by context.

Acts 19:32 (KJV)

32 Some therefore cried one thing, and some another: for the **assembly** was confused: and the more part knew not wherefore they were come together. (means a mob or crowd)

Acts 19:39 (KJV)

39 But if ye enquire any thing concerning other matters, it shall be determined in a lawful **assembly.**

Now, the word "Church" as it appears in Matthew 18:17 is believed that this is the church that Paul is speaking of in his letters. Is it? Let's examine this scripture. In this scripture The Messiah is explaining what to do if your brother should sin or trespass against you. His advice is to tell your brother their faults and if they do not listen bring more witnesses. If your brother continues to neglect you, you should tell the "CHURCH" but if he neglects the "CHURCH", the scriptures say "LET HIM BE UNTO THE HEATHEN MAN AND A PUBLICAN".

Does this sound like the church that Paul speaks about (The body of The Messiah)? No, because the church that Paul speaks about included the Heathens or Gentiles and in Matthews 18:17 it clearly makes a distinction or separation between the "CHURCH" and THE HEATHENS (GENTILES).

If Matthew 18:17 was not pointing towards the church of The Messiah (that included gentiles), what church did he mean? He was speaking of the Israelite "CHURCH", the assembly of the Israelites who believed the gospel of the Kingdom of God (Mark 1:14-15).

We must remember that the Messiah's ministry in the four gospels was limited to his people which were the Israelites (John 1:11, Matthew 10:5-6 & Matthew 1:21) and Gentiles were not included during this period of time. There were only a few occasions The Messiah interacted with other people from other nations.

- 1. The Samaritans: (John 4:1-42)
- 2. The Syrophoenician Woman: (Matthew 15:21-28), (Mark 7:24-30)
- 3. The Greeks: (John 12:20-36)

The children of Israel (Israelites) were called the church in the wilderness. Do the scriptures ever associate being in the wilderness with any other nation of people besides the Israelites? Acts 7:38 clearly supports it was only the Israelites in the wilderness being spoken to by an angel at Mt. Sanai receiving the oracles of The Most High God.

Acts 7:38 (KJV)

[38] This is he, that was in the **church** in the wilderness with the angel which spake to him in the mount Sina, and with our fathers: who received the lively oracles to give unto us:

Exodus 19:3 (KJV)

[3] And Moses went up unto God, and the LORD called unto him out of the mountain, saying, Thus shalt thou say to the house of Jacob, and tell the children of Israel;

Romans 3:2 (KJV)

[2] Much every way: chiefly, because that unto them were committed the oracles of God.

When reading the four gospels all of the disciples preached the Kingdom of God not the church of the body of The Messiah. The disciple Peter was an apostle of Israel and preached primarily to Israelites not Gentiles.

Galatians 2:7-9 (KJV)

[7] But contrariwise, when they saw that the gospel of the uncircumcision was committed unto me, as the gospel of the circumcision was unto Peter;

[8] (For he that wrought effectually in Peter to the apostleship of the circumcision, the same was mighty in me toward the Gentiles:)

[9] And when James, Cephas, and John, who seemed to be pillars, perceived the grace that was given unto me, they gave to me and Barnabas the right hands of fellowship; that we should go unto the heathen, and they unto the circumcision

Acts 11:19 (KJV)

[19] Now they which were scattered abroad upon the persecution that arose about Stephen travelled as far as Phenice, and Cyprus, and Antioch, preaching the word to none but unto the Jews only.

The twelve disciples did not hear of the church, the body of The Messiah until Paul told them about it because Paul was the apostle to the Gentiles. Paul was the one who began laying the foundation for this church or assembly among the Israelites and Gentiles.

Romans 11:13 (KJV)

[13] For I speak to you Gentiles, inasmuch as I am the apostle of the Gentiles, I magnify mine office:

1 Corinthians 3:10-11 (KJV)

[10] According to the grace of God which is given unto me, as a wise masterbuilder, I have laid the foundation, and another buildeth thereon. But let every man take heed how he buildeth thereupon.

[11] For other foundation can no man lay than that is laid, which is Jesus Christ.

Galatians 3:27-28 (KJV)

[27] For as many of you as have been baptized into Christ have put on Christ.

[28] There is neither Jew nor Greek, there is neither bond nor free, there is neither male nor female: for ye are all one in Christ Jesus.

Chapter 15

THE GENTILES

There is much information in the bible concerning the Gentiles and the part they played and still playing in the world today. We must have some understanding as to who are the Gentiles? How are they different from the Israelites?

The Most High God is clear and very specific about his plan and how he feels about the Gentile nations. There is a huge misconception that the Most High God looks at everyone the same and He doesn't separate people. But the scriptures are very clear that the Most High God not only looks at individuals but clearly looks at nations.

We know this because the true nation of Israel went into slavery or captivity over and over again under Gentile nations because of their sins against the Most High God. This punishment did not apply to the Gentile nations. However, the scriptures note that the Most High God has not dealt with any other nation other than True Israel and other nations do not know his true judgment as of yet.

Psalm 147:20 (KJV)

[20] He hath not dealt so with any nation: and as for his judgments, they have not known them. Praise ye the LORD.

We also know he separates people because Paul states a separation in I Corinthians 10:32. We should not be fooled to think the Most High God is looking at only individuals and not nations. The scriptures simply do not support it.

> **1 Corinthians 10:32 (KJV)**
>
> [32] Give none offence, neither to the Jews, nor to the Gentiles, nor to the church of God:

THE NATIONS

The word "nations" in Hebrew is "gôy" or "gôyim" and in Greek "ethnos" which is also rendered "Gentiles and Heathen". Although the word 'nations' means Gentiles and Heathen it can also be applied to the nation of Israel such as in Genesis 12:2 and Deuteronomy 32:28. This word "nations" usually applies to a non-Israelite nation.

> **Genesis 12:2 (KJV)**
>
> [2] And I will make of thee a great **nation,** and I will bless thee, and make thy name great; and thou shalt be a blessing:
>
> **Deuteronomy 32:28 (KJV)**
>
> [28] For they are a **nation** void of counsel, neither is there any understanding in them.

Now that we know the word "NATIONS" means "GENTILES", there is a rare translation of the word "GENTILES" in I Corinthians 12:2 (NIV version).

The NIV and the Amplified version of the bible translates the word to "PAGAN" and "HEATHEN" which is always associated in scriptures primarily with Gentile nations as demonstrated in I Corinthians 12:2. Please compare the three translations. You'll see that the word "NATIONS", "GENTILES", "PAGANS" and "HEAHTENS" are associated to have similar meanings as recorded in different versions of the bible. The word "STRANGERS" is another word that can be used for Gentiles in the scriptures.

---

1 Corinthians 12:2 (KJV)

[2] Ye know that ye were **Gentiles,** carried away unto these dumb idols, even as ye were led.

---

1 Corinthians 12:2 (NIV)

[2] You know that when you were **pagans,** somehow or other you were influenced and led astray to mute idols.

---

1 Corinthians 12:2 (AMPC) (Amplified)

[2] You know that when you were **heathen,** you were led off after idols that could not speak [habitually] as impulse directed *and* whenever the occasion might arise.

Most of the references concerning the nations in the Old Testament are negative. The bible describes them as vomit, source of slaves, a drop in the bucket and dust on the scales.

Leviticus 18:28 (KJV)

28 That the land spue not you out also, when ye defile it, as it spued out the nations that were before you.

Isaiah 40:15 (KJV)

15 Behold, the nations are as a drop of a bucket, and are counted as the small dust of the balance: behold, he taketh up the isles as a very little thing.

Leviticus 25:44 (KJV)

44 Both thy bondmen, and thy bondmaids, which thou shalt have, shall be of the heathen that are round about you; of them shall ye buy bondmen and bondmaids.

The Most High God have always used other nations to test True Israel's faith. The evil ways of other nations was used as a source of temptation to see if True Israel (the chosen people) will follow the Most High God's Laws, Statutes and Commandments.

Deuteronomy 12:30 (KJV)

30 Take heed to thyself that thou be not snared by following them, after that they be destroyed from before thee; and that thou enquire not after their gods, saying, How did these nations serve their gods? even so will I do likewise.

Deuteronomy 29:18 (KJV)

[18] Lest there should be among you man, or woman, or family, or tribe, whose heart turneth away this day from the LORD our God, to go and serve the gods of these nations; lest there should be among you a root that beareth gall and wormwood;

Deuteronomy 8:2 (KJV)

[2] And thou shalt remember all the way which the LORD thy God led thee these forty years in the wilderness, to humble thee, and to prove thee, to know what was in thine heart, whether thou wouldest keep his commandments, or no.

True Israel was never supposed to serve the gods of other nations. This confirms that there are other god's in the world and True Israel is still serving these god's today and is unaware that they are doing this against the God of Abraham, Isaac and Jacob. This will be a topic explored later in this book.

The other nations in the world have always been True Israel's enemy. They have always been associated with wickedness and their fate is not positive.

Psalm 9:17 (KJV)

[17] The wicked shall be turned into hell, and all the nations that forget God.

> **Isaiah 64:2 (KJV)**
>
> [2] As when the melting fire burneth, the fire causeth the waters to boil, to make thy name known to thine adversaries, that the nations may tremble at thy presence!

However, when The Most High God was angry with His chosen people Israel, He will use other nations to punish them such as in the many slaveries and captivities. This is why He always left a few people from other nations around the nation of Israel for a continual test to see if they would choose righteousness or wickedness. Unfortunately, True Israel chose wickedness which landed them in the current position on earth today.

> **Judges 2:21-22 (KJV)**
>
> [21] I also will not henceforth drive out any from before them of the nations which Joshua left when he died:
>
> [22] That through them I may prove Israel, whether they will keep the way of the LORD to walk therein, as their fathers did keep it, or not.

In the New Testament the Messiah's ministry was basically towards his own people of Israel. He did not have a ministry towards other people from other nations except on a few occasions mentioned earlier in this book. He practically called the Syrophenician woman (from another nation) a dog.

Why would The Messiah do such a thing? He is often promoted as a man of love, which is true, however he is also a man of war and of judgment that most so called biblical preachers totally choose to ignore today.

Mark 7:26-27 (KJV)

[26] The woman was a Greek, a Syrophenician by nation; and she besought him that he would cast forth the devil out of her daughter.

[27] But Jesus said unto her, Let the children first be filled: for it is not meet to take the children's bread, and to cast it unto the dogs.

Matthew 15:26 (KJV)

[26] But he answered and said, It is not meet to take the children's bread, and to cast it to dogs.

Matthew 10:34 (KJV)

[34] Think not that I am come to send peace on earth: I came not to send peace, but a sword.

The Messiah was very clear when he told his disciples do not go in the way of the Gentiles or nations but go rather to the lost sheep of the house of Israel.

Matthew 10:5-6 (KJV)

[5] These twelve Jesus sent forth, and commanded them, saying, Go not into the way of the **Gentiles,** and into any city of the Samaritans enter ye not:

[6] But go rather to the lost sheep of the house of Israel.

The nation of Israel was always separate from other nations in the Most High God's eyes and we must interpret the scriptures just as he sees the world. Now, that we have some understanding concerning the nations. Does the bible specifically record who is Gentile?

WHO IS A GENTILE?

The bible is very specific who the Gentiles are in the world today. We must go to the very beginning of the bible where The Most High God began to map out the lineage of people upon the earth.

Every human came from one of three people's left behind on earth after the great flood. Only eight people survived this flood. It was Noah, his wife and the three wives of Japheth, Shem and Ham (The sons of Noah). This was a total of eight people who survived the great flood.

Beginning in the book of Genesis chapter 10, the lineage of Noah sons are clearly laid out. Take notice of the lineage of Noah's son Japheth. He is the progenitor of the Gentile nations (Europeans), just as Ham is the progenitor of the dark races, except the Negroes (Africa) and Shem (the Hebrew lineage) in the Middle East.

Genesis 10:1-5 (KJV)

1 Now these are the generations of the sons of Noah, Shem, Ham, and Japheth: and unto them were sons born after the flood.

2 The sons of Japheth; Gomer, and Magog, and Madai, and Javan, and Tubal, and Meshech, and Tiras.

3 And the sons of Gomer; Ashkenaz, and Riphath, and Togarmah.

4 And the sons of Javan; Elishah, and Tarshish, Kittim, and Dodanim.

5 By these were the isles of the Gentiles divided in their lands; every one after his tongue, after their families, in their nations.

The book of Jasher (missing book from the bible) mentions the same lineage of Japheth as in the book of Genesis. Although the book of Jasher is missing from our bibles today it is mentioned in our bible (Joshua 10:13 and II Samuel 1:18).

Jasher 7:1-9

1 And these are the names of the sons of Noah: Japheth, Ham and Shem; and children were born to them after the flood, for they had taken wives before the flood.

2 These are the sons of Japheth; Gomer, Magog, Madai, Javan, Tubal, Meshech, and Tiras, seven sons.

3 And the sons of Gomer were Askinaz, Rephath and Tegarmah.

4 And the sons of Magog were Elichanaf and Lubal.

5 And the children of Madai were Achon, Zeelo, Chazoni and Lot.

6 And the sons of Javan were Elisha, Tarshish, Chittim and Dudonim.

7 And the sons of Tubal were Ariphi, Kesed and Taari.

8 And the sons of Meshech were Dedon, Zaron and Shebashni.

9 And the sons of Tiras were Benib, Gera, Lupirion and Gilak; these are the sons of Japheth according to their families, and their numbers in those days were about four hundred and sixty men

If the Europeans are considered to be Gentiles then how are the so-called black people or African Americans be Gentiles? This would be impossible and can only mean that the black people's lineage must come from one of Noah's other sons and in this case his son Shem. Shem's lineage leads right down to the children of Israel (The Hebrew Israelites).

The black people (Israelites) have been taught that they are Gentiles with absolutely no proof but accepted this belief system from the Roman Empire which created Christianity. Romans are considered to be Gentiles not Israelites from the biblical scriptures.

THE GENTILE DYNASTY

The Gentile Dynasty was always foretold in the bible and continues to come to pass in our day. The Most High God shared this vision with Nebuchadnezzar and it was interpreted by the prophet Daniel (An Israelite) in the book of Daniel.

One that studies World History concerning Nations will find that World History lines up perfectly with the bible. Every nation that ruled in the course of history is mentioned and foretold in the bible. It is no secret who will be in charge of the world if one was to read the scriptures. The scriptures clearly let us know that the Gentiles will be in charge until the times of the Gentiles be fulfilled. These were the words of the Messiah and Paul confirmed them.

Luke 21:24 (KJV)

[24] And they shall fall by the edge of the sword, and shall be led away captive into all nations: and Jerusalem shall be trodden down of the Gentiles, until the times of the Gentiles be fulfilled.

This means that True Israel is not in charge today but the Gentile nations are the ruling Kingdom of the world. Most of True Israel are still blinded but will awaken soon and realize their destiny as a nation that will rule the world once the Messiah returns to gather them from the four corners of the earth.

Romans 11:25 (KJV)

[25] For I would not, brethren, that ye should be ignorant of this mystery, lest ye should be wise in your own conceits; that blindness in part is happened to Israel, until the fulness of the Gentiles be come in.

In the book of Daniel chapter 2, tells of Nebuchadnezzar having a dream. He was troubled by this dream and wanted someone to interpret it. He could not remember the dream but knew it was troubling. He commanded to call on the magicians, astrologers and sorcerers to interpret the dream but none could.

Daniel was able to go before King Nebuchadnezzar and explain the dream. Daniel explained that King Nebuchadnezzar saw a great image with a head of fine gold, breast and arms of silver, belly and thighs of brass, legs of iron and feet part iron and part of clay.

Daniel 2:31-33 (KJV)

[31] Thou, O king, sawest, and behold a great image. This great image, whose brightness was excellent, stood before thee; and the form thereof was terrible.

[32] This image's head was of fine gold, his breast and his arms of silver, his belly and his thighs of brass,

[33] His legs of iron, his feet part of iron and part of clay.

After Daniel explained what he saw in the vision he began to give the interpretation of the vision. He explained that each part of this image represented a future coming kingdom upon the earth.

Daniel 2:36-45 (KJV)

[36] This is the dream; and we will tell the interpretation thereof before the king.

[37] Thou, O king, art a king of kings: for the God of heaven hath given thee a kingdom, power, and strength, and glory.

[38] And wheresoever the children of men dwell, the beasts of the field and the fowls of the heaven hath he given into thine hand, and hath made thee ruler over them all. Thou art this head of gold.

[39] And after thee shall arise another kingdom inferior to thee, and another third kingdom of brass, which shall bear rule over all the earth.

⁴⁰ And the fourth kingdom shall be strong as iron: forasmuch as iron breaketh in pieces and subdueth all things: and as iron that breaketh all these, shall it break in pieces and bruise.

⁴¹ And whereas thou sawest the feet and toes, part of potters' clay, and part of iron, the kingdom shall be divided; but there shall be in it of the strength of the iron, forasmuch as thou sawest the iron mixed with miry clay.

⁴² And as the toes of the feet were part of iron, and part of clay, so the kingdom shall be partly strong, and partly broken.

⁴³ And whereas thou sawest iron mixed with miry clay, they shall mingle themselves with the seed of men: but they shall not cleave one to another, even as iron is not mixed with clay.

⁴⁴ And in the days of these kings shall the God of heaven set up a kingdom, which shall never be destroyed: and the kingdom shall not be left to other people, but it shall break in pieces and consume all these kingdoms, and it shall stand for ever.

⁴⁵ Forasmuch as thou sawest that the stone was cut out of the mountain without hands, and that it brake in pieces the iron, the brass, the clay, the silver, and the gold; the great God hath made known to the king what shall come to pass hereafter: and the dream is certain, and the interpretation thereof sure.

The 1st Image Daniel Saw

Nebuchadnezzar's Dream

Daniel 2

606 BC
Babylonian
Empire

The Times

538 BC
Medo-Persian
Empire

333 BC
Grecian
Empire

of the

63 BC
Rome
(not named)

Gentiles

Approximately where we are,
today

Christ

In Daniel chapter 7, the prophet Daniel had another dream and
visions likening other kingdoms to animals. Each animal
represented a Gentile Kingdom just as the great image in Daniel
chapter 2. What Daniel saw was four great beasts coming out of
the sea (people). The first beast was a lion with eagle wings; the
second beast was like a bear with 3 ribs in its mouth, the third
beast was like a leopard which had four wings on its back and the
fourth beast was just named dreadful and terrible. Each beast
represented a ruling Gentile Kingdom just as Nebuchadnezzar's
statute.

Daniel 7:1-8 (KJV)

1 In the first year of Belshazzar king of Babylon Daniel had a dream and visions of his head upon his bed: then he wrote the dream, and told the sum of the matters.

2 Daniel spake and said, I saw in my vision by night, and, behold, the four winds of the heaven strove upon the great sea.

3 And four great beasts came up from the sea, diverse one from another.

4 The first was like a lion, and had eagle's wings: I beheld till the wings thereof were plucked, and it was lifted up from the earth, and made stand upon the feet as a man, and a man's heart was given to it.

5 And behold another beast, a second, like to a bear, and it raised up itself on one side, and it had three ribs in the mouth of it between the teeth of it: and they said thus unto it, Arise, devour much flesh.

6 After this I beheld, and lo another, like a leopard, which had upon the back of it four wings of a fowl; the beast had also four heads; and dominion was given to it.

7 After this I saw in the night visions, and behold a fourth beast, dreadful and terrible, and strong exceedingly; and it had great iron teeth: it devoured and brake in pieces, and stamped the residue with the feet of it: and it was diverse from all the beasts that were before it; and it had ten horns.

8 I considered the horns, and, behold, there came up among them another little horn, before whom there were three of the first horns plucked up by the roots: and, behold, in this horn were eyes like the eyes of man, and a mouth speaking great things.

The 2nd Image Daniel Saw

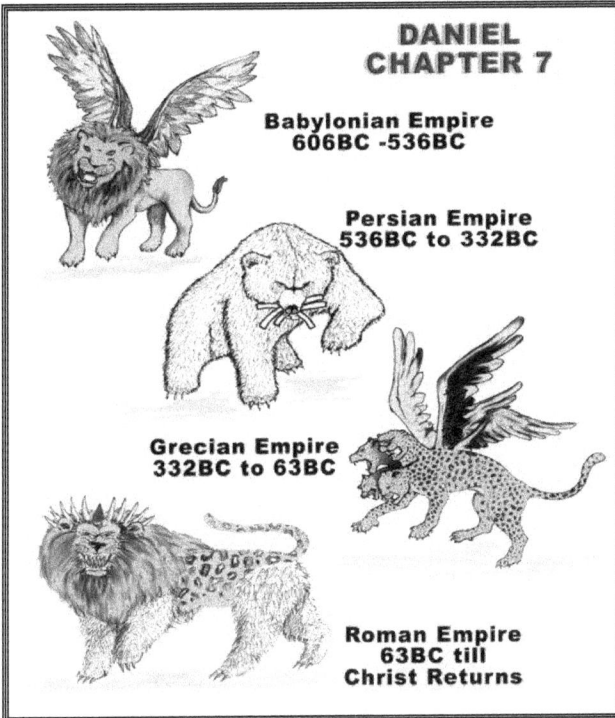

DANIEL CHAPTER 7

Babylonian Empire
606BC -536BC

Persian Empire
536BC to 332BC

Grecian Empire
332BC to 63BC

Roman Empire
63BC till
Christ Returns

King Nebuchadnezzar and Daniels Visions Compared

Daniel 2   **Daniel 7**

Babylon
605-539 BC

Medo-
Persia
539-331 BC

Grecia
331-168 BC

Rome
168 BC-476 AD

4 Kingdoms Who Scattered Judah

Daniel's Dream	Zechariah's Four Horns	Nebuchadnezzar's Dream
Lion	1. Babylon	Head of Gold
Bear	2. Medo-Persia	Chest and Arms of Silver
Leopard	3. Greece	Belly and Thighs of Bronze
Terrible Beast	4. Rome	Legs of Iron and Feet of Iron and Clay

Daniel's Dream of
4 Beasts (Daniel 7)

Nebuchadnezzar's Statue
(Daniel 2)

www.pictures4bibles.com

The Gentile Dynasty was told from the very beginning in the bible and when lined up with world history one can see it happened exactly as told in the scriptures. Please see chart.

Comparison between Daniel 2 (Statute Image) and Daniel 7 (The Beast)		
Daniel 2 (The Statute Image)	**Daniel 7 (The Beast)**	**Nation In Power**
Head of Gold	Lion with Eagle's Wings	Babylon = Iraq
Chest and Arms of Silver	Bear with 3 Ribs in Mouth	Medo-Persia = Russia + Iran
Belly and Thighs of Bronze	Leopard with Four Heads	Greek = Greece
Legs of Iron	Beast with Iron Teeth	Pagan Rome
Feet of Iron and Clay	10 Horns of The Beast	The 10 Gentile Nations Papal or Holy Roman Empire (E.U. European Union)

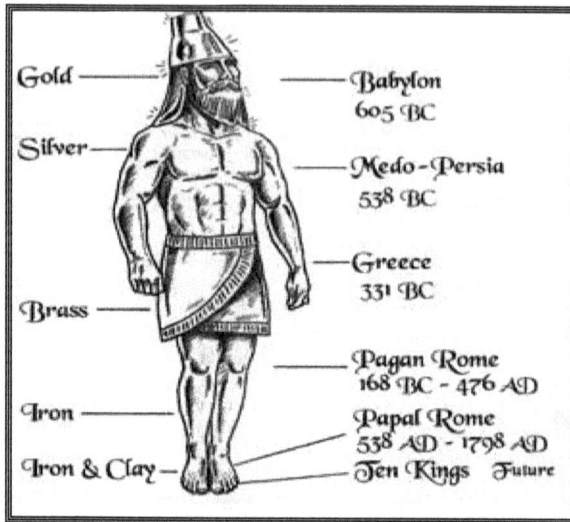

We are currently approaching the end of the last Gentile Kingdom on this earth before the Most High God, The Messiah and the children of Israel take rulership over the entire earth with the Kingdom of Israel being the nation in power. This power will be forever and ever.

Daniel 7:18 (KJV)

[18] But the saints of the most High shall take the kingdom, and possess the kingdom for ever, even for ever and ever.

There is a scripture in 2nd Esdras (Apocrypha) that says Esau (Gentiles) is the end of the world and Jacob (Israel) is the beginning that follows after Esau or Gentile reign. This would line up with other scriptures supporting this fact.

2nd Esdras 6:9 (KJV)
9 For Esau is the end of the world, and Jacob is the beginning of it that followeth.

The Apocrypha

This is just a note to say the Apocrypha books were in the original 1611 King James Bible and were taken out in 1885. This means the Apocrypha books were in the bible for 274 years before being removed.

The Image of Daniel Chapter 2

"Nebuchadnezzar had dreams...

The secret was revealed to Daniel...

[God] made known what will be in the latter days."

(Daniel 2:1, 19, 28)

The Image: Daniel 2:31–33

The head of gold = Nebuchadnezzar, king of Babylon

(verses 36–38)

Chest and arms of silver = Medo-Persia

(verse 32; Daniel 5: 30 31)

Belly of bronze = Greece

(Daniel 2.39, 8:21–22)

The Rock destroys the Image: Daniel 2: 34–35

Legs of iron = Rome

(Daniel 2:40)

The Rock = Jesus

(Matthew 21:42–44)

Feet and toes = Strong and weak governments of the Endtime

(Daniel 2:41–43)

The mountain fills the earth = The Kingdom of God

(Daniel 2:44; Micah 4:1)

GRAFTED IN (GENTILES)

Although there are Gentiles who were The Most High God's servants throughout scripture such as King Nebuchadnezzar and others. They were not the chosen people of the Most High God. They were not the lot of his inheritance.

We must take a look at the chronological order of the Gentiles being grafted into the fold with the Israelites. First, the bible describes Gentiles as the wild olive tree (Romans 11:17) and Israelites the good olive tree or natural branches (Romans 11:21, 24) (Jeremiah 11:16). The Gentiles were grafted into the natural olive tree and not the other way around (biblical fact).

This section will address the how, why and when concerning Gentiles being grafted in. The first time the bible records a Gentile being grafted in is in the book of Acts chapter 10. Notice that the book of Acts is after the Gospels of Matthew, Mark, Luke and John, after the death of The Messiah. This means that the Gentiles were not being addressed in the Gospels (something to think about).

In the book of Acts chapter 10 the subject matter is the Roman Centurion named Cornelius (Gentile). He had a vision from the Most High God where he saw an angel telling him to send for Peter (An Israelite Apostle). Why do we suppose The Most High God instructed Cornelius to send for Peter? Why couldn't the Most High God just give Cornelius the instructions he wanted him to have without calling for Peter?

Let's keep in mind that Cornelius was called after the death of the Messiah to seek out Peter (the Apostle). Why did Cornelius have to go to Peter? Why couldn't he just accept The Messiah as his Lord and personal savior without being instructed by an Israelite in which he was told by the angel of God to seek? Should this order or formula exist today? The answer is simply order.

The Most High God chose a people to do this job (True Israel). The Most High God is very organized and orderly and his chosen people are the salt of the earth to lead Gentile nations to righteousness but they fell (sinned) and now are subject to punishment in captivity because of it.

John 4:22 (KJV)

[22] Ye worship ye know not what: we know what we worship: for salvation is of the Jews.

This leads to the reason Gentiles got grafted in. When True Israel stumbled and fell the opportunity for salvation came unto to the Gentiles as stated in Romans 11:11. This was to provoke True Israel to jealously so they could be persuaded to come back to their own God and not the gods of the Gentiles. So, did Gentiles get grafted in because The Messiah died on the cross initially? (Something to think about).

Romans 11:11 (KJV)

[11] I say then, Have they stumbled that they should fall? God forbid: but rather through their fall salvation is come unto the Gentiles, for to provoke them to jealousy.

The Most High God is a jealous God and when his chosen people (True Israel) continued to sin and wanted to serve the god's of the Gentile nations, it was hurtful to Him, so in turn it seemed as thou he wanted True Israel to feel what He was feeling. Nevertheless, the Most High God did not cast his people away.

For a lack of a better phrase or word, True Israel is temporarily suspended until after their captivity is over.

Exodus 20:5 (KJV)

[5] Thou shalt not bow down thyself to them, nor serve them: for I the LORD thy God am a jealous God, visiting the iniquity of the fathers upon the children unto the third and fourth generation of them that hate me;

Deuteronomy 32:21 is a prophecy Paul was referring to from Romans 11:11

Deuteronomy 32:21 (KJV)

[21] They have moved me to jealousy with that which is not God; they have provoked me to anger with their vanities: and I will move them to jealousy with those which are not a people; I will provoke them to anger with a foolish nation.

In the meantime, the Most High God is pulling out a people that are not a people (Gentiles) for his name. This act does not annul any plan that the God of Abraham, Isaac and Jacob have for his chosen people (True Israel).

Acts 15:14-17 (KJV)

[14] Simeon hath declared how God at the first did visit the Gentiles, to take out of them a people for his name.

[15] And to this agree the words of the prophets; as it is written,

[16] After this I will return, and will build again the tabernacle of David, which is fallen down; and I will build again the ruins thereof, and I will set it up:

[17] That the residue of men might seek after the Lord, and all the Gentiles, upon whom my name is called, saith the Lord, who doeth all these things.

Amos 9:11-13 is the prophesy Simeon was referring to from Acts 15:14-17 (The words of the prophet as written).

Amos 9:11-13 (KJV)

[11] In that day will I raise up the tabernacle of David that is fallen, and close up the breaches thereof; and I will raise up his ruins, and I will build it as in the days of old:

[12] That they may possess the remnant of Edom, and of all the heathen, which are called by my name, saith the LORD that doeth this.

[13] Behold, the days come, saith the LORD, that the plowman shall overtake the reaper, and the treader of grapes him that soweth seed; and the mountains shall drop sweet wine, and all the hills shall melt.

> **Romans 11:1-2 (KJV)**
>
> 1 I say then, Hath God cast away his people? God forbid. For I also am an Israelite, of the seed of Abraham, of the tribe of Benjamin.
>
> [2] God hath not cast away his people which he foreknew. Wot ye not what the scripture saith of Elias? how he maketh intercession to God against Israel saying,

It appears the Gentiles were being grafted in after the death of the Messiah and not while the Messiah was on earth during his ministry. The Gentiles are being grafted in for three reasons:

I. To make True Israel jealous (Romans 11:11)

II. To take out of them a people for the Most High God's name (Acts 15:14)

III. To serve the nation of Israel in the Kingdom to come in righteousness (Isaiah 14:2)

Today, the Gentile nations are still being grafted into the fold. This will continue while True Israel is blinded in part and the fullness of the Gentiles comes in.

> **Romans 11:25 (KJV)**
>
> [25] For I would not, brethren, that ye should be ignorant of this mystery, lest ye should be wise in your own conceits; that blindness in part is happened to Israel, until the fulness of the Gentiles be come in.

THE GENTILES (CUT OFF)

While True Israel is in a place of slumber, sleep or punishment for the most part during these days of awakening, the Gentiles on the earth should have taken the Gospel in its true authentic form. Instead, it was polluted, changed and corrupted to fit a different narrative than what it was meant for.

For example:

I. The bible is probably about 95% written about the Israelites and modern-day Christianity rarcly speak of or mentions them as the true people of the book.

II. Nearly all of the **prophetic scriptures** in our bibles are written about the Israelites and modern-day Christianity does not speak or teach that True Israel will be gathered during the last days.

III. The bible is taught from a European perspective where everything and everyone is inclusive no matter whom they are and scriptures do not teach that at all.

IV. Gentiles did not share with True Israel who they were when taken as slaves through the Transatlantic Slave Trade. Instead, they used the bible to demonstrate that they were the masters and True Israel should obey and follow them.

There are many, many, many more examples of how the Gentile nations have taken the bible and distorted it to fit their agenda. Now, whether it was done on purpose or mistake is another argument.

However, when researched, one will find that many Gentiles know and can confirm who the real Israelites are today and those that do not know will eventually know that they inherited lies.

Jeremiah 16:19 (KJV)

[19] O LORD, my strength, and my fortress, and my refuge in the day of affliction, the Gentiles shall come unto thee from the ends of the earth, and shall say, Surely our fathers have inherited lies, vanity, and things wherein there is no profit.

There was a warning given to Gentiles from Paul in Romans 11:13

Romans 11:13 (KJV)

[13] For I speak to you Gentiles, inasmuch as I am the apostle of the Gentiles, I magnify mine office:

This warning to the Gentiles was to let them know that boasting against the natural branches (The Israelites) was prohibited. Let's take a moment and think about something. If the Most High God took his chosen people (True Israel) and put them into slavery after slavery because of their wickedness and constant disobedience. What more would he do to the Gentiles who are not a people?

Remember, the Gentiles have not received their full judgment or punishment as of yet. The Gentiles today are on top of the world being the leaders of the world. True Israel is receiving their punishment now, a little at a time through multiple slaveries and other challenges as stated in Deuteronomy Chapter 28:15-68.

Psalm 147:19-20 (KJV)

[19] He sheweth his word unto Jacob, his statutes and his judgments unto Israel.

[20] He hath not dealt so with any nation: and as for his judgments, they have not known them. Praise ye the LORD.

This warning to the Gentiles was to let them know they will be cut off due to their continual boasting and pride against the true Israelites of the bible. The Gentiles of today are uplifting and supporting the fake Jews (who are rich) and the real Israelites are being ignored and forgotten (who are cursed).

This is clearly stated in Romans chapter 11. If the Most High God did not spare the natural branches (True Israel), He will not spare others who are being grafted in that will continue to be high minded. The Gentiles must be in the Most High's God goodness to be grafted in or otherwise they will be cut off.

Romans 11:18-22 (KJV)

[18] Boast not against the branches. But if thou boast, thou bearest not the root, but the root thee.

[19] Thou wilt say then, The branches were broken off, that I might be grafted in.

²⁰ Well; because of unbelief they were broken off, and thou standest by faith. Be not highminded, but fear:

²¹ For if God spared not the natural branches, take heed lest he also spare not thee.

²² Behold therefore the goodness and severity of God: on them which fell, severity; but toward thee, goodness, if thou continue in his goodness: otherwise thou also shalt be cut off.

The scriptures go on to say that it would be easier for True Israel (Israelites) to be grafted back into their own natural Olive Tree than those who are considered to be the wild Olive Tree (Gentiles). Keep in mind; Gentiles are grafted into Israel's tree not the other way around.

There is a prophecy in the book of Zephaniah that mention nations being cut off. These nations will be gathered and the Most High God's indignation will be poured upon them in his jealous anger with fire. This prophecy could be what Paul was trying to say in the book of Romans.

Zephaniah 3:6-8 (KJV)

⁶ I have cut off the nations: their towers are desolate; I made their streets waste, that none passeth by: their cities are destroyed, so that there is no man, that there is none inhabitant.

⁷ I said, Surely thou wilt fear me, thou wilt receive instruction; so their dwelling should not be cut off, howsoever I punished them: but they rose early, and corrupted all their doings.

⁸ Therefore wait ye upon me, saith the LORD, until the day that I rise up to the prey: for my determination is to gather the nations,

that I may assemble the kingdoms, to pour upon them mine indignation, even all my fierce anger: for all the earth shall be devoured with the fire of my jealousy.

In the book of Joel there is another prophetic scripture that has not yet taken place. Joel mentions how the Most High God will call all nations down to the valley of Jehoshaphat and deal with them for the mistreatment of his chosen people (True Israel). This judgment on other nations is due to the scattering of Israelites, given a boy for a harlot and selling the girls for wine and all the other many things that the African American (Israelites) community has suffered.

Joel 3:1-3 (KJV)

1 For, behold, in those days, and in that time, when I shall bring again the captivity of Judah and Jerusalem,

[2] I will also gather all nations, and will bring them down into the valley of Jehoshaphat, and will plead with them there for my people and for my heritage Israel, whom they have scattered among the nations, and parted my land.

[3] And they have cast lots for my people; and have given a boy for an harlot, and sold a girl for wine, that they might drink.

The Most High God goes on to say concerning the Gentiles (heathens) that they should prepare for war. They should assemble themselves and get ready to be judged. This is amazing when you think that humans will try and fight with the Most High God and think they are going to win.

This is what the Most High God means about boasting, having such arrogance to think they are mightier than Him. If you read the story of Nimrod and Pharoah they had the same type of arrogance and this is why other nations will be held accountable for their actions. No one escapes God's judgment. Absolutely, no one!

Joel 3:9-12 (KJV)

[9] Proclaim ye this among the Gentiles; Prepare war, wake up the mighty men, let all the men of war draw near; let them come up:

[10] Beat your plowshares into' swords and your pruninghooks into spears: let the weak say, I am strong.

[11] Assemble yourselves, and come, all ye heathen, and gather yourselves together round about: thither cause thy mighty ones to come down, O LORD.

[12] Let the heathen be wakened, and come up to the valley of Jehoshaphat: for there will I sit to judge all the heathen round about.

David wrote in Psalm 110:6 which confirm that the Most High God will judge the heathen nations to the degree that there will be many dead bodies. As a matter of fact, in Ezekiel 39:11-12 it states that the house of Israel will be burying dead bodies for seven months. This burying speaks of Gog and Magog in which we know are Gentiles from Genesis 10: 2 and I Chronicles 1:5 from the son of Japheth. Gog and Magog is said to be today's Russia and southern Europe.

Psalm 110:6 (KJV)

[6] He shall judge among the heathen, he shall fill the places with the dead bodies; he shall wound the heads over many countries.

Ezekiel 39:11-12 (KJV)

[11] And it shall come to pass in that day, that I will give unto Gog a place there of graves in Israel, the valley of the passengers on the east of the sea: and it shall stop the noses of the passengers: and there shall they bury Gog and all his multitude: and they shall call it The valley of Hamongog.

[12] And seven months shall the house of Israel be burying of them, that they may cleanse the land.

The Gentile nations are required to fall in line with the Most High God just as the true Israelites of the bible with no exceptions. The Gentiles should not be fooled by continuing the boasting, the arrogance and not recognizing the true children of Israel. This behavior will only bring upon judgment because they have taken away from the word of God and taught a narrative that is not true. The bible says we should not add or take away from it or we would be in jeopardy of having our part out of the book of life.

Deutcronomy 4:2 (KJV)

[2] Ye shall not add unto the word which I command you, neither shall ye diminish ought from it, that ye may keep the commandments of the LORD your God which I command you.

Revelation 22:19 (KJV)

[19] And if any man shall take away from the words of the book of this prophecy, God shall take away his part out of the book of life, and out of the holy city, and from the things which are written in this book.

We'll end this section by saying keep the commandments. Do not despise the word of the Most High God in its authentic form because there is life in it and only truth will make you free.

Proverbs 13:13 (KJV)

[13] Whoso despiseth the word shall be destroyed: but he that feareth the commandment shall be rewarded.

John 8:32 (KJV)

[32] And ye shall know the truth, and the truth shall make you free.

Chapter 16
PAGANISM

This chapter is going to be one of the most compelling chapters in this book because of the subject matter which is "PAGANISM". Do we really know what it means to be "PAGAN" or be involved in paganism?

This is a very important matter to those who authentically say they believe in the bible but is challenged by the fine line of knowing what is pagan and what is bible. Many centuries ago, these two worlds collided and mixed.

Remember the bible had an origin before Christianity was ever founded. Christianity was not founded until approximately 30 AD. However, it was followed in its authentic form because you had the Israelite Apostles / Disciples spreading its authentic message about the MESSIAH and the KINGDOM of GOD from the biblical scriptures. Another note to remember is that the apostles never called themselves Christians. They were called Christians first in ANTIOCH (Acts 11:26) by another nation of people.

The word Christian is only used three times in the whole King James Version of the bible (Acts 11:26, Acts 26:28, I Peter 4:16). The disciples never called themselves Christians but brethren, which were more common during that time. The disciples constantly preached and taught the true message of the biblical scriptures during their reign on the earth.

The scriptures that were being taught during the disciples' time on the earth was from the Old Testament because the New Testament had not been written or was being written during this time. We know this because Paul often quoted from the Old Testament. So, the New Testament preaching and teaching derived from the Old Testament.

So, what changed? According to today's interpretation of the biblical scriptures, it is taught that The Messiah who died on the cross had done away with so many things, mainly the laws of The Most High God. What most people don't realize is that during the time of the disciples on earth, there was a constant battle for people to live right according to the biblical scriptures and throughout time people were persecuted for following the scriptures.

This leads to our subject matter at hand "PAGANISM". While there were people trying to live biblically correct there were always people living contrary to the biblical scriptures that we call pagan practices today. It was Emperor Constantine of Rome who legalized the religion of Christianity as we know it today around 313 AD. This movement came with serious altercations to the authentic form of Christianity or the scriptures. It is said that Emperor Constantine converted to being a Christian; however, he never stopped his pagan practices or the worshipping of other gods (mainly the sun). He convinced those who wanted to become a Christian that they can worship other gods and be labeled as a Christian.

This was a huge problem for the authentic form of Christianity because it completely destroyed the authentic version of the scriptures. Remember Rome (a Gentile nation) was in power during this time of Constantine (a Roman Emperor) and had control of all politics and religion belief systems during this time.

As we move forward into history today, this Roman dominated belief system has not changed. Modern Day Christianity has taken on other forms of beliefs contrary to the bible. This was because Roman Emperor Constantine allowed pagan practices to be mixed with the belief system of Authentic Christianity or just simply authentic bible belief.

When Roman Catholicism was created all other forms of Christianity that followed adapted the ways of Roman Catholicism. This includes all forms of Christianity such as:

Baptist	Pentecostal / Charismatic	Dutch Reform
Episcopalian	Lutheran	Church of the Nazarene
Non-Denominational	Angelican	Disciples of Christ
Evangelist	Evangelical	United Church of Christ
Methodist	Assemblies of God	Mennonite
Presbyterian	Christian Reform	Christian Science
Quaker	Seventh-Day Adventist	Church of God In Christ

It doesn't matter what denomination of Christianity that has been founded or developed, it all stems from Roman Catholicism. It is biblical fact that the bible belief system came from God whose name is YAH (Psalm 68:4). His word or oracles was only given to the Israelites to share with other nations because this was the Most High's divine order and still his order today.

Psalm 147:19 (KJV)

[19] He sheweth his word unto Jacob, his statutes and his judgments unto Israel.

Romans 3:1-2 (KJV)

1 What advantage then hath the Jew? or what profit is there of circumcision?

[2] Much every way: chiefly, because that unto them were committed the oracles of God.

The Roman interpretation of the scriptures must be re-examined because they were not the original people to deliver this message of the scriptures to the world. In fact, they were the heathens who took the book (bible) and began interpreting as they saw fit which in turn created the many false doctrines, we receive today in modern day Christianity.

There is a scripture in the book of Revelation that notes "THE MOTHER OF HARLOTS AND ABOMINATIONS OF THE EARTH". Many associate this scripture to mean the Roman Catholic Church or the religious system that comes out of Rome.

If this is the case then the Roman Catholic Church is the mother of all Christian churches that follow the doctrines created by them. This would give proof and indicate that the modern-day Christian Church as we know it today is not biblical and follows after another god and not the God of Abraham, Isaac and Jacob.

Revelation 17:3-5 (KJV)

[3] So he carried me away in the spirit into the wilderness: and I saw a woman sit upon a scarlet coloured beast, full of names of blasphemy, having seven heads and ten horns.

[4] And the woman was arrayed in purple and scarlet colour, and decked with gold and precious stones and pearls, having a golden cup in her hand full of abominations and filthiness of her fornication:

[5] And upon her forehead was a name written, MYSTERY, BABYLON THE GREAT, THE MOTHER OF HARLOTS AND ABOMINATIONS OF THE EARTH.

In the book of Daniel chapter 7, a horn will rise out of a kingdom and speak great words against the Most High God and think to change times and laws. We know Daniel chapter 7 is speaking of a Gentile Kingdom and the only Gentile Kingdom that has change the laws and times of the Most High God is the Roman Catholic Church (Rome the Kingdom). The Roman Catholic Church is guilty and admits their role in changing the biblical scriptures to fit their narrative.

This may be a hard pill to swallow for some people but the proof is in the in the scriptures when proper understanding is obtained. We will explore some of those differences as we move along in this chapter.

Daniel 7:25 (KJV)

²⁵ And he shall speak great words against the most High, and shall wear out the saints of the most High, and think to change times and laws: and they shall be given into his hand until a time and times and the dividing of time.

If the word "PAGAN" can mean "NATION", "HEATHEN", then that means PAGANISM comes from another nation other than Israel and since the God of Abraham, Isaac and Jacob told True Israel to stay away from the ways of others nations, it must have been important for a very good reason. The reason being is that the ways of the heathen does not come from The Most High God of the bible and should be avoided at all cost.

The word "PAGANISM" is derived from the Latin word "PAGANUS" and a basic definition could be: Anyone involved in any religious act, practice or ceremony which is not biblical. Paganism usually refers to the authentic religions of ancient Greece, Rome, Egypt and Scandinavia etc. Those who believe and worship many gods are considered PAGAN.

This introduction to" PAGANISM" is a general overview and not all of the specifics. There is much more information to share concerning this topic but of course we cannot put it all in one book. However, this author will share more of the specifics on paganism in the upcoming pages. "PAGANISM" was one of the main reasons True Israel went into captivity wanting to serve other gods other than their own. Let's find out what they did and still doing to this day.

PAGANS
ADDITIONAL SCRIPTURES

Deuteronomy 17:2-7 (Worship the Moon & Sun)	Deuteronomy 18:9-12 (Divination, Witchcraft)	Judges 2:11 (Serving Ba'-a-lim)
Acts 8:9-13 (Sorcery & Witchcraft)	Jeremiah 10:1-5 (Vain Christmas Practice)	Acts 17:16-23 (City in Idolatry)
II Kings 23:5 (Incense unto Ba'al, Sun, Moon & Planets)	Numbers 25:1-5 (Bowed down to gods)	Exodus 7:10-12 (Sorcerers, Magicians & Enchantments)

TRADITIONS OF MEN
(THE HOLIDAYS)

The holidays would be a perfect example of what we call traditions of men. There is not one scripture in the bible to remotely support any of the holidays that are celebrated today. Nearly all of the holidays have very dark and satanic roots. There are several scriptures that warn us to stay away from traditions of men and only keep The Most High God's commandments which include the holy days not holidays. We cannot keep our own tradition and reject the commandments of God.

Colossians 2:8 (KJV)

[8] Beware lest any man spoil you through philosophy and vain deceit, after the tradition of men, after the rudiments of the world, and not after Christ.

Mark 7:7-9 (KJV)

[7] Howbeit in vain do they worship me, teaching for doctrines the commandments of men.

[8] For laying aside the commandment of God, ye hold the tradition of men, as the washing of pots and cups: and many other such like things ye do.

[9] And he said unto them, Full well ye reject the commandment of God, that ye may keep your own tradition.

The Messiah himself said why do you transgress the commandments of God by your own tradition? Just as the Messiah followed the law, he expects the rest of mankind to live the same way, especially True Israel and their descendants.

Matthew 15:3 (KJV)

[3] But he answered and said unto them, Why do ye also transgress the commandment of God by your tradition?

John 7:19 (KJV)

[19] Did not Moses give you the law, and yet none of you keepeth the law? Why go ye about to kill me?

True Israel for a long time has followed traditions of men and the things that Satan introduced to the whole world. It has become very difficult to distinguish what is real and what is not. However, when we measure or compare the scriptures to the traditions or (holidays) that are celebrated today they fall short of the reality of the scriptures. When we think we're praising the Most High God of the bible, are we really?

The scriptures let us know we can praise him with our lips but our hearts are far from him. This is because we're doing it our own way and not the way of the Most High God's instructions, so therefore we are worshipping in vain because we follow the commandments of men by celebrating pagan holidays that have nothing to do with the God of the bible. The holidays were created to go against the laws of the Most High God simply because they did not come from him.

Matthew 15:8-9 (KJV)

[8] This people draweth nigh unto me with their mouth, and honoureth me with their lips; but their heart is far from me.

[9] But in vain they do worship me, teaching for doctrines the commandments of men.

We are living in the days where most people will not endure sound doctrine or teachings but rather believe fables such as Santa Clause and Easter bunnies etc. As for the religion of Christianity that adopted the false belief system that the Messiah has something to do with Christmas and Easter is one of the biggest misleading unbiblical doctrines that have been believed for centuries.

But after careful research one will find each one of the holidays derived from a different source other than the bible. The only true and sound doctrine of the bible is the Most High God's Laws, Statutes and Commandments, period. Any other doctrine that is taught is false and not biblical and those who teach anything other than the Laws, Statutes and Commandments of the Most High God of the bible are considered to be a false prophet. The Laws must be on the lips of priest, preachers and ministers to be considered a true messenger of the Most High God of the bible. This following of the law concept have been demonstrated from Genesis to Revelation without exceptions.

---

2 Timothy 4:2-4 (KJV)

[2] Preach the word; be instant in season, out of season; reprove, rebuke, exhort with all long suffering and doctrine.

[3] For the time will come when they will not endure sound doctrine; but after their own lusts shall they heap to themselves teachers, having itching ears;

[4] And they shall turn away their ears from the truth, and shall be turned unto fables.

Proverbs 4:2 (KJV)

[2] For I give you good doctrine, forsake ye not my law.

Malachi 2:7 (KJV)

[7] For the priest's lips should keep knowledge, and they should seek the law at his mouth: for he is the messenger of the LORD of hosts

Traditions of men have been a huge deception not only to True Israel but to the whole world and now that True Israel is awakening to who they really are (people of color). It is a must that True Israel starts stripping away the things that displeases the Most High God and start seeking the God of Abraham, Isaac and Jacob in spirit and in truth. True Israel must return to honoring the holy days and not the holidays.

True Israel should not serve or seek after the gods of other nations. This act was forbidden and considered an abomination unto the God of Abraham, Isaac and Jacob.

Deuteronomy 12:29-32 (KJV)

[29] When the LORD thy God shall cut off the nations from before thee, whither thou goest to possess them, and thou succeedest them, and dwellest in their land;

[30] Take heed to thyself that thou be not snared by following them, after that they be destroyed from before thee; and that thou enquire not after their gods, saying, How did these nations serve their gods? even so will I do likewise.

[31] Thou shalt not do so unto the LORD thy God: for every abomination to the LORD, which he hateth, have they done unto their gods; for even their sons and their daughters they have burnt in the fire to their gods.

[32] What thing soever I command you, observe to do it: thou shalt not add thereto, nor diminish from it.

What/Who is Paganism?

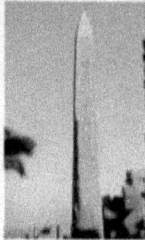

Washington Memorial   Pagan Egyptian Obelisk

"Nimrod shed innocent blood and Rebelled against Jehovah God."

- Let us start with a clear definition of what the term means from 3 different sources. 1st from the perspective of a Pagan "Collectively, Paganism is one of the most rapidly growing religions in the world. It is beautiful, life-affirming faith that honors the land and all its creatures. Because it has revived the old gods, it is sometimes called the old Religion. Whatever the name, many people have found that the faith fills a void they've long carried. Have you ever wondered what happened to the ancient gods you learned about in grade school?" (pg. xi The Everything Paganism Book by Selene Silverwind).

- Now from http://www.merriamwebster.com paganism: a religion that has many gods or goddesses, considers the earth holy, and does not have a central authority

- Finally, from a Christian point of view: God clearly commanded the descendants of Abraham not to have any other gods besides him (Exod 20:3). This strict, undivided loyalty was the basis of the covenant relationship God established between himself and the people of Israel. http://www.biblestudytools.com

- I often wondered who was Yaweh referencing when He stated about the "other gods". I am putting forth that He was mainly referencing an ancient anti-christ figure named Nimrod! After the evidence is put forth you will decide for yourself.

THE HOLIDAYS

Christmas

Christmas is one of the most celebrated holidays on earth today. It is said this celebration represents the birth of Jesus Christ or the Messiah. The date in question is December 25. How do we know that the Messiah was born on this day? As a matter of fact, the bible does not reveal the birthdates of anyone, neither prophets, disciples nor any other biblical patriarchs.

How important is birthdays to the Most High God? According to the biblical scriptures the Most High God appears to be more concern with the remembering of the Messiah's death than his birth. So where do we get this notion to celebrate the Messiah's birth? It certainly didn't come from the bible.

Luke 22:19-20 (KJV)

[19] And he took bread, and gave thanks, and brake it, and gave unto them, saying, This is my body which is given for you: this do in remembrance of me.

[20] Likewise also the cup after supper, saying, This cup is the new testament in my blood, which is shed for you.

1 Corinthians 11:24-25 (KJV)

[24] And when he had given thanks, he brake it, and said, Take, eat: this is my body, which is broken for you: this do in remembrance of me.

[25] After the same manner also he took the cup, when he had supped, saying, this cup is the new testament in my blood: this do ye, as oft as ye drink it, in remembrance of me.

2 Timothy 2:8 (KJV)

[8] Remember that Jesus Christ of the seed of David was raised from the dead according to my gospel:

Job and Jeremiah complained about their birth and wish they were never born.

Job 3:1-3 (KJV)

1 After this opened Job his mouth, and cursed his day.

[2] And Job spake, and said,

[3] Let the day perish wherein I was born, and the night in which it was said, There is a man child conceived.

Jeremiah 20:14 (KJV)

[14] Cursed be the day wherein I was born: let not the day wherein my mother bare me be blessed.

To tell the truth Christmas is one of those pagan holidays that is based on religious tradition and is completely pagan in nature. All of the rituals associated with Christmas celebrations are definitely not in the bible which includes Yule Logs, Mistletoes, Holly, Santa Claus, Wreaths and the Christmas tree were all associated with satanic rituals.

There are bumper stickers that exist saying "Put Christ Back Into Christmas". This would be impossible because Christ never was in Christmas to begin with. It was the other Christ Paul talked about in II Corinthians 11:4 that would be in Christmas, perhaps the one born on December 25. This Christmas celebration was celebrated long before the Messiah was even born and therefore could not stem from him.

---

2 Corinthians 11:4 (KJV)

[4] For if he that cometh preacheth another Jesus, whom we have not preached, or if ye receive another spirit, which ye have not received, or another gospel, which ye have not accepted, ye might well bear with him.

True Israel was always given specific instructions on how to conduct themselves; and the rituals of traditional Christmas celebrations are prohibited. Jeremiah chapter 10 is an example of what the children of Israel or True Israel was instructed not to do as it pertains to cutting a tree and decorating it with silver and gold.

This was the way of the heathens and their customs were vain in the eyes of the Most High God. A Christmas celebration has no biblical roots and strictly comes from an unholy foundation and should be avoided by those who believe the bible.

This Christmas ritual was always pagan in nature and considered to be idolatry or idol worship in the eyes of the Most High God. It was and still is an abomination unto the Most High God of the bible. This type of worship or ritual is definitely not approved due to the first commandment (Thou Shalt Have No Other gods Before

Me). True Israel was instructed to have absolutely no other god's or graven images whatsoever.

Jeremiah 10:1-4 (KJV)

1 Hear ye the word which the LORD speaketh unto you, O house of Israel:

[2] Thus saith the LORD, Learn not the way of the heathen, and be not dismayed at the signs of heaven; for the heathen are dismayed at them.

[3] For the customs of the people are vain: for one cutteth a tree out of the forest, the work of the hands of the workman, with the axe.

[4] They deck it with silver and with gold; they fasten it with nails and with hammers, that it move not.

Deuteronomy 7:25-26 (KJV)

[25] The graven images of their gods shall ye burn with fire: thou shalt not desire the silver or gold that is on them, nor take it unto thee, lest thou be snared therin: for it is an abomination to the LORD thy God.

[26] Neither shalt thou bring an abomination into thine house, lest thou be a cursed thing like it: but thou shalt utterly detest it, and thou shalt utterly abhor it; for it is a cursed thing.

A reliable bible dictionary would tell you that Christmas is celebrated by most Protestants and Roman Catholics on December 25; by Eastern Orthodox churches on January 6; and by Armenian churches on January 19. Notice that there is no mentioning of True

Israel or Israelites involvement in the development of Christmas, it is always pointed towards other nations, mainly Rome.

The definition goes on to say that the first mention of the Christmas observance on December 25 is in the time of Constantine (Roman Emperor) about 325 A.D.; Why after nearly 300 years after the Messiah's death it's decided that The Messiah's birth should be celebrated? The bible definition will tell you that Christmas celebration or observance derived from pagan origins and has nothing to do with the birth of the Messiah. As a matter of fact, Christmas was illegal in the United States up until 1836. It was considered an ancient pagan holiday. The first state that declared Christmas a legal holiday was Alabama (1836) and then Louisiana and Arkansas followed in (1838). It was not a federal holiday until 1870.

The true history of Christmas is attached to the Roman Saturnalia (a harvest festival) that marked the Winter Solstice (the return of the sun) that was celebrated in the Northern hemisphere. The characters involved with this celebration would be Nimrod (The ancient Babylonian ruler and his son Tammuz). Nimrod was said to be born on December 25 and when he died became the sun god. This celebration could also be known as Mithraic, Feast of the Sun-God.

The Roman festival of Saturnalia was celebrated in the following way:
- Decorating homes with greens and lights
- The giving and the exchanges of gifts to children and the poor
- Indulging of food

As one can see this celebration resembles what we know today as Christmas celebration. This celebration was later Christianized as a day to celebrate the birth of the Messiah. This Saturnalia celebration (the god Saturn) started as a two-day affair on December 17 and eventually became a seven-day event. The climax of this celebration eventually ended on December 25th, around the time of the Winter Solstice. These celebrations date back as far as 217 B.C., way before the Messiah was even born.

Around the 4th century the Roman Catholic Church adopted the Saturnalia festival hoping to take the pagan masses in with it. Also, about 312 AD it is believed that Roman Emperor Constantine converted to Christianity and ended the persecution of Christians and began imperial patronage of the Christian churches. Before Constantine supposed conversion to Christianity, he was first brought up in the Sol Invicta Cult and he did not release all of his old belief system but instead brought some of those cultic belief systems into authentic Christianity.

History eventually replaced the Saturnalia / Winter Soltice celebration with the celebration of the birth of the Messiah. This transition took place by chatolic leaders successfully convincing a large number of pagans to convert to "Christianity" but they were promised they could continue celebrating Saturnalia as Christmas.

The history of Christmas is more detailed than this book can expound on but the general picture is that Christmas is not a biblical doctrine and lines up more with satanic rituals and should not be practiced by those who are true bible believers.

Every practice of Christmas ritual is derived from another source other than the biblical scriptures. Such as the Christmas Tree, Yule Logs, Christmas Presents, Christmas Ham, Holly Wreaths, Santa Claus, Mistletoe etc. When practicing these Christmas rituals, you're actually practicing pagan customs that's usually giving praise to another god other than the God of Abraham, Isaac and Jacob. It is Idolatry!

Although celebrating Christmas gives most people a good feeling but doesn't necessarily mean it's a good thing. This just goes to show you everything that feels good is not good. Most of the sinful things man and Satan has created certainly can produce a feeling of fun and enjoyment. But in the end sin only produces death according to the bible (Romans 6:23).

Please continue to research this holiday and its rituals. You'll be amazed at the deception that has generated throughout history concerning the holiday of Christmas.

Who Is Actually Said To Be Born On December 25th (Other god's)

<u>NAME</u>
Nimrod
Hermes
Prometheus
Adonis
Horus
Attis of Phrygia
Osiris
Krishna
Zoroaster
Mithra of Persia
Heracles
Tammuz
Dionysus

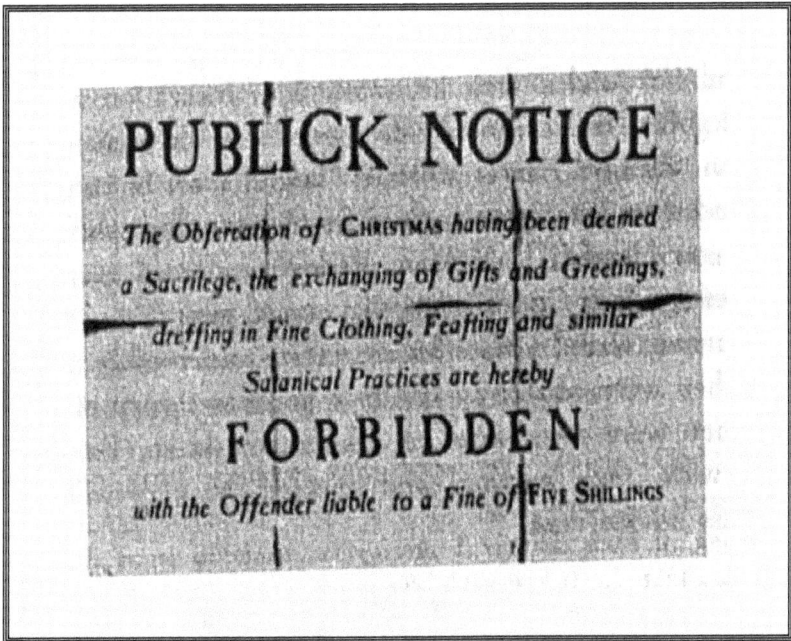

PUBLICK NOTICE

The Obfervation of Christmas having been deemed a Sacrilege, the exchanging of Gifts and Greetings, dreffing in Fine Clothing, Feafting and similar Satanical Practices are hereby

FORBIDDEN

with the Offender liable to a Fine of Five Shillings

17th century puritan public notice
Christmas
A satanic practice
May 11, 1659
17th-century public notice in <u>Boston</u> deeming the celebration of Christmas forbidden and <u>sacrilegious</u>

Where Did the Dec. 25th Celebration Start?

•It is of Pagan origin! (Not from the Bible)

•The first evidence of the feast is from Egypt. Pagan customs centering around the January calends [the pagan calendar] gravitated to Christ-mas." *(Catholic Encyclopedia, 1911 ed.)*

• They (Roman Catholics) copied it from the pagan Roman sun-god, ...following Saturnalia, was the Brumalia festival (birth of sun god) on Dec. 25th *(New Shaff-Herzog Ency. of Religious Knowledge)*

•Christmas was first celebrated in the 3rd century in Rome 354, and Constantinople in 379, and Antioch in 388 *(Gospel of Luke Commentary, Norval Geldenhuys, p. 102).*

SATURNALIA

Yule love it

ORIGIN OF CHRISTMAS: a quick summary for those who don't know, Christmas derived from the Pagan holiday Saturnalia which the Romans held on the 17th of December that lasted seven days, it was a time of equality & lawlessness, they started the holiday to honor the king Saturnus who ruled during the golden age, during the week long period of Saturnalia they held rituals where they sacrificed infants & animals & had orgies & since the Roman empire didn't like that they were losing people to Paganism they adopted the idea & decided to have December 25th as the day of Christ being born to help people convert easier from Paganism to Christianity.

Easter

Easter is known as a day in modern Christianity as a day for celebrating the resurrection of the Messiah. For others it means rabbits, colored eggs and Easter baskets etc. Now, how could this holiday mean both, it's either one or the other. We discovered that Christmas comes from pagan roots and Easter is no different. The deception continues as many are made to believe Easter derived from the resurrection of the Messiah.

Easter has nothing to do with the Messiah's resurrection; it's another celebration or festival celebrated before the Messiah was even born or died. Mostly all holidays can be researched back to the days of the Babylonian times involving Nimrod, Semiramis and Tammuz.

Nimrod was the great great grandson of Noah known as a mighty hunter (Genesis 10:8-9). The story says he married his mother Semiramis who first husband was Cush (Noah's grandson and father of Nimrod). Both Cush and Semiramis were king and queen of Babylon. After Nimrod died his mother wife believed he ascended to the sun, making him a sun god. He also became known as Baal, Mithra, Osiris (Egypt), Adonis (Syria) and the beginning of sun worship (Rome).

Nimrod's mother wife Semiramis over the course of time had many changes to her name such as: Ishtar (pronounced Easter), Ashtoreth, Isis, Astarte, Ostara, the moon goddess, the **queen of heaven** and the goddess of spring. She was also known as the sex or fertility goddess. It is said Semiramis believed she descended down from the moon on an egg.

Semiramis eventually had a son named Tammuz who likes rabbits and was killed by a wild boar or pig while hunting. Tammuz supposed blood spilled on a tree stump and an Evergreen tree grew overnight which symbolized Tammuz coming back to life as a tree (The Christmas Tree). Also, the "T" in Tammuz is used on Hot Cross Buns and on the foreheads during the time of Lent. Many people think this "T" is the cross of the Messiah but history shows this is the "T" in the name TAMMUZ. (Ezekiel 8:14). The cross is not a symbol of the Messiah but it is a graven image that should not be worn by True Israel or those who choose to follow the scriptures of the bible. (Deuteronomy 5:8) and (Exodus 20:4).

Jeremiah 7:18 (KJV)

[18] The children gather wood, and the fathers kindle the fire, and the women knead their dough, to make cakes to the **queen of heaven**, and to pour out drink offerings unto other gods, that they may provoke me to anger.

2 Kings 23:5 (KJV)

[5] And he put down the idolatrous priests, whom the kings of Judah had ordained to burn incense in the high places in the cities of Judah, and in the places round about Jerusalem; them also that **burned incense unto Baal, to the sun, and to the moon**, and to the planets, and to all the host of heaven.

The origin of the word Easter appears to stem from a Germanic origin related to German Ostern. It appears to derive from Eastre, the name of a goddess associated with spring (An Anglo-Saxon pagan goddess).

The Bible (King James Version) uses the word Easter only once in Acts 12:4. However, this was a mistranslation error in the King James Version of the bible. The word "PASSOVER" should have been used. Many other versions of the bible use the word "PASSOVER" instead of Easter.

Acts 12:4 (KJV)

[4] And when he had apprehended him, he put him in prison, and delivered him to four quaternions of soldiers to keep him; intending after **Easter** to bring him forth to the people.

Bible Versions of Acts 12:4 (Easter should be "PASSOVER")

Bible Version	Scripture
Amplified	[4] When he had seized Peter, he put him in prison, turning him over to four squads of soldiers of four each to guard him [in rotation throughout the night], planning after the **Passover** to bring him out before the people [for execution].
New American Standard Bible	[4] When he had seized him, he put him in prison, delivering him to four [a]squads of soldiers to guard him, intending after the **Passover** to bring him out before the people.
Revised Standard Version	[4] And when he had seized him, he put him in prison, and delivered him to four squads of soldiers to guard him, intending after the **Passover** to bring him out to the people.
New International Version (NIV)	[4] After arresting him, he put him in prison, handing him over to be guarded by four squads of four soldiers each. Herod intended to bring him out for public trial after the **Passover.**
The Living Bible	[4] and imprisoned him, placing him under the guard of sixteen soldiers. Herod's intention was to deliver Peter to the Jews for execution after the **Passover.**
1599 Geneva Bible	[4] [a]And when he had caught him, he put him in prison, and delivered him to four quaternions of soldiers to be kept, intending after the **Passover** to bring him forth to the people.

Thus far the origins of Easter have absolutely nothing to do with the resurrection of the Messiah but everything to do with Nimrod (Baal), Semiramis (Ashtoreth) and Tammuz, which by the way is mentioned in the scriptures.

Walking after these gods was an abomination to the Most High God of Israel and still is to this day. It had become more difficult to identify these deities due to the changing of names and other factors throughout history. Nevertheless, it's the same gods that was worshipped during the times of ancient Israel. We have been fooled to think that we're worshipping or celebrating the God of Abraham, Isaac and Jacob in so many ways it is astonishing. The deception is GREAT!

Nimrod (Baal)	Semiramis (Ashtoreth)	Tammuz
Hosea 2:8	I Kings 11:5	Ezekiel 8:14
Hosea 13:1	I Kings 11:33	
Romans 11:4	II Kings 23:13	
Zephaniah 1:4		
I Kings 18:19		
Romans 11:4		

Some final thoughts on Easter would be that the Easter bunny and other rituals associated with Easter are older than Christianity.

These rituals were injected into true biblical beliefs and distorted the true meaning of the bible concerning the resurrection of the Messiah.

Easter shows its pagan roots dating back to the old lunar calendar. It has been established on the first Sunday after the first full moon after the spring equinox, which is the pregnant phrase of Eostre passing into fertile season. This festival was not called Easter until the Goddess name was given in the late Middle Ages.

The bottom line is when one celebrates Easter, they are celebrating the sex / fertility goddess of ancient Babylon and not the resurrection of the Messiah. Please research further…

It's amazing what Christians will do; who they will worship; because they love their traditions.

Easter   *Ishtar*
EOSTRE   Ashtoreth

"EASTER" – goddess of Fertility

Rabbit – Symbol of Fertility

The goddess "Easter"

Semiramis & Tammuz of Babel were worshipped as a divine mother and son under many different manes. They became:

- Ishtar & Tammuz of Assyria
- Ashtaroth & Baal of Phoenicia
- Isis & Horus of Egypt
- Aphrodite & Eros of Greece
- Venus & Cupid of Rome

The "Entire" Earth is Lying in the Power of Ancient Babylon and the spell cast by Nimrod and his mother.

Thanksgiving

The Thanksgiving holiday is another one of those festivals that most people are unaware of the real reason it's celebrated. It's not celebrated to give thanks to the Most High God of the bible. Thanksgiving was first celebrated nationally in 1789 being declared by George Washington but it was not officially a federal holiday until 1863 declared by Abraham Lincoln.

It is said Thanksgiving was suppose to have been a note of thanks from the Pilgrims (Puritans) to Squanto and the Wampanoag Indians for helping them learn how to grow corn and fish etc. However, when the English Colonialist got word that the new world was public domain, they decided to seize the land by enslaving and killing the native Indians.

This thanksgiving celebration was generated by a brutal attack or the genocide of a people (The Indians). When we celebrate this holiday, we are promoting acceptance of genocide and land theft. This genocide was implemented by zealots called puritans who were Europeans. The next time Thanksgiving come around think about all the Indians who died. This is something the Most High God does not approve. When the children of Israel (True Israel) were in great calamity and in deep distressed by their enemies, Esau (Edom) was guilty for standing with the enemies of Israel and for that the Most High God will punish and judge this nation of people harshly.

> **Obadiah 12-14 (KJV)**
>
> [12] But thou shouldest not have looked on the day of thy brother in the day that he became a stranger; neither shouldest thou have rejoiced over the children of Judah in the day of their destruction; neither shouldest thou have spoken proudly in the day of distress.
>
> [13] Thou shouldest not have entered into the gate of my people in the day of their calamity; yea, thou shouldest not have looked on their affliction in the day of their calamity, nor have laid hands on their substance in the day of their calamity;
>
> [14] Neither shouldest thou have stood in the crossway, to cut off those of his that did escape; neither shouldest thou have delivered up those of his that did remain in the day of distress.

In other words, we should never celebrate or rejoice when people are being murdered and treated unjustly. The Most High God sees it all and the consequences of such actions are noted by the God of Israel. True Israel need not celebrate Thanksgiving but participate in the holy days instead.

ALL HOLIDAYS

All of the popular holidays celebrated today stem from the same source reaching back to ancient Babylon. The word "HOLIDAY", itself reveals according to the online etymology dictionary is nothing but a "religious festival" and is no way connected to the doctrines of the bible.

1500s, earlier *haliday* (c. 1200), from Old English *haligdæg* "holy day, consecrated day, **religious anniversary**; Sabbath," from *halig* "holy" (see **holy**) + *dæg* "day" (see **day**); in 14c. meaning both **"religious festival"** and "day of exemption from labor and recreation," but pronunciation and sense diverged 16c. As an adjective mid-15c. *Happy holidays* is from mid-19c., in British English, with reference to summer vacation from school. As a Christmastime greeting, by 1937, American English, in Camel cigarette ads.

https://www.etymonline.com/word/holiday

The biblical scriptures repeat over and over again that these practices or festivals are forbidden because this was the ways of the heathens only. True Israel was instructed to destroy all the heathen's graven images of their god's. The bible addresses who the false images and gods were by their names in ancient times. Their names were Baal, Ashtaroth and Tammuz.

Deuteronomy 12:2-4 (KJV)

[2] Ye shall utterly destroy all the places, wherein the nations which ye shall possess served their gods, upon the high mountains, and upon the hills, and under every green tree:

[3] And ye shall overthrow their altars, and break their pillars, and burn their groves with fire; and ye shall hew down the graven images of their gods, and destroy the names of them out of that place.

[4] Ye shall not do so unto the LORD your God.

Exodus 34:13 (KJV)

[13] But ye shall destroy their altars, break their images, and cut down their groves:

Leviticus 26:1 (KJV)

26 Ye shall make you no idols nor graven image, neither rear you up a standing image, neither shall ye set up any image of stone in your land, to bow down unto it: for I am the LORD your God.

Deuteronomy 7:5 (KJV)

[5] But thus shall ye deal with them; ye shall destroy their altars, and break down their images, and cut down their groves, and burn their graven images with fire.

Judges 2:13 (KJV)

[13] And they forsook the LORD, and served Baal and Ashtaroth.

The instructions again were to keep the commandments of the Most High God and not worship the heathen god's which include any traditions and / or holiday festivals or customs.

Deuteronomy 4:2 (KJV)

2 Ye shall not add unto the word which I command you, neither shall ye diminish ought from it, that ye may keep the commandments of the LORD your God which I command you.

We cannot take Satan rituals and turn them around to use them for the God of Abraham, Isaac and Jacob. This concept won't and will not work according to the biblical scriptures.

Leviticus 18:30 (KJV)

30 Therefore shall ye keep mine ordinance, that ye commit not any one of these abominable customs, which were committed before you, and that ye defile not yourselves therein: I am the LORD your God.

Deuteronomy 12:29-30 (KJV)

29 When the LORD thy God shall cut off the nations from before thee, whither thou goest to possess them, and thou succeedest them, and dwellest in their land;

30 Take heed to thyself that thou be not snared by following them, after that they be destroyed from before thee; and that thou enquire not after their gods, saying, How did these nations serve their gods? even so will I do likewise.

It will please the Most High God if True Israel and those who choose to follow the biblical scriptures turn away from worshipping traditions of men and all deep rooted satanic rituals which include all holidays etc.

1 Kings 11:5-6 (KJV)

[5] For Solomon went after Ashtoreth the goddess of the Zidonians, and after Milcom the abomination of the Ammonites.

[6] And Solomon did evil in the sight of the LORD, and went not fully after the LORD, as did David his father.

1 Samuel 7:3 (KJV)

[3] And Samuel spake unto all the house of Israel, saying, If ye do return unto the LORD with all your hearts, then put away the strange gods and Ashtaroth from among you, and prepare your hearts unto the LORD, and serve him only: and he will deliver you out of the hand of the Philistines.

All holidays are wicked including Valentine's Day, Halloween, New Year's Day, Mother's Day and Father's Day. They all seem so innocent on the surface but after careful research and inquiry concerning the roots of these holidays, one will find them to be pagan, evil and wicked. True Israel was forbidden to take part in these rituals and festivals because they all had heathen or /and satanic roots.

All these holidays have one thing in common. They all can be traced back to Babylon in one form or another involving Nimrod, Semiramis and Tammuz. The names have changed over the many years but nevertheless the roots are the same.

Samhain Blessing

PAGAN HOLIDAYS
Wicked Customs

CHRISTMAS One of the most celebrated "holidays" on earth. Based on religious traditions, this non-Biblical celebration is completely pagan in nature. (Jeremiah 10:2-6; Amos 5:21; Jeremiah 7:18; Luke 2:1-8)

THANKSGIVING Another highly celebrated "holiday" that is rooted in wickedness and the destruction of the Lord's Chosen People. (Isaiah 5:20; Leviticus 11:7; Amos 5:21; Micah 2:1-2; Amos 5:15; Colossians 2:8)

NEW YEAR'S DAY This day is a complete inaccurate celebration of the modern day Gregorian Calendar. The "New Year" celebration is celebrating the Roman God Janus who was their god of new beginnings and transisitions. (Daniel 7:25; 1 Corinthians 6:9; Colossians 2:8)

VALENTINE'S DAY Valentines Day also has pagan roots steeming from the Roman God Lupercus who was the Roman god of fertility, and Juno Februrata or the godess of fever. (Jeremiah 10:2; John 14:15; Galatians 5:19; Leviticus 18:24-30)

EASTER Modern Easter is named after the Babylonian Godess Ishthar who was the Mother and Wife of Nimrod, and Mother of their son Tammuz. (Jeremiah 10:2; Leviticus 11:7; Amos 5:21; Mark 7:6-9; Genesis 10:8-10; Exodus 20:4; Acts 5:29)

HALLOWEEN Clearly nothing is "hallowed" or Holy during this day. (Jeremiah 10:2; Isaiah 8:20; Mark 12:27; Mark 7:6-9; Amos 5:21; Exodus 20:4; Deuteronomy 18:10; Psalms 78:5-8; Zepheniah 1:8)

MOTHER'S DAY AND FATHER'S DAY We know that the Most High commanded that we honor our Father and Mother (Exodus 20:12), but he did not ordain there to be two specific holidays of the year to honor them. (Acts 19:24-35; 1 Maccabees 1:11-12; Colossians 2:8; Mark 7:6-8)

"Lupercalia"

Chapter 17

THE LESSONS

THE RESURRECTION: SATURDAY OR SUNDAY?

This lesson is an extension of the Easter tradition belief system from chapter 16 (Paganism). One of the most popular beliefs in modern day Christianity is that The Messiah was crucified on Friday and rose on Sunday. This topic must be explored to uncover the lie in this doctrine by using plain scriptures. The scriptures are very clear that this cannot be possible which will give more validity to the fact that Easter is pagan and Sunday worship is pagan. Both stem from pagan roots and not the bible.

Let's began by starting with one scripture that can end this lesson in its track. The scripture is Matthew 12:38-40. This scripture states that the Messiah will be in the grave three days and three nights just as Jonah was in the belly of the whale or fish three days and three nights.

Already there's a problem with the Messiah being crucified on Friday and rising on Sunday. Question: How do you get three days and three nights from Friday to Sunday? Mathematically it's impossible. So, this doctrine concerning the Messiah being crucified on Friday and rising on Sunday is definitely flawed.

Matthew 12:38-40 (KJV)

[38] Then certain of the scribes and of the Pharisees answered, saying, Master, we would see a sign from thee.

[39] But he answered and said unto them, An evil and adulterous generation seeketh after a sign; and there shall no sign be given to it, but the sign of the prophet Jonas:

[40] For as Jonas was three days and three nights in the whale's belly; so shall the Son of man be three days and three nights in the heart of the earth.

Jonah 1:17 (KJV)

[17] Now the LORD had prepared a great fish to swallow up Jonah. And Jonah was in the belly of the fish three days and three nights.

Jonah 2:1-2 (KJV)

1 Then Jonah prayed unto the LORD his God out of the fish's belly,

[2] And said, I cried by reason of mine affliction unto the LORD, and he heard me; out of the belly of hell cried I, and thou heardest my voice.

Some may say the hours of the days were different during that time period in history. However, when we look at how the Most High God calculates a day, he is very specific. It was man who changed the meaning of a day and not the Most High God. Man say a new day starts at twelve midnight (12:00 AM) but The Most High God does not calculate or start his day at twelve midnight. His day starts in the evening according to the scriptures. You'll see that when the Most High divided the light from darkness, he called the light day and darkness night and starting in the evening until the morning was and still one whole day. This is repeated in Genesis 1:4-5, 8, and 13. In Leviticus 23:32 is another example that a day is from evening to evening, in this scripture example it's referring to the Sabbath day.

Genesis 1:4-5 (KJV)

[4] And God saw the light, that it was good: and God divided the light from the darkness.

[5] And God called the light Day, and the darkness he called Night. And the evening and the morning were the first day.

Genesis 1:8 (KJV)

[8] And God called the firmament Heaven. And the evening and the morning were the second day.

Genesis 1:13 (KJV)

[13] And the evening and the morning were the third day.

Leviticus 23:32 (KJV)

[32] It shall be unto you a sabbath of rest, and ye shall afflict your souls: in the ninth day of the month at even, from even unto even, shall ye celebrate your sabbath.

The Messiah also knew how many hours were in a day because he made it known in John 11:8-10. He stated, "Are there not twelve hours in the day". So, if there's twelve hours in a day, then there must be twelve hours in the night. This would mean the Messiah knew about time and how many hours would make a whole day.

John 11:8-10 (KJV)

[8] His disciples say unto him, Master, the Jews of late sought to stone thee; and goest thou thither again?

[9] Jesus answered, Are there not twelve hours in the day? If any man walk in the day, he stumbleth not, because he seeth the light of this world.

[10] But if a man walk in the night, he stumbleth, because there is no light in him.

The Messiah also knew how many days he would be in the grave because he quoted it several times in the scriptures. The Messiah knew he had to be in the grave for at least 72 hours to make three days and three nights. Again, Friday through Sunday falls short of 72 hours in the grave and therefore cannot be true.

John 2:19-21 (KJV)

[19] Jesus answered and said unto them, Destroy this temple, and in three days I will raise it up.

[20] Then said the Jews, Forty and six years was this temple in building, and wilt thou rear it up in three days?

[21] But he spake of the temple of his body.

Mark 9:31 (KJV)

31 For he taught his disciples, and said unto them, The Son of man is delivered into the hands of men, and they shall kill him; and after that he is killed, he shall rise the third day.

Matthew 27:63 (KJV)

63 Saying, Sir, we remember that that deceiver said, while he was yet alive, After three days I will rise again.

Mark 8:31 (KJV)

31 And he began to teach them, that the Son of man must suffer many things, and be rejected of the elders, and of the chief priests, and scribes, and be killed, and after three days rise again.

The Messiah's death was prophesied in the book of Daniel and it supports the three days and three night's conclusion. Daniel wrote that the Messiah will be cut off in the midst of the week and the word Midst mean the middle position. This could not be Friday but Wednesday which falls in the middle of the week. If we calculate three days and three nights from Wednesday it will take you to Saturday not Sunday.

Daniel 9:26-27 (KJV)

26 And after threescore and two weeks shall Messiah be cut off, but not for himself: and the people of the prince that shall come shall destroy the city and the sanctuary; and the end thereof shall be with a flood, and unto the end of the war desolations are determined.

> ²⁷ **And he shall confirm the covenant with many for one week: and in the midst of the week he shall cause the sacrifice and the oblation to cease,** and for the overspreading of abominations he shall make it desolate, even until the consummation, and that determined shall be poured upon the desolate.

The bible even gives a specific time the Messiah was being crucified. The bible says it was about the sixth hour (12:00 PM) that darkness was over the whole earth until the ninth hour (3:00 PM) before he gave up the ghost or died.

Luke 23:44-46 (KJV)

⁴⁴ And it was about the sixth hour, and there was a darkness over all the earth until the ninth hour.

⁴⁵ And the sun was darkened, and the veil of the temple was rent in the midst.

⁴⁶ And when Jesus had cried with a loud voice, he said, Father, into thy hands I commend my spirit: and having said thus, he gave up the ghost.

Mark 15:34-37 (KJV)

³⁴ And at the ninth hour Jesus cried with a loud voice, saying, Eloi, Eloi, lama sabachthani? which is, being interpreted, My God, my God, why hast thou forsaken me?

³⁵ And some of them that stood by, when they heard it, said, Behold, he calleth Elias.

³⁶ And one ran and filled a spunge full of vinegar, and put it on a reed, and gave him to drink, saying, Let alone; let us see whether Elias will come to take him down.

³⁷ And Jesus cried with a loud voice, and gave up the ghost.

Matthew 27:46-50 (KJV)

⁴⁶ And about the ninth hour Jesus cried with a loud voice, saying, Eli, Eli, lama sabachthani? that is to say, My God, my God, why hast thou forsaken me?

⁴⁷ Some of them that stood there, when they heard that, said, This man calleth for Elias.

⁴⁸ And straightway one of them ran, and took a spunge, and filled it with vinegar, and put it on a reed, and gave him to drink.

⁴⁹ The rest said, Let be, let us see whether Elias will come to save him.

⁵⁰ Jesus, when he had cried again with a loud voice, yielded up the ghost.

The Messiah eventually died and rose on the third day just as the scriptures said he would according to I Corinthians 15:3-4.

---

1 Corinthians 15:3-4 (KJV)

³ For I delivered unto you first of all that which I also received, how that Christ died for our sins according to the scriptures;

⁴ And that he was buried, and that he rose again the third day according to the scriptures:

It is appropriate to say the Messiah died on that Wednesday instead of Friday for several reasons supported by the scriptures.

One, the Messiah represented the Lamb of God. Why? He was sent to be that sacrificial lamb for Israel and eventually other nation's sins of the past. This was the law that was done away with (The sacrificial law) (Hebrews 10:1-10). The nation of Israel need not kill anymore Lambs because The Messiah replaced it with his death. When he said it was finished this is what he meant.

---

1 Corinthians 5:7 (KJV)

[7] Purge out therefore the old leaven, that ye may be a new lump, as ye are unleavened. For even Christ our passover is sacrificed for us:

John 1:29 (KJV)

[29] The next day John seeth Jesus coming unto him, and saith, Behold the Lamb of God, which taketh away the sin of the world.

Two, when the Messiah was crucified, he was actually crucified right before one of Israel's high holy days (The Feast of Unleavened Bread) (Thursday) which means he died on the Passover (Preparation Day) (Wednesday) which would have been appropriate since he was the Lamb to be sacrificed. The Messiah needed to be removed off the cross due to the High Sabbath Day that was approaching (Feast of Unleavened Bread) (Thursday).

John 19:31 (KJV)

31 The Jews therefore, because it was the preparation, that the bodies should not remain upon the cross on the sabbath day, (for that sabbath day was an high day,) besought Pilate that their legs might be broken, and that they might be taken away.

John 19:14 (KJV)

14 And it was the preparation of the passover, and about the sixth hour: and he saith unto the Jews, Behold your King!

John 19:42 (KJV)

42 There laid they Jesus therefore because of the Jews' preparation day; for the sepulchre was nigh at hand.

Mark 15:42 (KJV)

42 And now when the even was come, because it was the preparation, that is, the day before the sabbath,

This is part of the equation that modern day or Roman Christianity gets confused. It's not understood that there were two Sabbath Days the week of the Messiah's crucifixion or death. There was a Sabbath Day on Thursday (High Sabbath) and on Saturday (Weekly Sabbath). This is one reason why modern-day Christianity chooses to believe the crucifixion was on Friday instead of Wednesday, in spite of the biblical and historical evidence. They do not take into account the High Sabbath Day the scriptures mention.

This could be because modern day Christianity focuses on holidays and not the Most High holy days which include (Passover, Feast of Unleavened Bread, Pentecost, Feast of Trumpets, Day of Atonement and Feasts of tabernacles). All these days have a meaning to the Most High God of the scriptures.

Since Wednesday was the preparation (Passover)(Leviticus 23:4-50) day and Thursday was the High Sabbath day (Unleavened Bread)(Leviticus 23:6-9). We now come to Friday which was the only day True Israel (Israelites) was able to work, buy and sell before the weekly Sabbath (Saturday). The fact that True Israel was still under the laws, statutes and commandments of the Most High God, they understood and knew once the Sabbath (Saturday) came in they were unable to buy, sell and cook etc. True Israel followed Exodus 20:8, even during the week of the crucifixion of the Messiah.

Since Friday was the only day True Israel (Israelites) was able to buy, sell and cook etc. for the week of the crucifixion, this would have been the only day that Mary Magdalene and Mary the mother of James could have bought and prepared spices to anoint the body of the Messiah. Luke 23:56 states they rested on the Sabbath Day according to the commandment. If we read Mark 16:1-2 you'll read that in verse one that the Sabbath was passed. This was the weekly Sabbath, not the High Sabbath Day which was Thursday of that week.

Luke 23:56 (KJV)

[56] And they returned, and prepared spices and ointments; and rested the sabbath day according to the commandment.

By verse two the first day of the week (Sunday) is mentioned. So, this means that both of the Mary's would have bought the spices and prepared them on Friday, rested on the weekly Sabbath Day (Saturday) and brought the spices to anoint the body of the Messiah on Sunday morning.

Mark 16:1-2 (KJV)

1 And when the sabbath was past, Mary Magdalene, and Mary the mother of James, and Salome, had bought sweet spices, that they might come and anoint him.

^{2} And very early in the morning the first day of the week, they came unto the sepulchre at the rising of the sun.

Most of us know the first day of the week is named Sunday, the day in which the Messiah is alleged to have risen from the dead. There is a huge problem with this theory according to the scriptures. The scriptures clearly state that on the first day of the week, the Messiah's body was gone. So, this would have meant The Messiah had already risen before both Marys' brought the spices to anoint the body. As a matter of fact, it was still dark when they brought the spices and when they looked at the sepulcher the stone was rolled away. He was already gone.

Mark 16:1-6 (KJV)

1 And when the sabbath was past, Mary Magdalene, and Mary the mother of James, and Salome, had bought sweet spices, that they might come and anoint him.

^{2} And very early in the morning the first day of the week, they came unto the sepulchre at the rising of the sun.

^{3} And they said among themselves, Who shall roll us away the stone from the door of the sepulchre?

⁴ And when they looked, they saw that the stone was rolled away: for it was very great.

⁵ And entering into the sepulchre, they saw a young man sitting on the right side, clothed in a long white garment; and they were affrighted.

⁶ And he saith unto them, Be not affrighted: Ye seek Jesus of Nazareth, which was crucified: he is risen; he is not here: behold the place where they laid him.

Luke 24:1-6 (KJV)

1 Now upon the first day of the week, very early in the morning, they came unto the sepulchre, bringing the spices which they had prepared, and certain others with them.

² And they found the stone rolled away from the sepulchre.

³ And they entered in, and found not the body of the Lord Jesus.

⁴ And it came to pass, as they were much perplexed thereabout, behold, two men stood by them in shining garments:

⁵ And as they were afraid, and bowed down their faces to the earth, they said unto them, Why seek ye the living among the dead?

⁶ He is not here, but is risen: remember how he spake unto you when he was yet in Galilee,

John 20:1 (KJV)

1 The first day of the week cometh Mary Magdalene early, when it was yet dark, unto the sepulchre, and seeth the stone taken away from the sepulchre.

When both Mary's noticed the body of the Messiah was gone it was also confirmed by the angels saying "He is not here: for he is risen".

Matthew 28:5-6 (KJV)

5 And the angel answered and said unto the women, Fear not ye: for I know that ye seek Jesus, which was crucified.

6 He is not here: for he is risen, as he said. Come, see the place where the Lord lay.

So, if the Messiah was already risen by Sunday morning (The first day of the week), why do modern Christianity celebrate resurrection on Sunday morning? We must ask ourselves these questions and seek answers so that we can correctly fall in line with the scriptures.

It is a clear biblical fact that the Messiah had to be in the grave 3 days and 3 nights (72 hours). This could not have been accomplished from Friday through Sunday. However, this is definitely possible from Wednesday through Saturday. The Messiah had to have been risen on Saturday, probably between 3pm to 6pm which would have made 3 days and 3 nights (72 hours). This would account for The Messiah being missing or gone by the time both Marys' came with the spices on Sunday morning.

INCORRECT

Bible Definition of 3 Days: (Friday Crucifixion)

Monday	Tuesday	Wednesday	Thursday	Friday		Saturday		Sunday	
Day				Night	Day	Day	Night	Day	Night
12				12	12	12	12	12	12
12 Hours		72 Hours				60 Hours			

A Friday crucifixion would have left the Messiah in the grave until Monday if we count 3 days and 3 nights according to bible time.

CORRECT

Bible Definition of 3 Days: (Wednesday Crucifixion)

Monday	Tuesday	Wednesday		Thursday		Friday		Saturday		Sunday
		3PM To 6PM	Day	Day		Day		Day	3PM To 6PM	
		Night		Night		Night				
		12	12	12	12	12	12	12	12	
		72 Hours								

A Wednesday crucifixion perfectly lines up with all the biblical scriptures concerning his crucifixion and resurrection.

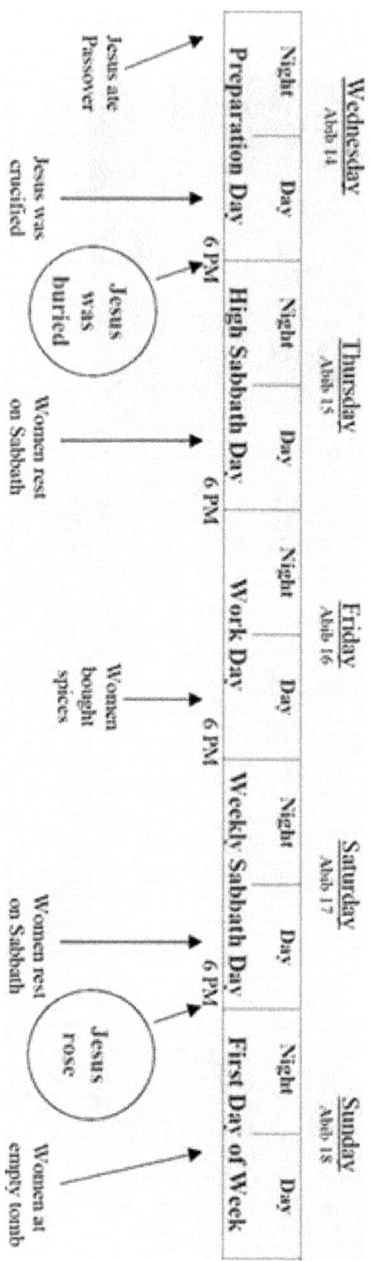

Wednesday Abib 14		Thursday Abib 15		Friday Abib 16		Saturday Abib 17		Sunday Abib 18
Night	Day	Night	Day	Night	Day	Night	Day	Night	Day
Preparation Day		High Sabbath Day		Work Day		Weekly Sabbath Day		First Day of Week

6 PM · 6 PM · 6 PM · 6 PM

Jesus ate Passover

Jesus was crucified

Jesus was buried

Women rest on Sabbath

Women bought spices

Women rest on Sabbath

Jesus rose

Women at empty tomb

In spite of clear plain scriptures many will continue to believe The Messiah rose on Sunday, falsely celebrating a resurrection that never took place on that day. This is why we should study to show ourselves approved and prove all things as the scriptures suggest. Sunday worship and Sunday Resurrection services both have pagan roots and should be avoided for those who choose to follow the true and living God of the scriptures.

This practice of Resurrection Sunday started with the Roman Catholic Church who changed the gathering on the Sabbath Day (Saturday) (biblical) to gathering on Sunday (pagan) to honor their Sun god. The Catholic Church proudly admits this fact and has boldly changed many of the laws of the Most High God of Abraham, Isaac and Jacob to suite their own agenda.

There is not one scripture in the entire bible to suggest the Sabbath Day (Saturday) changed to Sunday, (the first day of the week). The Pictorial Bible Dictionary pg. 846 defines Sunday as being derived from pagan sources which means the days of the week is named after pagan gods. When the Babylonian astrologers divided the calendar into seven-day weeks, the plan went into Egypt where days were named for planets.

However, Sunday is named after the Sun and Roman Emperor Constantine by royal decree in 321 AD made it Solis Day, (day of the sun). This was the god that Constantine worshiped and Christianity adopted this practice and kept it ever since.

The bible never once states remember to keep Sunday (the first day of the week) but Remember the Sabbath day, to keep it holy. This is the only day he hallowed and sanctified for his people to keep throughout their generations but his chosen people were taught to keep Sunday by pagans who worshipped other gods instead of the God of Israel.

Exodus 20:8 (KJV)

[8] Remember the sabbath day, to keep it holy.

Deuteronomy 5:12 (KJV)

[12] Keep the sabbath day to sanctify it, as the LORD thy God hath commanded thee.

Genesis 2:3 (KJV)

[3] And God blessed the seventh day, and sanctified it: because that in it he had rested from all his work which God created and made.

Exodus 20:11 (KJV)

[11] For in six days the LORD made heaven and earth, the sea, and all that in them is, and rested the seventh day: wherefore the LORD blessed the sabbath day, and hallowed it.

Exodus 31:16 (KJV)

[16] Wherefore the children of Israel shall keep the sabbath, to observe the sabbath throughout their generations, for a perpetual covenant.

IN HEAVEN NOW OR LATER

Another lesson worth exploring is the kingdom of heaven. Where is heaven going to be? When one dies, do they go directly to heaven or hell? Where are the patriarchs of the bible now such as King David? Is your soul separate from your body? The answers to these questions and others will amaze you.

Once again in modern day Christianity we are taught that when we die our souls go to heaven or hell. We hear this preached especially at funerals, you'll hear statements like "he or she is in a better place" or "they are not in pain anymore" etc. How is it that everyone goes to heaven when pastors preach funeral messages but nobody is stated as going to hell? It is understood that it gives comfort to the living when they lose a love one to tell them their lost is in heaven. However, is it biblical truth? Let's explore…

The first thing is to find a scripture that directly states whether there's anybody in heaven now or not. Is there a scripture stating such a thing exist? Can one be found? The answers to those questions are yes. This lesson will begin with the scripture John 3:13 that states no man has ascended up to heaven. This lesson could end right here because this scripture is plain and right to the point. No one means, no one, so where did the notion come from that people are in heaven today? You guessed it, another pagan belief system.

John 3:13 (KJV)

[13] And no man hath ascended up to heaven, but he that came down from heaven, even the Son of man which is in heaven.

THE SOUL / THE BREATH OF LIFE

This is a lesson that needs to be broken down into smaller pieces to obtain an understanding and a good place to start is with the soul. Since most believe the soul is separate from the body, let's explore some scriptures to help us understand this soul concept. If we go back to the beginning starting with Adam this is what the scripture says concerning Adam's soul. In Genesis 2:7 it states that the Most High God breathed into his nostrils the breath of life and he became a living soul.

Genesis 2:7 (KJV)

[7] And the LORD God formed man of the dust of the ground, and breathed into his nostrils the breath of life; and man became a living soul.

Genesis 2:7 does not say Adam was given a soul but he was the soul, he became the living soul. When the King James Version of this scripture compared with other translations of the same scripture it simply supports the same thing. Man is a living soul, a creature, a living being, a living person.

Genesis 2:7

- King James Version = A Living Soul
- English Standard version = A Creature
- New King James Version = A Living Being
- New International Version = A Living Being
- New American Standard Bible = A Living Being
- New Living Translation = A Living Person
- The New Jerusalem Bible = A Living Being
- Today's English Version = Man Began to Live
- The Living Bible = A Living Person
- Good News Bible = Man Began to Live

The word "SOUL" by definition in Hebrew is (nephesh) which means being or creature or a breathing creature. When the breath of life or the spirit of life (spirit meaning breath) enters a body it becomes a living soul.

> **Job 33:4 (KJV)**
>
> [4] The spirit of God hath made me, and the breath of the Almighty hath given me life.

The bottom line is the body and the Most High's breathe of life or spirit equals a living soul. Examples of this can be found throughout scriptures. Let's start with Leviticus 5:1-6. Here it is clear the soul can sin, hear, talk, touch, swear and have lips to do evil and can be guilty. This description describes a person not something that separates from your body.

> **Leviticus 5:1-6 (KJV)**
>
> 5 And if a soul sin, and hear the voice of swearing, and is a witness, whether he hath seen or known of it; if he do not utter it, then he shall bear his iniquity.
>
> [2] Or if a soul touch any unclean thing, whether it be a carcase of an unclean beast, or a carcase of unclean cattle, or the carcase of unclean creeping things, and if it be hidden from him; he also shall be unclean, and guilty.
>
> [3] Or if he touch the uncleanness of man, whatsoever uncleanness it be that a man shall be defiled withal, and it be hid from him; when he knoweth of it, then he shall be guilty.
>
> [4] Or if a soul swear, pronouncing with his lips to do evil, or to do good, whatsoever it be that a man shall pronounce with an oath, and it be hid from him; when he knoweth of it, then he shall be guilty in one of these.

⁵ And it shall be, when he shall be guilty in one of these things, that he shall confess that he hath sinned in that thing:

⁶ And he shall bring his trespass offering unto the LORD for his sin which he hath sinned, a female from the flock, a lamb or a kid of the goats, for a sin offering; and the priest shall make an atonement for him concerning his sin.

Souls can have blood…

Jeremiah 2:34 (KJV)

³⁴ Also in thy skirts is found the blood of the souls of the poor innocents: I have not found it by secret search, but upon all these.

Fish are souls…

Revelation 16:3 (KJV)

³ And the second angel poured out his vial upon the sea; and it became as the blood of a dead man: and every living soul died in the sea.

In the book of Exodus chapter 1 we see Jacob coming into the land of Egypt with his family. Notice in verse 5 it says that seventy souls came out of the loins of Jacob. Does this mean that Jacob had seventy souls inside of him or was their seventy people who came into Egypt with him? No, it was seventy people that were called souls.

> **Exodus 1:5 (KJV)**
>
> [5] And all the souls that came out of the loins of Jacob were seventy souls: for Joseph was in Egypt already

This also can be applied to Paul in the New Testament where it states in Acts 27:37 that there were 276 souls in a ship. Did Paul have 276 souls inside of him or was there 276 people on the ship? It was people...

> **Acts 27:37 (KJV)**
>
> [37] And we were in all in the ship two hundred threescore and sixteen souls.

The soul can go to the grave not heaven according to Psalm 49:15

> **Psalm 49:15 (KJV)**
>
> [15] But God will redeem my soul from the power of the grave: for he shall receive me. Selah.

When fasting it usually means one will go without food for any length of time. The scriptures address this as fasting. How can a soul be afflicted if it is immortal and becomes separate from the body? When fasting you are afflicting your body which is the soul. It is not separate from your body.

Leviticus 23:26-27 (KJV)

[26] And the LORD spake unto Moses, saying,

[27] Also on the tenth day of this seventh month there shall be a day of atonement: it shall be an holy convocation unto you; and ye shall afflict your souls, and offer an offering made by fire unto the LORD.

A soul can also die…if it is immortal how could this happen? It is clear in Ezekiel 18:4, if a soul sinneth it shall die. This means if a person sin it will and can die because the wages of sin is death.

Ezekiel 18:4 (KJV)

[4] Behold, all souls are mine; as the soul of the father, so also the soul of the son is mine: the soul that sinneth, it shall die.

Ezekiel 18:20 (KJV)

[20] The soul that sinneth, it shall die. The son shall not bear the iniquity of the father, neither shall the father bear the iniquity of the son: the righteousness of the righteous shall be upon him, and the wickedness of the wicked shall be upon him.

If the Most High God takes his breath or spirit out of man, they die and turn back to dust. In other words without God's breath or spirit you are a dead soul.

James 2:26 (KJV)

[26] For as the body without the spirit is dead, so faith without works is dead also

> **Psalm 104:29 (KJV)**
>
> [29] Thou hidest thy face, they are troubled: thou takest away their breath, they die, and return to their dust.

The bible does not appear to give any evidence that when one dies, they go immediately to heaven. It is suspected that when one dies the spirit separates from the body and goes to heaven when all the spirit is by definition is God's breath. Let's make it clear that the spirit in man does not belong to man, it belongs to the Most High God, so when man dies his breath returns back to him. Many believe the breath or spirit is us when it's in fact The Most High's.

> **Job 34:14-15 (KJV)**
>
> [14] If he set his heart upon man, if he gather unto himself his spirit and his breath;
>
> [15] All flesh shall perish together, and man shall turn again unto dust.

The word "SPIRIT" is defined according to Strong's Concordance #H5397 means Wind, Breath or life –force, such as in John 3:8 and Genesis 2:7. As long as one is alive the spirit or breath of God is in them. Without this breath or spirit, you are a dead soul. But you are the soul.

> **Job 27:3 (KJV)**
>
> [3] All the while my breath is in me, and the spirit of God is in my nostrils;

BACK TO DUST

What really happens when one dies according to the scriptures? If we don't go straight to heaven upon death where do we go? The scriptures clearly teach we return to dust and dust only. The scriptures never say we go straight to heaven or anywhere else other than dust. The bible teaches that from the very beginning in Genesis 3:19 that dust thou art and dust shalt thou return.

Genesis 3:19 (KJV)

[19] In the sweat of thy face shalt thou eat bread, till thou return unto the ground; for out of it wast thou taken: for dust thou art, and unto dust shalt thou return.

Psalm 104:29 (KJV)

[29] Thou hidest thy face, they are troubled: thou takest away their breath, they die, and return to their dust.

Ecclesiastes 12:7 is a scripture that is used to say our spirit goes to heaven but if we read this scripture very carefully it never says man goes to heaven. It says man returns to dust and the spirit returns to God who gave it. Once again, the spirit is his breath and should not be portrayed that it's a man that went to heaven.

Ecclesiastes 12:7 (KJV)

[7] Then shall the dust return to the earth as it was: and the spirit shall return unto God who gave it.

Daniel understood when a man dies, he returns to dust because he stated "many of them that sleep in the dust of the earth shall awake, some to everlasting life, and some to shame and everlasting contempt". Daniel knew if one is sleep, he is dead and will not wake until the resurrection.

Daniel 12:2 (KJV)

2 And many of them that sleep in the dust of the earth shall awake, some to everlasting life, and some to shame and everlasting contempt.

Job also knew there will be a resurrection of the dead because he states in Job 14:13-14 that he wanted to be kept secret in the grave and did not want to appear again until his change come. What change? He's speaking of the resurrection when he will have a new body.

Job 14:10-15 (KJV)

10 But man dieth, and wasteth away: yea, man giveth up the ghost, and where is he?

11 As the waters fail from the sea, and the flood decayeth and drieth up:

12 So man lieth down, and riseth not: till the heavens be no more, they shall not awake, nor be raised out of their sleep.

13 O that thou wouldest hide me in the grave, that thou wouldest keep me secret, until thy wrath be past, that thou wouldest appoint me a set time, and remember me!

14 If a man die, shall he live again? all the days of my appointed time will I wait, till my change come.

¹⁵ Thou shalt call, and I will answer thee: thou wilt have a desire to the work of thine hands.

Psalm 13:3 (KJV)

³ Consider and hear me, O LORD my God: lighten mine eyes, lest I sleep the sleep of death;

It appears David agrees with Daniel and Job that sleep means dead and awaking will be the resurrection. He even states waking in the likeness of the Most High. If he was already spirit and in heaven, why would he suggest waking up in his likeness?

Psalm 17:15 (KJV)

¹⁵ As for me, I will behold thy face in righteousness: I shall be satisfied, when I awake, with thy likeness.

So, out of the mouth of Daniel, Job and David all knew sleep meant dead and waking up refers to the resurrection, then why didn't either one of them mention being in heaven or waking up in heaven? That's because everyone who ever died or sleep is still dead or sleep. The bible makes it clear sleep means one is dead. The Messiah taught that's what it meant.

Matthew 9:24 (KJV)

²⁴ He said unto them, Give place: for the maid is not dead, but sleepeth. And they laughed him to scorn.

Mark 5:39 (KJV)

39 And when he was come in, he saith unto them, Why make ye this ado, and weep? the damsel is not dead, but sleepeth

Luke 8:51-52 (KJV)

51 And when he came into the house, he suffered no man to go in, save Peter, and James, and John, and the father and the mother of the maiden.

52 And all wept, and bewailed her: but he said, Weep not; she is not dead, but sleepeth.

John 11:11-14 (KJV)

11 These things said he: and after that he saith unto them, Our friend Lazarus sleepeth; but I go, that I may awake him out of sleep.

12 Then said his disciples, Lord, if he sleep, he shall do well.

13 Howbeit Jesus spake of his death: but they thought that he had spoken of taking of rest in sleep.

14 Then said Jesus unto them plainly, Lazarus is dead.

As a matter of fact, the bible informs us that King David is still in his sepulcher or grave until this day and did not ascend into heaven. How can these plain and straight forward scriptures be ignored? David is not in heaven but still in his grave like everyone else that ever died.

> **Acts 2:29 (KJV)**
>
> [29] Men and brethren, let me freely speak unto you of the patriarch David, that he is both dead and buried, and his sepulchre is with us unto this day.

> **Acts 2:34 (KJV)**
>
> [34] For David is not ascended into the heavens: but he saith himself, The Lord said unto my Lord, Sit thou on my right hand,

What happened to Moses? Did he go to heaven when he died? The scriptures say The Most High himself buried him in the land of Moab. Why didn't the Most High take him to heaven?

> **Deuteronomy 34:5-7 (KJV)**
>
> [5] So Moses the servant of the LORD died there in the land of Moab, according to the word of the LORD.
>
> [6] And he buried him in a valley in the land of Moab, over against Bethpeor: but no man knoweth of his sepulchre unto this day.
>
> [7] And Moses was an hundred and twenty years old when he died: his eye was not dim, nor his natural force abated.

THE DEAD KNOWS NOTHING

If people believe the dead goes immediately to heaven upon death, then they must believe one will know they are in heaven or have some sort of consciousness. The bible teaches quite the opposite. The bible lets us know that when people die, they know nothing because their sleep without consciousness, their thoughts is perished, they do not praise the Most High God and they have no remembrance while their dead. They know absolutely nothing until the resurrection according to the scriptures.

Psalm 146:3-4 (KJV)

[3] Put not your trust in princes, nor in the son of man, in whom there is no help.

[4] His breath goeth forth, he returneth to his earth; in that very day his thoughts perish.

Ecclesiastes 9:3-6 (KJV)

[3] This is an evil among all things that are done under the sun, that there is one event unto all: yea, also the heart of the sons of men is full of evil, and madness is in their heart while they live, and after that they go to the dead.

[4] For to him that is joined to all the living there is hope: for a living dog is better than a dead lion.

[5] **For the living know that they shall die: but the dead know not any thing,** neither have they any more a reward; for the memory of them is forgotten.

⁶ Also their love, and their hatred, and their envy, is now perished; neither have they any more a portion for ever in any thing that is done under the sun.

Psalm 6:5 (KJV)

⁵ For in death there is no remembrance of thee: in the grave who shall give thee thanks?

SOMETHING TO THINK ABOUT

If we are to believe when one dies, they will go immediately to heaven, then how could the Messiah come back and raise the dead as the scriptures proclaims? Shouldn't they be in heaven already? Who is in the grave to be resurrected if everyone who died is already in heaven?

The scripture plainly states in I Thessalonians 4:16-17 that the Messiah will descend from heaven with a shout, with the voice of an archangel and the dead in Christ shall rise first, then we which are alive and remain shall be caught up to meet him in the air. Nowhere in this passage of scripture indicates those who died are coming back with him. He is coming to resurrect from the grave not bring back those who has already died from heaven. The Messiah even mentions in verse 14-15 of I Thessalonians 4th chapter that those who sleep (died) in the Messiah are the ones who will be raised. If they are already in heaven then they would have already been raised with consciousness. Think about that for a minute???????????????

> **1 Thessalonians 4:13-17 (KJV)**
>
> [13] But I would not have you to be ignorant, brethren, concerning them which are asleep, that ye sorrow not, even as others which have no hope.
>
> [14] For if we believe that Jesus died and rose again, even so them also which sleep in Jesus will God bring with him.
>
> [15] For this we say unto you by the word of the Lord, that we which are alive and remain unto the coming of the Lord shall not prevent them which are asleep.
>
> [16] For the Lord himself shall descend from heaven with a shout, with the voice of the archangel, and with the trump of God: and the dead in Christ shall rise first:
>
> [17] Then we which are alive and remain shall be caught up together with them in the clouds, to meet the Lord in the air: and so shall we ever be with the Lord.

One of the major problems that throws off the true biblical belief that there is no one in heaven is the false "RAPTURE DOCTRINE". There will be no one leaving this earth during the tribulation period as taught in the rapture doctrine. As a matter of fact, the scripture says that the son of man (The Messiah) will not return until after the tribulation as stated in Matthew 24:29-30. Question: Did Noah and his family get raptured up when the Most High God destroyed the earth by water? Or did they stay on the earth?

> **Matthew 24:29-30 (KJV)**
>
> [29] Immediately after the tribulation of those days shall the sun be darkened, and the moon shall not give her light, and the stars shall fall from heaven, and the powers of the heavens shall be shaken:
>
> [30] And then shall appear the sign of the Son of man in heaven: and then shall all the tribes of the earth mourn, and they shall see the Son of man coming in the clouds of heaven with power and great glory.

The rapture doctrine was created by a man named John Nelson Darby in the 1800's. He was an Anglo-Irish supposed bible teacher and considered to be the father of modern Dispensationalism and Futurism. There was no teaching about the rapture before the 1800's but John Nelson Darby made this false doctrine apart of Christianity. Now, nearly the whole world believes there will be a rapture instead of the wilderness teaching.

WHERE IS HEAVEN?

The first scripture presented in this chapter to debunk that there are people in heaven right now is John 3:13. This verse established that there is no one in heaven right now and according to the scriptures, there will never be anyone in heaven where the Most High God lives.

The bible makes it perfectly clear that heaven will be on earth not in the dwelling place of the Most High God. The earth is the place man will dwell and it's called the "Kingdom of heaven" a phase mostly used in the book of Matthew and 'Kingdom of God" in the book of Mark, Luke and John.

One of the most popular scriptures that indicate heaven will be on earth is in "The Lord's Prayer". How is this missed? It says, "Thy Kingdom come, thy will be done in earth, as it is in heaven", which means his kingdom to come will be on earth.

Matthew 6:9-10 (KJV)

[9] After this manner therefore pray ye: Our Father which art in heaven, Hallowed be thy name.

[10] Thy kingdom come, Thy will be done in earth, as it is in heaven.

This view is supported throughout the scriptures in the Old and New Testament. In the book of Zechariah 14:9 it is prophesied the Lord will be king over all the earth.

Zechariah 14:9 (KJV)

[9] And the LORD shall be king over all the earth: in that day shall there be one LORD, and his name one.

All prophesies concerning the Messiah coming never indicates he's coming to take man to heaven. Only that he's coming to set up his kingdom on the earth or reign on the earth.

Revelation 5:10 (KJV)

[10] And hast made us unto our God kings and priests: and we shall reign on the earth.

The book of Revelation is filled with promises of heaven being on earth. Actually, one of the last prophecies in the book of Revelation is when the father himself brings the new city down from heaven to earth.

> **Revelation 21:2 (KJV)**
>
> [2] And I John saw the holy city, new Jerusalem, coming down from God out of heaven, prepared as a bride adorned for her husband.

During the pagan Christmas season one of the most popular scriptures used is Isaiah 9:6-7. This scripture explains that the Messiah, the son of God will be called wonderful counselor and the government shall be upon his shoulder, meaning that he will rule. What government? Is this a government in heaven? The Messiah is chosen to rule over people in an earthy government.

> **Isaiah 9:6-7 (KJV)**
>
> [6] For unto us a child is born, unto us a son is given: and the government shall be upon his shoulder: and his name shall be called Wonderful, Counsellor, The mighty God, The everlasting Father, The Prince of Peace.
>
> [7] Of the increase of his government and peace there shall be no end, upon the throne of David, and upon his kingdom, to order it, and to establish it with judgment and with justice from henceforth even for ever. The zeal of the LORD of hosts will perform this.

In Revelation 22:12-13 the Messiah clearly states that he will come quickly and his reward is with him to give every man according as his work shall be. If he is coming with a reward, then nobody could be in heaven because he's bringing his reward to the earth which is the kingdom of heaven.

Revelation 22:12-13 (KJV)

[12] And, behold, I come quickly; and my reward is with me, to give every man according as his work shall be.

[13] I am Alpha and Omega, the beginning and the end, the first and the last

One of the Messiah's messages when he was on earth was preaching the Kingdom of Heaven or God. This message was taught to his disciples who also preached this same message. This is a message that is totally lost today and no one is expecting the kingdom of God to be on earth, but instead most believe that man will be swooped up to the Most High's dwelling place in the rapture which is not biblically sound.

Mark 1:14 (KJV)

[14] Now after that John was put in prison, Jesus came into Galilee, preaching the gospel of the kingdom of God,

Luke 9:1-2 (KJV)

[1] Then he called his twelve disciples together, and gave them power and authority over all devils, and to cure diseases.

[2] And he sent them to preach the kingdom of God, and to heal the sick.

One scripture in the Old and New Testament repeats the same phrase which is "the meek shall inherent the earth". The meek will eventually inherent the earth after the end times fulfills itself. These verses are not speaking of now but a future to come. But the point is all about earth which is the focus, not heaven (God's dwelling place).

Matthew 5:5 (KJV)

5 Blessed are the meek: for they shall inherit the earth.

Psalm 37:11 (KJV)

11 But the meek shall inherit the earth; and shall delight themselves in the abundance of peace.

To reinforce the meek inheriting the earth, there is a scripture that will give some context of what will be done with the meek of the earth and that is reproof which means the meek of the earth has not been reproof as of yet because the scriptures go on the say that during this time the wolf will dwell with the lamb and the leopard shall lie down with kid. We know this is not happening nowhere in the earth today and there's never any mentioning of animals going to heaven (The Most High's Dwelling place) so this must mean that this kingdom to come is referring to the earth.

John 14: 1-3 informs us that when the Messiah comes again (to earth), we will be there also. No mention that anyone will be taken into heaven (God's dwelling place).

John 14:1-3 (KJV)

1 Let not your heart be troubled: ye believe in God, believe also in me.

2 In my Father's house are many mansions: if it were not so, I would have told you. I go to prepare a place for you.

3 And if I go and prepare a place for you, I will come again, and receive you unto myself; that where I am, there ye may be also.

Several times in the prophetic book of Daniel 7:18, 22, 27 it mentions the saints will take the kingdom forever. What kingdom is Daniel referring? The one in God's dwelling place or an earthy kingdom? If we read Daniel 7: 27 it specifically mentions a kingdom under the whole heaven. What's under the heaven? The earth…

Daniel 7:18 (KJV)

[18] But the saints of the most High shall take the kingdom, and possess the kingdom for ever, even for ever and ever.

Daniel 7:22 (KJV)

[22] Until the Ancient of days came, and judgment was given to the saints of the most High; and the time came that the saints possessed the kingdom.

Daniel 7:27 (KJV)

[27] And the kingdom and dominion, and the greatness of the kingdom under the whole heaven, shall be given to the people of the saints of the most High, whose kingdom is an everlasting kingdom, and all dominions shall serve and obey him.

Revelation 2:26-27 is in the Messiah's own words saying that those who overcome in the end will have power over nations and rule with a rod of iron. The nations are referring to the nations of this world, not nations in heaven (God's dwelling place).

> **Revelation 2:26-27 (KJV)**
>
> [26] And he that overcometh, and keepeth my works unto the end, to him will I give power over the nations:
>
> [27] And he shall rule them with a rod of iron; as the vessels of a potter shall they be broken to shivers: even as I received of my Father.

Jeremiah 23:5 proclaims that a righteous king will be raised and will execute judgment and justice in the earth. This doesn't indicate judgment and justice will be in heaven (God's dwelling) but on earth.

> **Jeremiah 23:5 (KJV)**
>
> [5] Behold, the days come, saith the LORD, that I will raise unto David a righteous Branch, and a King shall reign and prosper, and shall execute judgment and justice in the earth.

When examining the scriptures concerning this topic of heaven and whether people go there when they die, it falls short of the facts. There is not one single scripture in the entire bible that gives any indication that when people die, they go to heaven (God's dwelling place).

One would think out of all the people that died in the bible there would be at least one scripture directly indicating someone is in heaven (God's dwelling place). But when the scriptures are analyzed not one can be found. As a matter of fact, there is more evidence that shows no one is in heaven such as in the case of David who is mention as not ascending into heaven in the book of Acts 2:34. So, if David didn't make it into heaven then who did?

THE RESURRECTION

The true biblical version of what really happens when one dies is generally not taught in modern day Christianity today. The religion itself relies on fantasies and false doctrines that rarely if at all line up with biblical scriptures. Instead of believing that when one dies, they go directly to heaven, it should be taught that there will be a resurrection.

The bible is clear that only one resurrection has taken place to date, although there is indication in scripture there could have been another. Let's explore the one and only resurrection that took place and actually where someone went to heaven (God's dwelling place). This person would be the Messiah who actually rose and went to sit on the right-hand side of his father. Notice in the following scriptures two are speaking, it's the father and the son. The father is telling his son to sit on his right-hand side until he makes his enemies his footstool. Who are his enemies? Those who refuse to follow his commandments. He won't make his enemies his footstool until the **DAY of The LORD**, when he returns, after the tribulation.

Psalm 110:1 (KJV)

1 The LORD said unto my Lord, Sit thou at my right hand, until I make thine enemies thy footstool.

Matthew 22:44 (KJV)

44 The LORD said unto my Lord, Sit thou on my right hand, till I make thine enemies thy footstool?

There are several scriptures to support that the Messiah was raised and is sitting on his father's right-hand side. It definitely does not support anyone else besides the Messiah and the angels in heaven by the Most High's side at this time. Here are several other scriptures to support this claim.

Romans 8:34	Hebrews 1:13	Heb 10:12-13	Colossians 3:1
I Pet 3:21-22	Acts 2:34-35	Lk 22:69-70	Eph 1:20-21

Shortly after the Messiah was raised from the dead, something else happened. The scripture gives clear indication that during The Messiah's resurrection other saints who slept (dead) was also raised from the dead. They were even seen by others in Jerusalem (The Holy City).

Matthew 27:52-53 (KJV)

[52] And the graves were opened; and many bodies of the saints which slept arose,

[53] And came out of the graves after his resurrection, and went into the holy city, and appeared unto many.

The question is who were these saints? Did these saints go to heaven where The Most High God lives? The bible does not give any information as to their identities or where they are located today. But we do know they did not go to Heaven (The Most High's dwelling place). However, the scriptures do indicate generally who the saints were. The saints by biblical definition in this context are the Israelites, so those who were raised had to be from the nation of Israel.

Most believe if you are a saint, you have accepted the Messiah as your Lord and personal savior and this could be anyone. However, The Messiah was just crucified and nobody had a chance to accept him as Lord and savior immediately after his death. The bible is very clear the true saints are the Israelites (God's chosen people). The Old Testament confirms this on multiple occasions. The Israelites objectively are the true saints and others could be subjectively saints. So, from this analysis we know the saints that were raised from their graves had to be from the nation of Israel.

Psalm 50:5 (KJV)

[5] Gather my saints together unto me; those that have made a covenant with me by sacrifice.

Psalm 148:14 (KJV)

[14] He also exalteth the horn of his people, the praise of all his saints; even of the children of Israel, a people near unto him. Praise ye the LORD.

Psalm 106:16 (KJV)

[16] They envied Moses also in the camp, and Aaron the saint of the LORD.

Since these particular saints did not go to heaven (The Most High's dwelling place). This still leaves only the Father, The Messiah and the angels currently in heaven at this moment. The Apostle Paul and Luke both mentioned that The Messiah was the first to be raised from sleep (dead) and was the first fruit from the dead. So, if this is the case then where is the argument that people who died before The Messiah made it to heaven (The Most High's dwelling place)? The scripture clearly states The Messiah is the only one who has immortality after death.

Acts 26:22-23 (KJV)

[22] Having therefore obtained help of God, I continue unto this day, witnessing both to small and great, saying none other things than those which the prophets and Moses did say should come:

[23] That Christ should suffer, and that he should be the first that should rise from the dead, and should shew light unto the people, and to the Gentiles.

---

1 Corinthians 15:20-22 (KJV)

[20] But now is Christ risen from the dead, and become the firstfruits of them that slept.

[21] For since by man came death, by man came also the resurrection of the dead.

[22] For as in Adam all die, even so in Christ shall all be made alive.

---

1 Timothy 6:14-16 (KJV)

[14] That thou keep this commandment without spot, unrebukable, until the appearing of our Lord Jesus Christ:

[15] Which in his times he shall shew, who is the blessed and only Potentate, the King of kings, and Lord of lords;

[16] Who only hath immortality, dwelling in the light which no man can approach unto; whom no man hath seen, nor can see: to whom be honour and power everlasting. Amen.

As a matter of fact, those who are still sleep or dead in their graves cannot be resurrected until they hear the Messiah's voice to come out of the grave.

---

1 Thessalonians 4:16-17 (KJV)

[16] For the Lord himself shall descend from heaven with a shout, with the voice of the archangel, and with the trump of God: and the dead in Christ shall rise first:

[17] Then we which are alive and remain shall be caught up together with them in the clouds, to meet the Lord in the air: and so shall we ever be with the Lord.

John 5:28-29 (KJV)

[28] Marvel not at this: for the hour is coming, in the which all that are in the graves shall hear his voice,

[29] And shall come forth; they that have done good, unto the resurrection of life; and they that have done evil, unto the resurrection of damnation.

Question: If the dead are still in the grave, how could they be in heaven with consciousness?

All of the saints who ever died are awaiting their change to put on immortality and this has not taken place as of yet. Everyone who has ever died is still in the grave and therefore no one is in heaven (The Most High's dwelling place). It is unknown who those saints were that was raised in Matthew 27:52 and where they are today (we can only speculate). But we know from other scriptures they did not go to heaven.

1 Corinthians 15:50-54 (KJV)

[50] Now this I say, brethren, that flesh and blood cannot inherit the kingdom of God; neither doth corruption inherit incorruption.

[51] Behold, I shew you a mystery; We shall not all sleep, but we shall all be changed,

[52] In a moment, in the twinkling of an eye, at the last trump: for the trumpet shall sound, and the dead shall be raised incorruptible, and we shall be changed.

[53] For this corruptible must put on incorruption, and this mortal must put on immortality.

[54] So when this corruptible shall have put on incorruption, and this mortal shall have put on immortality, then shall be brought to pass the saying that is written, Death is swallowed up in victory.

THE DIETARY LAW

The Dietary Law is another law not recognized in modern day Christianity. It is taught one can eat anything as long as they pray over it. This belief is taken from I Timothy 4:4. Again, this is another writing of Paul in which Peter warns how Paul letters can be misinterpreted. If Paul's letters are incorrectly interpreted it can lead to one's destruction (II Peter 3:16).

We will get to I Timothy 4 in a second but let's first find out what is the dietary law. The dietary law is a law that the God of Abraham, Isaac and Jacob instituted for the children of Israel and eventually for all humans to follow. This law was instituted to keep the children of Israel from unclean foods and not be defiled. This law was and still a perpetual statute unto the nation of Israel and strangers who choose to follow the laws of the God of Abraham, Isaac and Jacob.

Paul, the writer of most of the New Testament would never have told people they could eat anything if they just prayed over it. Why? He was a supporter of following all the laws of the Most High God. He often quoted from the Old Testament and admitted he followed the law or Torah of the Most High God.

Romans 7:25 (KJV)

25 I thank God through Jesus Christ our Lord. So then with the mind I myself serve the law of God; but with the flesh the law of sin.

Let's go back to the beginning where the law was instituted. There were several reasons the Most High God told his chosen people to stick to his dietary law. One is because they were to be the model nation for the whole world and should be set apart from every other nation. Two, this included what the nation of True Israel was suppose to be eating.

If True Israel were to eat anything outside of the dietary law, they were considered to be unclean or defiled. The Most High God instructions stated, "Thou shalt not eat any abominable thing". This was a commandment that should never have been broken.

Deuteronomy 14:2-3 (KJV)

[2] For thou art an holy people unto the LORD thy God, and the LORD hath chosen thee to be a peculiar people unto himself, above all the nations that are upon the earth.

[3] Thou shalt not eat any abominable thing.

Leviticus 20:25-26 (KJV)

[25] Ye shall therefore put difference between clean beasts and unclean, and between unclean fowls and clean: and ye shall not make your souls abominable by beast, or by fowl, or by any manner of living thing that creepeth on the ground, which I have separated from you as unclean.

[26] And ye shall be holy unto me: for I the LORD am holy, and have severed you from other people, that ye should be mine.

Leviticus 11:44-47 (KJV)

[44] For I am the LORD your God: ye shall therefore sanctify yourselves, and ye shall be holy; for I am holy: neither shall ye

defile yourselves with any manner of creeping thing that creepeth upon the earth.

45 For I am the LORD that bringeth you up out of the land of Egypt, to be your God: ye shall therefore be holy, for I am holy.

46 This is the law of the beasts, and of the fowl, and of every living creature that moveth in the waters, and of every creature that creepeth upon the earth:

47 To make a difference between the unclean and the clean, and between the beast that may be eaten and the beast that may not be eaten.

The Most High God was always concerned about what humans ate. This can be seen as far back as Noah. During the gathering of all animals upon Noah's Ark as we know were gathered by male and female. But they needed to gather extra food to eat and the food that was extra was only the food that was clean not unclean.

Genesis 6:17-22 (KJV)

17 And, behold, I, even I, do bring a flood of waters upon the earth, to destroy all flesh, wherein is the breath of life, from under heaven; and every thing that is in the earth shall die.

18 But with thee will I establish my covenant; and thou shalt come into the ark, thou, and thy sons, and thy wife, and thy sons' wives with thee.

19 And of every living thing of all flesh, two of every sort shalt thou bring into the ark, to keep them alive with thee; they shall be male and female.

> ²⁰ Of fowls after their kind, and of cattle after their kind, of every creeping thing of the earth after his kind, two of every sort shall come unto thee, to keep them alive.
>
> ²¹ And take thou unto thee of all food that is eaten, and thou shalt gather it to thee; and it shall be for food for thee, and for them.
>
> ²² Thus did Noah; according to all that God commanded him, so did he.

If we go to Genesis 7:1-2 notice that the clean beast that were gathered were by sevens not by twos. This was a clue that they needed clean food to eat and clean food for burnt offerings.

> **Genesis 7:1-2 (KJV)**
>
> 1 And the LORD said unto Noah, Come thou and all thy house into the ark; for thee have I seen righteous before me in this generation.
>
> ² **Of every clean beast thou shalt take to thee by sevens**, the male and his female: and of beasts that are not clean by two, the male and his female.

> **Genesis 8:15-20 (KJV)**
>
> ¹⁵ And God spake unto Noah, saying,
>
> ¹⁶ Go forth of the ark, thou, and thy wife, and thy sons, and thy sons' wives with thee.
>
> ¹⁷ Bring forth with thee every living thing that is with thee, of all flesh, both of fowl, and of cattle, and of every creeping thing that creepeth upon the earth; that they may breed abundantly in the earth, and be fruitful, and multiply upon the earth.

¹⁸ And Noah went forth, and his sons, and his wife, and his sons' wives with him:

¹⁹ Every beast, every creeping thing, and every fowl, and whatsoever creepeth upon the earth, after their kinds, went forth out of the ark.

²⁰ And Noah builded an altar unto the LORD; and took of every clean beast, and of every clean fowl, and offered burnt offerings on the altar.

The Dietary Law in scripture is located in Leviticus 11:1-32, 39-43 and in Deuteronomy (Please read). It gives specific instructions what we should eat and what we should not eat.

- Fish you can eat = (Leviticus 11:9) and (Deut. 14:9)
- Birds and Fowls, you can eat = Deuteronomy 14:11, 20
- Insects you can eat = (Leviticus 11:22)
- Beast you can eat = (Deuteronomy 14:4-6)

In Leviticus 3:17 we are also instructed not to eat any fat or blood. The dietary law is perpetual and should be followed.

Leviticus 3:17 (KJV)

¹⁷ It shall be a perpetual statute for your generations throughout all your dwellings, that ye eat neither fat nor blood.

In the book of Job there is a scripture that clearly states an unclean thing cannot be made clean. So, praying over unclean food and thinking that the Most High God is blessing it is false. It cannot be done according to the scripture.

Job 14:4 (KJV)

[4] Who can bring a clean thing out of an unclean? not one.

It is a serious offense to eat unclean foods. It is against The Most High God's law that still exists and is not done away. If we seek prophetic scriptures concerning this matter you'll see when the Messiah returns to earth during the **Day of The Lord** he is coming back angry to kill all those who are breaking or transgressing The Most High God's law. This includes the dietary law and eating swine's flesh (Pig or Pork) will not be tolerated. If this dietary law was done away with then why would the Messiah kill those who are breaking it? He intends on coming back for war on all those who are breaking it.

Revelation 19:11-15 (KJV)

[11] And I saw heaven opened, and behold a white horse; and he that sat upon him was called Faithful and True, and in righteousness he doth judge and make war.

[12] His eyes were as a flame of fire, and on his head were many crowns; and he had a name written, that no man knew, but he himself.

[13] And he was clothed with a vesture dipped in blood: and his name is called The Word of God.

[14] And the armies which were in heaven followed him upon white horses, clothed in fine linen, white and clean.

[15] And out of his mouth goeth a sharp sword, that with it he should smite the nations: and he shall rule them with a rod of iron: and he treadeth the winepress of the fierceness and wrath of Almighty God.

2 Thessalonians 1:6-10 (KJV)

[6] Seeing it is a righteous thing with God to recompense tribulation to them that trouble you;

[7] And to you who are troubled rest with us, when the Lord Jesus shall be revealed from heaven with his mighty angels,

[8] In flaming fire taking vengeance on them that know not God, and that obey not the gospel of our Lord Jesus Christ:

[9] Who shall be punished with everlasting destruction from the presence of the Lord, and from the glory of his power;

[10] When he shall come to be glorified in his saints, and to be admired in all them that believe (because our testimony among you was believed) in that day.

Isaiah 66:14-17 (KJV)

[14] And when ye see this, your heart shall rejoice, and your bones shall flourish like an herb: and the hand of the LORD shall be known toward his servants, and his indignation toward his enemies.

[15] For, behold, the LORD will come with fire, and with his chariots like a whirlwind, to render his anger with fury, and his rebuke with flames of fire.

[16] For by fire and by his sword will the LORD plead with all flesh: and the slain of the LORD shall be many.

¹⁷ They that sanctify themselves, and purify themselves in the gardens behind one tree in the midst, **eating swine's flesh, and the abomination, and the mouse, shall be consumed together, saith the LORD.**

I TIMOTHY 4:1-5 EXPLAINED

1 Timothy 4:1-5 (KJV)

1 Now the Spirit speaketh expressly, that in the latter times some shall depart from the faith, giving heed to seducing spirits, and doctrines of devils;

² Speaking lies in hypocrisy; having their conscience seared with a hot iron;

³ Forbidding to marry, and commanding to abstain from meats, which God hath created to be received with thanksgiving of them which believe and know the truth.

⁴ For every creature of God is good, and nothing to be refused, if it be received with thanksgiving:

⁵ For it is sanctified by the word of God and prayer.

I Timothy 4:1-5 are verses used as proof to say that any type of food can be eaten as long as one prays over it. Is this what Paul really meant? If this is the case then Paul is contradicting himself in many scriptures throughout the bible (New Testament) because he clearly says he follows the law which includes the **Dietary Law.**

Please Read: Romans 7:25, Acts 21:24, Acts 28:23 and Acts 24:14 to support that Paul was an advocate of the laws of the Most High God in the scriptures.

Another point to make is Paul believed in the Old Testament because he quoted from it frequently to support his points of believe. For example: Paul wrote I Corinthians and I Timothy but if you read I Corinthians 9:8-9 and I Timothy 5:18 you'll see he quoted this exact scripture from Deuteronomy 25:4 verbatim on both of these occasions. Also read Galatians 3:12 / Leviticus 18:5 and II Corinthians 9:9 / Psalm 112:9 for more examples. (There are plenty more).

EXAMPLE 1

1 Corinthians 9:8-9 (KJV)

[8] Say I these things as a man? or saith not the law the same also?

[9] For it is written in the law of Moses, **thou shalt not muzzle the mouth of the ox that treadeth out the corn**. Doth God take care for oxen?

Deuteronomy 25:4 (KJV)

[4] Thou shalt not muzzle the ox when he treadeth out the corn.

EXAMPLE 2

> **Galatians 3:12 (KJV)**
>
> [12] And the law is not of faith: but, **The man that doeth them shall live in them.**
>
> --
>
> **Leviticus 18:5 (KJV)**
>
> [5] Ye shall therefore keep my statutes, and my judgments: **which if a man do, he shall live in them:** I am the LORD

EXAMPLE 3

> **2 Corinthians 9:9 (KJV)**
>
> [9] (As it is written, He hath dispersed abroad; he **hath given to the poor: his righteousness remaineth for ever.**
>
> --
>
> **Psalm 112:9 (KJV)**
>
> [9] He hath dispersed, **he hath given to the poor; his righteousness endureth for ever;** his horn shall be exalted with honour.

The breakdown of I Timothy 4:1-5 verse by verse.

> **1 Timothy 4:1 (KJV)**
>
> [1] Now the Spirit speaketh expressly, that in the latter times some shall depart from the faith, giving heed to seducing spirits, and doctrines of devils;

Paul began this 4th chapter of I Timothy by identifying doctrines originating with demons and giving heed to seducing spirits. In other words, Paul is beginning to warn against false heretical teachings or doctrines in latter times. Paul is not starting out addressing the laws or doctrines of the Most High God but of devils. Keep this in mind as we continue with the rest of the verses.

1 Timothy 4:2 (KJV)

2 Speaking lies in hypocrisy; having their conscience seared with a hot iron;

The 2nd verse continues to support the idea that these seducing spirits, false teachings and the speaking of lies in the latter days will be seared in the conscience with a hot iron. Meaning, the lies and hypocrisy would be so great that truth will not be recognized. The false doctrines or teachings will make people insensitive, dulled to what's right and wrong.

1 Timothy 4:3 (KJV)

3 Forbidding to marry, and commanding to abstain from meats, which God hath created to be received with thanksgiving of them which believe and know the truth.

The beginning of the 3rd verse expounds on two specific false teachings which are forbidding marriage and abstaining from meats. There are no laws from the Most High God to abstain from either marrying or abstaining from meats. There is an organization on earth today that supports these doctrines. The organization is the Roman Catholic Church. They promote not getting married (Priest) and abstaining from meats (Lent). This is not a rule of the bible but the organization of the Roman Catholic Church. So, these are the doctrines of devils.

The 2nd part of the verse takes a turn where Paul is saying we can eat meats because the Most High God had created it to be received with Thanksgiving but he ends the verse by saying "to those who believe and know the truth". What is the truth Paul is suggesting?

If you know the truth about what you can eat, then you'll know that Paul is pointing towards the dietary law, simply because he supports the law of the Most High God and would never suggest one can eat anything if you just pray over it. Paul knows that the law is the truth.

Psalm 119:142 (KJV)

¹⁴² Thy righteousness is an everlasting righteousness, and thy law is the truth

---

1 Timothy 4:4 (KJV)

⁴ For every creature of God is good, and nothing to be refused, if it be received with thanksgiving:

In this 4th verse Paul is stating that every creature of The Most High God is good and nothing should be refused if it is received with thanksgiving. This verse does not state that one can eat anything because it was created by the Most High God. It is apparent that what the Most High God creates is good but is everything he created is good for food? The Most High God created Rats, leeches, flies, poisonous frogs and cockroaches. Does this mean we should eat them? Absolutely not, this is why the Most High God instituted a law of what we should eat and not eat. If we ate anything whether we prayed over it or not we could die. All creatures are good for God's purpose not all for consumption or for food.

> **1 Timothy 4:5 (KJV)**
>
> [5] For it is sanctified by the word of God and prayer.

This 5th verse tops it off with Paul stating "sanctified by the word of God and prayer". The only foods that were sanctified or set apart were those foods mentioned in the dietary law. Those foods are listed in Leviticus 11:1-32, 39-43.

In conclusion of this topic, Paul is not promoting anyone to eat anything if it's created by the Most High God but only those foods that are sanctified by the word of God.

Chapter 18

THE SABBATH

The Sabbath…What is it? How important is it? Should we observe it today? There are many questions concerning the Sabbath observance. Is it possible to find answers in the bible? Today, we know most of Christianity gathers on the first day of the week. Is this biblical? This chapter will explore scriptures on this topic of the Sabbath to see if this is a biblical event or not. There is much information in the scriptures and no one should be confused about the Sabbath day.

First, the word Sabbath comes from the Hebrew word "Shabat", meaning cessation or time of rest. This Sabbath day was instituted at the very beginning of creation when the Most High God took it upon himself to rest on the Sabbath day; this day is known in modern times as Saturday. The Most High God rest was a rest of completion not because he was tired or exhausted but because his work was finished. We know the Most High God does not get tired or weary.

Isaiah 40:28 (KJV)

[28] Hast thou not known? hast thou not heard, that the everlasting God, the LORD, the Creator of the ends of the earth, fainteth not, neither is weary? there is no searching of his understanding.

The first account of the Most High's Sabbath appears in Genesis 2:1-3

Genesis 2:1-3 (KJV)

1 Thus the heavens and the earth were finished, and all the host of them.

2 And on the seventh day God ended his work which he had made; and he rested on the seventh day from all his work which he had made.

3 And God blessed the seventh day, and sanctified it: because that in it he had rested from all his work which God created and made.

Exodus 20:11 (KJV)

11 For in six days the LORD made heaven and earth, the sea, and all that in them is, and rested the seventh day: wherefore the LORD blessed the sabbath day, and hallowed it.

Hebrews 4:4 (KJV)

4 For he spake in a certain place of the seventh day on this wise, And God did rest the seventh day from all his works.

Notice, this seventh day (Saturday) was blessed, sanctified and hallowed by the Most High God. Can we say this about the first day of the week (Sunday)? Absolutely not. There is not one scripture in the entire bible from Genesis to Revelation or the Apocrypha to say the Sabbath Day is no longer relevant.

The word blessed could mean "divine", sanctify mean "set apart" and hallowed mean "to render and treat holy". So, the Most High God took the seventh day of the week and blessed it, sanctified it, and hallowed it. When did the Most High God undo this blessed, sanctified and hollowed day? If one is looking in the scriptures for this answer it will not be found. Only in man's history or tradition of men will one find how the Sabbath day (Saturday) was changed to Sunday (first day of the week) but not in the scriptures.

This Sabbath Day was so important it was instituted into the Ten Commandments of the Most High God. It became the fourth commandment which says "Remember the Sabbath Day, to keep it holy". It is mentioned in Exodus 20:8 and Deuteronomy 5:12.

Exodus 20:8 (KJV)

[8] Remember the sabbath day, to keep it holy.

Deuteronomy 5:12 (KJV)

[12] Keep the sabbath day to sanctify it, as the LORD thy God hath commanded thee.

This was a law that should have never been broken and should stand today. Although this law was instituted at creation and all men were to follow it. It was again given to True Israel (Israelites) to be kept forever. This is why the Most High God reminded them to keep it by saying" Remember the Sabbath" in Exodus 20:8.

THE CONSEQUENCES

It was a struggle for True Israel (Israelites) to keep the Sabbath and when they didn't it was serious consequences. For example: The Most High instructed the children of Israel to gather two times as much manna on the sixth day when they were in the wilderness because he was not going to rain down manna (bread) on the seventh day due to the law of rest (The Sabbath).

Exodus 16:22-27 (KJV)

22 And it came to pass, that on the sixth day they gathered twice as much bread, two omers for one man: and all the rulers of the congregation came and told Moses.

23 And he said unto them, This is that which the LORD hath said, To morrow is the rest of the holy sabbath unto the LORD: bake that which ye will bake to day, and seethe that ye will seethe; and that which remaineth over lay up for you to be kept until the morning.

24 And they laid it up till the morning, as Moses bade: and it did not stink, neither was there any worm therein.

25 And Moses said, Eat that to day; for to day is a sabbath unto the LORD: to day ye shall not find it in the field.

26 Six days ye shall gather it; but on the seventh day, which is the sabbath, in it there shall be none.

27 And it came to pass, that there went out some of the people on the seventh day for to gather, and they found none.

There were Israelites that were killed due to not keeping or following the law of keeping the Sabbath. For example: There was a man in the wilderness with the children of Israel that were gathering sticks on the Sabbath Day and the Most High God instructed Moses that this man should be put to death. This man was stoned to death because he was working or picking up sticks on the Sabbath Day.

Numbers 15:32-36 (KJV)

[32] And while the children of Israel were in the wilderness, they found a man that gathered sticks upon the sabbath day.

[33] And they that found him gathering sticks brought him unto Moses and Aaron, and unto all the congregation.

[34] And they put him in ward, because it was not declared what should be done to him.

[35] And the LORD said unto Moses, The man shall be surely put to death: all the congregation shall stone him with stones without the camp.

[36] And all the congregation brought him without the camp, and stoned him with stones, and he died; as the LORD commanded Moses.

In the book of Nehemiah there is another example of the importance of keeping the Sabbath Day. Those who kept the Sabbath Day were not able to buy or sell on that day. Nehemiah had to rebuke those who were working, selling and buying on the Sabbath Day. These were basically other nations of people selling to the Children of True Israel.

Nehemiah was very upset that the children of Israel were involved in this law-breaking practice. He knew the children of Israel was doing an evil thing by profaning the Sabbath and feared The Most High God will bring some sort of judgment upon them for profaning the Sabbath Day.

Nehemiah instructed that the gates to Jerusalem be closed before the Sabbath Day and should not be open until after the Sabbath Day was over. Nehemiah did not want any more burdens to be brought upon them by profaning the keeping of the Sabbath Day. Nehemiah threatened to beat them up or lay hands on them if they continued to buy or sell on the Sabbath Day.

Nehemiah 10:31 (KJV)

[31] And if the people of the land bring ware or any victuals on the sabbath day to sell, that we would not buy it of them on the sabbath, or on the holy day: and that we would leave the seventh year, and the exaction of every debt.

Nehemiah 13:15-22 (KJV)

[15] In those days saw I in Judah some treading wine presses on the sabbath, and bringing in sheaves, and lading asses; as also wine, grapes, and figs, and all manner of burdens, which they brought into Jerusalem on the sabbath day: and I testified against them in the day wherein they sold victuals.

[16] There dwelt men of Tyre also therein, which brought fish, and all manner of ware, and sold on the sabbath unto the children of Judah, and in Jerusalem.

[17] Then I contended with the nobles of Judah, and said unto them, What evil thing is this that ye do, and profane the sabbath day?

[18] Did not your fathers thus, and did not our God bring all this evil upon us, and upon this city? yet ye bring more wrath upon Israel by profaning the sabbath.

¹⁹ And it came to pass, that when the gates of Jerusalem began to be dark before the sabbath, I commanded that the gates should be shut, and charged that they should not be opened till after the sabbath: and some of my servants set I at the gates, that there should no burden be brought in on the sabbath day.

²⁰ So the merchants and sellers of all kind of ware lodged without Jerusalem once or twice.

²¹ Then I testified against them, and said unto them, Why lodge ye about the wall? if ye do so again, I will lay hands on you. From that time forth came they no more on the sabbath.

²² And I commanded the Levites that they should cleanse themselves, and that they should come and keep the gates, to sanctify the sabbath day. Remember me, O my God, concerning this also, and spare me according to the greatness of thy mercy.

Profaning the Sabbath Day was always prohibited. The Most High God despises the thought and notion of breaking of any of his Sabbaths. The following scriptures will give more insight as to how displeasing the breaking of the Most High Sabbaths was and still is today.

Ezekiel 20:13	Ezekiel 20:16	Ezekiel 20:21
Ezekiel 20:24	Ezekiel 23:38	Ezekiel 22:8
Isaiah 56:2-5	Isaiah 58:13	Jeremiah 17:21-27

The keeping of the Sabbath Day was commanded by the Most High's voice and finger.

> **Deuteronomy 4:12-13 (KJV)**
>
> [12] And the LORD spake unto you out of the midst of the fire: ye heard the voice of the words, but saw no similitude; only ye heard a voice.
>
> [13] And he declared unto you his covenant, which he commanded you to perform, even ten commandments; and he wrote them upon two tables of stone.

When the Laws, Statutes and Commandments were given to the children of Israel it included the keeping of the Sabbath Day. It was supposed to be kept for all generations and as a **perpetual covenant** for the children of Israel. The word perpetual means "lasting for an eternity", which suggest this covenant of keeping the Sabbath Day will never end.

> **Exodus 31:13 (KJV)**
>
> [13] Speak thou also unto the children of Israel, saying, Verily my sabbaths ye shall keep: for it is a sign between me and you throughout your generations; that ye may know that I am the LORD that doth sanctify you.

> **Exodus 31:16 (KJV)**
>
> [16] Wherefore the children of Israel shall keep the sabbath, to observe the sabbath throughout their generations, for a perpetual covenant.

Ezekiel 20:20 (KJV)

[20] And hallow my sabbaths; and they shall be a sign between me and you, that ye may know that I am the LORD your God.

Isaiah 40:8 (KJV)

[8] The grass withereth, the flower fadeth: but the word of our God shall stand for ever.

Malachi 3:6 (KJV)

[6] For I am the LORD, I change not; therefore ye sons of Jacob are not consumed.

Luke 16:17 (KJV)

[17] And it is easier for heaven and earth to pass, than one tittle of the law to fail.

1 Peter 1:25 (KJV)

[25] But the word of the Lord endureth for ever. And this is the word which by the gospel is preached unto you.

Matthew 5:18 (KJV)

[18] For verily I say unto you, Till heaven and earth pass, one jot or one tittle shall in no wise pass from the law, till all be fulfilled.

Psalm 119:44 (KJV)

[44] So shall I keep thy law continually for ever and ever.

If we fast forward into the future you'll see that the Sabbath Day will never be abolished, eventually all righteous people will be keeping it whether they want to or not according to prophecy. Most biblical scholars believe that Isaiah 66:23 and Zechariah 14:16 reflect future law keeping of the Sabbath and Feast Days etc. If this is true, then this would be proof that the Sabbath day will never end.

Isaiah 66:23 (KJV)

[23] And it shall come to pass, that from one new moon to another, and from one sabbath to another, shall all flesh come to worship before me, saith the LORD.

Zechariah 14:16 (KJV)

[16] And it shall come to pass, that every one that is left of all the nations which came against Jerusalem shall even go up from year to year to worship the King, the LORD of hosts, and to keep the feast of tabernacles.

Zechariah further explains if the laws are not kept concerning The Feast Days and Sabbaths, nations such as Egypt will not receive any rain. This is an indication that no one will be able to break any of The Most High's Laws without any consequences including the Sabbath Day.

Zechariah 14:17-18 (KJV)

[17] And it shall be, that whoso will not come up of all the families of the earth unto Jerusalem to worship the King, the LORD of hosts, even upon them shall be no rain.

[18] And if the family of Egypt go not up, and come not, that have no rain; there shall be the plague, wherewith the LORD will smite the heathen that come not up to keep the feast of tabernacles

---

THE BLESSINGS

The keeping of the Sabbath Day is not a bad or grievous thing. According to the scriptures it's a blessing to keep and observe it. None of the laws or commandments of The Most High God are grievous which includes the keeping of the Sabbath Day. It may be inconvenience to some people but certainly not grievous.

---

1 John 5:3 (KJV)

[3] For this is the love of God, that we keep his commandments: and his commandments are not grievous.

Psalm 1 expresses how blessed one is when following the laws of The Most High God. It lets us know that we should delight ourselves in the law and meditate in it day and night. The law also includes the Sabbath Day.

Psalm 1:1-6 (KJV)

1 Blessed is the man that walketh not in the counsel of the ungodly, nor standeth in the way of sinners, nor sitteth in the seat of the scornful.

2 But his delight is in the law of the LORD; and in his law doth he meditate day and night.

3 And he shall be like a tree planted by the rivers of water, that bringeth forth his fruit in his season; his leaf also shall not wither; and whatsoever he doeth shall prosper.

4 The ungodly are not so: but are like the chaff which the wind driveth away.

5 Therefore the ungodly shall not stand in the judgment, nor sinners in the congregation of the righteous.

6 For the LORD knoweth the way of the righteous: but the way of the ungodly shall perish.

Psalm 112:1 (KJV)

1 Praise ye the LORD. Blessed is the man that feareth the LORD, that delighteth greatly in his commandments.

Psalm 119:92 (KJV)

92 Unless thy law had been my delights, I should then have perished in mine affliction.

It will always be a blessing to follow the Most High's Laws, Statutes and Commandments and no one should deviate to the left or right of it. This includes the Sabbath Day because it's part of the commandments.

Deuteronomy 5:32 (KJV)

[32] Ye shall observe to do therefore as the LORD your God hath commanded you: ye shall not turn aside to the right hand or to the left.

Joshua 23:6 (KJV)

[6] Be ye therefore very courageous to keep and to do all that is written in the book of the law of Moses, that ye turn not aside therefrom to the right hand or to the left;

---

2 Chronicles 34:2 (KJV)

[2] And he did that which was right in the sight of the LORD, and walked in the ways of David his father, and declined neither to the right hand, nor to the left.

To honor the Sabbath Day is a blessing in so many ways according to Isaiah 58:13-14

Isaiah 58:13-14 (KJV)

[13] If thou turn away thy foot from the sabbath, from doing thy pleasure on my holy day; and call the sabbath a delight, the holy of the LORD, honourable; and shalt honour him, not doing thine own ways, nor finding thine own pleasure, nor speaking thine own words:

[14] Then shalt thou delight thyself in the LORD; and I will cause thee to ride upon the high places of the earth, and feed thee with the heritage of Jacob thy father: for the mouth of the LORD hath spoken it.

Isaiah 56:2 (KJV)

[2] Blessed is the man that doeth this, and the son of man that layeth hold on it; that keepeth the sabbath from polluting it, and keepeth his hand from doing any evil.

THE MESSIAH AND OTHERS ON THE SABBATH

THE MESSIAH

Many believe that the Sabbath Day was abolished once The Messiah died on the cross or that those in the New Testament did not follow the law of the Most High God. In fact the Messiah himself observed and followed all of the laws of the Most High God. This is what made him sinless.

John 15:10 (KJV)

[10] If ye keep my commandments, ye shall abide in my love; even as I have kept my Father's commandments, and abide in his love

---

If the Messiah would have broken the law of the Sabbath Day, he would not have been blameless because he would have sinned. Just as 'Thou shalt not steal", "Thou shalt not kill", "Thou shalt not commit adultery and "thou shalt not covet" etc. are all a part of the Ten Commandments / Law and most of the religious people or leaders of today are convinced that stealing and committing adultery is wrong. So why is the fourth commandment so hard to believe where it states, "Remember the Sabbath Day, To Keep It Holy". Isn't this commandment relevant to? Peter said The Messiah suffered for his people and became an example of how we should follow in his steps and that included observing the Sabbath Day.

---

1 Peter 2:21-22 (KJV)

[21] For even hereunto were ye called: because Christ also suffered for us, leaving us an example, that ye should follow his steps:

[22] Who did no sin, neither was guile found in his mouth:

The Messiah is caught on several occasions reading scriptures on the Sabbath Day, which was his custom to do.

Luke 4:16 (KJV)

[16] And he came to Nazareth, where he had been brought up: and, as his custom was, he went into the synagogue on the sabbath day, and stood up for to read.

The Messiah was often challenged by the Pharisees on various matters and the Sabbath Day was no different. The Pharisees followed their own traditions and lacked understanding as to what the Sabbath Day was all about. For example:
When the Messiah and his disciples were caught by the Pharisees plucking and eating corn, the Pharisees thought it was unlawful to do so and the Messiah needed to correct them by letting them know there were an immediate need to eat because they were hungry and doing the work of the Most High God.

Matthew 12:1-8 (KJV)

[1] At that time Jesus went on the sabbath day through the corn; and his disciples were an hungred, and began to pluck the ears of corn and to eat.

[2] But when the Pharisees saw it, they said unto him, Behold, thy disciples do that which is not lawful to do upon the sabbath day.

[3] But he said unto them, Have ye not read what David did, when he was an hungred, and they that were with him;

[4] How he entered into the house of God, and did eat the shewbread, which was not lawful for him to eat, neither for them which were with him, but only for the priests?

⁵ Or have ye not read in the law, how that on the sabbath days the priests in the temple profane the sabbath, and are blameless?

⁶ But I say unto you, That in this place is one greater than the temple.

⁷ But if ye had known what this meaneth, I will have mercy, and not sacrifice, ye would not have condemned the guiltless.

⁸ For the Son of man is Lord even of the sabbath day.

Mark 2:23 (KJV)

²³ And it came to pass, that he went through the corn fields on the sabbath day; and his disciples began, as they went, to pluck the ears of corn.

We must remember that the Sabbath Day was made for man and not man for the Sabbath.

Mark 2:27-28 (KJV)

²⁷ And he said unto them, The sabbath was made for man, and not man for the sabbath:

²⁸ Therefore the Son of man is Lord also of the sabbath.

This means under certain circumstances there are reasons to do good on the Sabbath Day but only in extreme emergencies. For example:

The Messiah gave the Pharisees a scenario of an Ox falling into a pit and would it be lawful to pull it out on the Sabbath Day? The answer is yes, The Messiah was making the point that it would not make sense to leave the Ox in the pit all day to suffer because it happened on the Sabbath Day.

> **Luke 14:5 (KJV)**
>
> [5] And answered them, saying, Which of you shall have an ass or an ox fallen into a pit, and will not straightway pull him out on the sabbath day?

In other words, good deeds and efforts for sustaining life can be done on the Sabbath Day such as healing etc.

> **Luke 14:1-4 (KJV)**
>
> 14 And it came to pass, as he went into the house of one of the chief Pharisees to eat bread on the sabbath day, that they watched him.
>
> [2] And, behold, there was a certain man before him which had the dropsy.
>
> [3] And Jesus answering spake unto the lawyers and Pharisees, saying, Is it lawful to heal on the sabbath day?
>
> [4] And they held their peace. And he took him, and healed him, and let him go;

Other scriptures pertaining to good deeds, sustaining life and necessity on the Sabbath Day are:

Mark 3:1-5	Healing of a Man's Hand
Matthew 12:11-12	Pulling Sheep Out of the Pit
Luke 6:9-10	Healing of the Hand
Luke 13:10-13	Healing a Woman with the Spirit of Infirmity
John 5:8-16	Healing a Man whole to walk
John 9:14	Healing of a Man's Eyes

The Messiah continued to honor the Sabbath Day throughout the scriptures by teaching on this day.

Mark 6:2 (KJV)

[2] And when the sabbath day was come, he began to teach in the synagogue: and many hearing him were astonished, saying, From whence hath this man these things? and what wisdom is this which is given unto him, that even such mighty works are wrought by his hands?

Luke 4:31 (KJV)

[31] And came down to Capernaum, a city of Galilee, and taught them on the sabbath days.

The first day of the week is never mentioned pertaining to meeting, worshipping or the reading of the scriptures by the Messiah or Disciples.

THE DISCIPLES AND PAUL

All of the disciples and Paul honored and observed the Sabbath Day without question. There are many debates that Paul was teaching against the law or the commandments of The Most High God. This argument cannot be true because the scriptures say Paul believed what was written in the law. He also believed what the prophets of the Old Testament stood for as well.

If this is the case then Paul had to have believed in the keeping of the Sabbath Day since it was part of the Law / Commandments of the Most High God.

Acts 24:14 (KJV)

[14] But this I confess unto thee, that after the way which they call heresy, so worship I the God of my fathers, believing all things which are written in the law and in the prophets:

Acts 13:27 (KJV)

[27] For they that dwell at Jerusalem, and their rulers, because they knew him not, nor yet the voices of the prophets which are read every sabbath day, they have fulfilled them in condemning him.

Paul always read, prayed and preached the scriptures on the Sabbath Day and he definitely kept the law and this was after the Messiah's death.

Acts 17:2-3 (KJV)

[2] And Paul, as his manner was, went in unto them, and three sabbath days reasoned with them out of the scriptures,

[3] Opening and alleging, that Christ must needs have suffered, and risen again from the dead; and that this Jesus, whom I preach unto you, is Christ.

Acts 16:13 (KJV)

[13] And on the sabbath we went out of the city by a river side, where prayer was wont to be made; and we sat down, and spake unto the women which resorted thither.

Acts 25:8 (KJV)

[8] While he answered for himself, Neither against the law of the Jews, neither against the temple, nor yet against Caesar, have I offended any thing at all.

Acts 13:14 (KJV)

[14] But when they departed from Perga, they came to Antioch in Pisidia, and went into the synagogue on the sabbath day, and sat down.

Acts 15:21 (KJV)

[21] For Moses of old time hath in every city them that preach him, being read in the synagogues every sabbath day.

During the days of the disciples and Paul there is scripture after scripture that supports The Sabbath Day was still in play, even the Gentiles needed to observe this day. This only concludes that the Sabbath Day continued to be observed after the death of the Messiah and all the laws was not nailed to the cross.

Acts 13:44 (KJV)

[44] And the next sabbath day came almost the whole city together to hear the word of God.

Acts 18:4 (KJV)

⁴ And he reasoned in the synagogue every sabbath, and persuaded the Jews and the Greeks.

Acts 13:42 (KJV)

⁴² And when the Jews were gone out of the synagogue, the Gentiles besought that these words might be preached to them the next sabbath.

THE TWO MARY'S

During the time of the Messiah's crucifixion a few things happened, The Messiah's body could not be on the cross and therefore needed to be taken down before the Sabbath Day. What most people don't realize is this particular week had two Sabbath Days. The first one was a High Sabbath meaning it was the (Feast of Unleavened Bread) and the second one was the regular Sabbath Day we know as (Saturday) today.

John 19:31 (KJV)

³¹ The Jews therefore, because it was the preparation, that the bodies should not remain upon the cross on the sabbath day, **(for that sabbath day was an high day,)** besought Pilate that their legs might be broken, and that they might be taken away.

During the first day of the **Feast of Unleavened Bread** the law states there should be no cooking, buying, selling or trading etc. This was the day after The Passover and The Messiah had to be off the cross before evening.

Leviticus 23:2-6 (KJV)

[2] Speak unto the children of Israel, and say unto them, Concerning the feasts of the LORD, which ye shall proclaim to be holy convocations, even these are my feasts.

[3] Six days shall work be done: but the seventh day is the sabbath of rest, an holy convocation; ye shall do no work therein: it is the sabbath of the LORD in all your dwellings.

[4] These are the feasts of the LORD, even holy convocations, which ye shall proclaim in their seasons.

[5] In the fourteenth day of the first month at even is the LORD's passover.

[6] And on the fifteenth day of the same month is the feast of unleavened bread unto the LORD: seven days ye must eat unleavened bread.

Leviticus 23:39 (KJV)

[39] Also in the fifteenth day of the seventh month, when ye have gathered in the fruit of the land, ye shall keep a feast unto the LORD seven days: on the first day shall be a sabbath, and on the eighth day shall be a sabbath.

The two Mary's wanted to bring spices to the grave of The Messiah after he was put in the tomb, but they could not do so because the law of keeping the Sabbath Day prevented them from buying, selling or working.

Mark 16:1-2 (KJV)

1 And when the sabbath was past, Mary Magdalene, and Mary the mother of James, and Salome, had bought sweet spices, that they might come and anoint him.

2 And very early in the morning the first day of the week, they came unto the sepulchre at the rising of the sun.

Luke 24:1-6 (KJV)

1 Now upon the first day of the week, very early in the morning, they came unto the sepulchre, bringing the spices which they had prepared, and certain others with them.

2 And they found the stone rolled away from the sepulchre.

3 And they entered in, and found not the body of the Lord Jesus.

4 And it came to pass, as they were much perplexed thereabout, behold, two men stood by them in shining garments:

5 And as they were afraid, and bowed down their faces to the earth, they said unto them, Why seek ye the living among the dead?

6 He is not here, but is risen: remember how he spake unto you when he was yet in Galilee,

Since that first High Sabbath Day of the week was after the Passover (Wednesday), then Thursday was the first day of **The Feast of Unleavened Bread.** The two Mary's could not have purchased or worked to prepare the spices for the Messiah's grave on Thursday because they believed in resting on the Sabbath according to the commandment.

Luke 23:56 (KJV)

[56] And they returned, and prepared spices and ointments; and rested the sabbath day according to the commandment.

The only day left to prepare the spices was on Friday and obviously they did not get the spices to the body until Sunday morning because that Saturday was another Sabbath Day which prevented them from working or preparing the spices.
How do we know it was that Sunday? Because the bible says in Mark 16:2 that it was early in the morning on the first day of the week the two Mary's brought the spices. However, the Messiah was gone by this time which means he rose prior to the first day of the week.

This story of the two Mary's is just an example of how during the time of The Messiah's reign on earth and after his death how the two Mary's were still following the Sabbath Day Law as it is written in the Old Testament.

THE FIRST DAY OF THE WEEK

This chapter is all about the Sabbath Day but some attention is needed in how the bible addresses the first day of the week. The first thing that should be noted is that the bible never addresses the first day of the week from Genesis to Revelation as being sanctified, hollowed or holy. It simply addresses the first day of the week as the first day of the week.

If this is the case then why is it in religious circles such as in Christianity the first day of the week (Sunday) is held to the standard as the Sabbath Day in which the Sabbath Day is the only day The Most High named? The other days of the week were just numbered 1, 2, 3, 4, 5, 6 and Sabbath.

Technically, all days of the week in today's society were named by the Babylonians then later adopted by the Romans. The days of the week are named after pagan gods / or deities, primarily after the planets, moon and the sun. This should add more support on how pagan the world is today.

DAY	CORRESPONDS TO
Sunday	The sun, in honor of the Sun god
Monday	The moon, in honor of the moon god
Tuesday	The planet Mars, in honor of the god Mars. The Saxons named this day after their god Tiw and called it Tiw's day. "Tuesday" comes from the name of this Saxon god.
Wednesday	The planet Mercury, later named in honor of the Teutinic god Wedn or Woden or Odin
Thursday	The planet Jupiter, later named in honor of Teutonic god Thor
Friday	The planet Venus, later named in the honor of the Teutonic goddess Frigg or Freia.
Saturday	The planet Saturn, in honor of the Roman god Saturn.

Let's explore some scriptures that mentions the first day of the week and see if this took the place of the Sabbath Day. The phrase "first day of the week" is only mentioned eight times in the New Testament and the Sabbath is mentioned sixty times. The word "Sunday' is never mentioned.

In the book of Genesis when The Most High was creating the world the first day of the week was mentioned. He called it "The first day of the week". But by the time he got to the seventh day of the week He called it the seventh day; however the seventh day became known as the Sabbath throughout the scriptures.

Exodus 16:26 (KJV)

[26] Six days ye shall gather it; but on the seventh day, which is the sabbath, in it there shall be none.

Exodus 20:10 (KJV)

[10] But the seventh day is the sabbath of the LORD thy God: in it thou shalt not do any work, thou, nor thy son, nor thy daughter, thy manservant, nor thy maidservant, nor thy cattle, nor thy stranger that is within thy gates:

There are several scriptures from the New Testament that are used to say that Sunday, the first day of the week, took the place of the Sabbath Day (Saturday). Let's examine more closely to see if this is true. The first scripture is Acts 20:7.

Acts 20:7 (KJV)

⁷ And upon the first day of the week, when the disciples came together to break bread, Paul preached unto them, ready to depart on the morrow; and continued his speech until midnight.

This verse appears to be saying that there was a worship gathering on the first day of the week because Paul was preaching and the disciples were breaking bread. How could we be sure this is what was happening? Let's take a closer look. First, notice it was a meeting at night and the next verse supports this statement (Acts 20:8).

Acts 20:8 (KJV)

⁸ And there were many lights in the upper chamber, where they were gathered together.

Because they were gathering or meeting on the first day of the week, does not necessarily mean the Sabbath (Saturday) was changed to Sunday. If we read (Acts 2:46 and Acts 20:11), you'll notice this was a daily act with the disciples to break bread together and talked for long periods of time.

Acts 2:46 (KJV)

⁴⁶ And they, continuing daily with one accord in the temple, and breaking bread from house to house, did eat their meat with gladness and singleness of heart,

---

> **Acts 20:11 (KJV)**
>
> [11] When he therefore was come up again, and had broken bread, and eaten, and talked a long while, even till break of day, so he departed.

If we were to take (Acts 20:7) to mean Sunday replaced the Sabbath because the disciples gathered with preaching and breaking of bread, then those who observe Sunday worship today should be having church services at night, every night and until the break of dawn. We know this does not happen, so how can we believe (Acts 20:7) give proof that the "first day of the week" replaced the Sabbath day.

I CORINTHIANS 16:2

> **1 Corinthians 16:2 (KJV)**
>
> [2] Upon the first day of the week let every one of you lay by him in store, as God hath prospered him, that there be no gatherings when I come.

There is absolutely no reference or indication of a public meeting or gathering service in this verse for when Paul arrives; so why this verse is typically used to defend worship on the first day of the week is baffling. This verse never declares that Sunday or the first day of the week took the place of The Sabbath Day (Saturday). Maybe the assumption could be from Paul gathering gifts on this day? But if we read the next verse (I Corinthians 16:3) it may become clearer what is being said in this context.

1 Corinthians 16:3 (KJV)

³ And when I come, whomsoever ye shall approve by your letters, them will I send to bring your liberality unto Jerusalem.

The key word in I Corinthians 16:3 is **"liberality"** because this word describes the type of offering Paul was collecting which mean gifts according to Strong's Concordance. This was not the tithe because in verse (I Corinthians 16:2) it mentions they were giving from what they had in store from what The Most High God had prospered them. It appears this was just love offerings and had nothing to do with changing the Sabbath Day to Sunday (first day of the week).

In a nutshell all this verse is saying is that Paul is stopping by on his way to Jerusalem picking up gifts for those who were in financially distress in Jerusalem. It was a special circumstance being part of a wider famine-relief effort aimed at providing those in Jerusalem with gifts or food supplies. This type of gift giving appears in other scriptures as well, please read Romans 15:26 and Acts 11:26-30.

Romans 15:26 (KJV)

²⁶ For it hath pleased them of Macedonia and Achaia to make a certain contribution for the poor saints which are at Jerusalem.

Acts 11:26-30 (KJV)

²⁶ And when he had found him, he brought him unto Antioch. And it came to pass, that a whole year they assembled themselves with the church, and taught much people. And the disciples were called Christians first in Antioch.

²⁷ And in these days came prophets from Jerusalem unto Antioch.

²⁸ And there stood up one of them named Agabus, and signified by the Spirit that there should be great dearth throughout all the world: which came to pass in the days of Claudius Caesar.

²⁹ Then the disciples, every man according to his ability, determined to send relief unto the brethren which dwelt in Judaea:

³⁰ Which also they did, and sent it to the elders by the hands of Barnabas and Saul.

Again, in retrospect there is nothing to suggest or indicate in I Corinthians 16:2 that there was a gathering or service to proclaim that the first day of the week was changed to represent The Sabbath Day.

MATTHEW 28:1

Matthew 28:1 (KJV)

1 In the end of the sabbath, as it began to dawn toward the first day of the week, came Mary Magdalene and the other Mary to see the sepulchre.

This verse only proves that there was still a Sabbath Day and the first day of the week followed. This verse does not prove that the Sabbath Day was changed to the first day of the week and therefore cannot be used to say the bible approves that Sunday (the first day of the week) as a day of worship and rest.

MARK 16:2

> **Mark 16:2 (KJV)**
>
> [2] And very early in the morning the first day of the week, they came unto the sepulchre at the rising of the sun.

This verse gives no account that the Sabbath Day was replaced by the first day of the week. It only indicates that the two Mary's brought sweet spices to the sepulcher early on the first day of the week (Sunday).

> **Mark 16:1 (KJV)**
>
> [1] And when the sabbath was past, Mary Magdalene, and Mary the mother of James, and Salome, had bought sweet spices, that they might come and anoint him.

MARK 16:9

> **Mark 16:9 (KJV)**
>
> [9] Now when Jesus was risen early the first day of the week, he appeared first to Mary Magdalene, out of whom he had cast seven devils.

The verses (Mark 16:9-20) present a controversy concerning its authenticity. Many biblical scholars are torn between this verse being authentic or not. In the fourth century nearly all the Greek manuscripts or Greek codices available lacked the longer ending in the book of Mark. There are many reasons experts believe these verses are not authentic.

1. The transition from verse 8-9 is very awkward

2. The vocabulary changes greatly in the Greek language

3. The ancient church fathers reveal no knowledge of these verses such as Clement, Origen, Eusebius and Jerome

In many commentaries and / or study bibles there is generally a footnote at the bottom of the page supporting that Mark verses 9-20 is not authentic. You'll read something like this:

The most reliable early manuscripts and other ancient witnesses do not have Mark 16:9-20

The following commentary is copied verbatim from the **NIV Disciples Study Bible** concerning Mark 16:9-20.

16:9-20, Holy Scriptures, Collection – Through the generations dedicated people copied God's inspired Word and produced hundreds of manuscripts of the bible. With their human freedom and limits, these people copied the text with amazing accuracy. Occasionally, a few differences crept into the text. Mk 16:9-20 is one significant addition present in the manuscript used for King James Version but not in the earliest or most reliable manuscripts. Some manuscripts add a brief missionary commission after v. 8. Some manuscripts with vv 9-20 also contain an extensive addition to v 14. Obviously, from the third century on readers thought v 8 was not a satisfactory ending to Mark, particularly because it ended abruptly with a Greek conjunction. The original ending of mark remains uncertain. Some have thought Mark was prevented from finishing the Gospel. Others accept v 8 as the original ending. Others think the original scroll was damaged or torn. This difference in thought indicates 16:9-20 should not be used as the sole basis of doctrine. The foundation of doctrine is well established from biblical texts that appear in the earliest

---

manuscripts. Compare John 7:53-8:11. Conclusions about the doctrine of revelation or Scripture should be based on the clear teachings which appear throughout the Bible. Scripture texts whose proper interpretation is difficult to establish should not form the foundation of the doctrine.

In any case Mark 16:9 does not provide any evidence or support that the Sabbath Day was changed from Saturday to Sunday.

LUKE 24:1

Luke 24:1 (KJV)

1 Now upon the first day of the week, very early in the morning, they came unto the sepulchre, bringing the spices which they had prepared, and certain others with them.

This verse is a repeat with the same contextual meaning as in Matthew 28:1 and Mark 16:2 in which it gives no indication of The Sabbath Day being changed to Sunday (First day of the week).

JOHN 20:1

John 20:1 (KJV)

1 The first day of the week cometh Mary Magdalene early, when it was yet dark, unto the sepulchre, and seeth the stone taken away from the sepulchre.

This verse is the same explanation as in verses Matthew 28:1, Luke 24:1 and Mark 16:2. No indication or meaning that the Sabbath Day (Saturday) is now Sunday.

JOHN 20:19

John 20:19 (KJV)

¹⁹ Then the same day at evening, being the first day of the week, when the doors were shut where the disciples were assembled for fear of the Jews, came Jesus and stood in the midst, and saith unto them, Peace be unto you.

This verse states that the disciples assembled for fear of the Jews. The reason for the assembling does not indicate they were assembling for worship, prayer, singing or reading of scripture. There is nothing in this verse to indicate the first day of the week (Sunday) took the place of the Sabbath Day (Saturday).

REVELATION 1:10

One more verse in question is Revelation 1:10. In this verse it uses the phrase "The Lord's Day". It is a very popular phase in today's Christian world to mean "Sunday". How does this verse automatically mean it's referring to "Sunday"?

Revelation 1:10 (KJV)

¹⁰ I was in the Spirit on the Lord's day, and heard behind me a great voice, as of a trumpet,

This verse does not specify what day of the week it's referring; neither does it gives a number of the week it's referring. So, how does one determine its meaning? First, we must look to see if this phrase appears anywhere else in the bible and in this case, it only appears once in the New Testament (Rev. 1:10). However, the phrase "The Lord's Day" does not appear in the Old Testament but the phase "The Day of the Lord" does. Could this be what

Revelation 1:10 is referring? If this is the case then the phrase "The Lord's Day" would refer to the Day of Judgment or Wrath of the Messiah.

Joel 2:1 (KJV)

1 Blow ye the trumpet in Zion, and sound an alarm in my holy mountain: let all the inhabitants of the land tremble: for the **day of the LORD** cometh, for it is nigh at hand;

Joel 2:31 (KJV)

31 The sun shall be turned into darkness, and the moon into blood, before the great and terrible **day of the LORD** come.

Acts 2:20 (KJV)

20 The sun shall be turned into darkness, and the moon into blood, before the great and notable **day of the Lord** come:

The Encyclopedia of Britannica (Sabbath, Vol. xxi, Pg 126) offer a statement that reads. "The first writer who mentions the name of Sunday as it connects to the first day of the week is Justin Martyr (Christian Apologist) (AD 140) and others such as Theophilus of Antioch (AD 168), Dionysius of Corinth (AD 170), Melito of Sardis (AD 177) and Irenaeus (AD 178) also make such claims. In every case the bible is clear that the first day of the week is a day of work not rest.

Exodus 23:12 (KJV)

[12] Six days thou shalt do thy work, and on the seventh day thou shalt rest: that thine ox and thine ass may rest, and the son of thy handmaid, and the stranger, may be refreshed.

Exodus 31:15 (KJV)

[15] Six days may work be done; but in the seventh is the sabbath of rest, holy to the LORD: whosoever doeth any work in the sabbath day, he shall surely be put to death.

Exodus 34:21 (KJV)

[21] Six days thou shalt work, but on the seventh day thou shalt rest: in earing time and in harvest thou shalt rest.

Exodus 35:2 (KJV)

[2] Six days shall work be done, but on the seventh day there shall be to you an holy day, a sabbath of rest to the LORD: whosoever doeth work therein shall be put to death.

Leviticus 23:3 (KJV)

[3] Six days shall work be done: but the seventh day is the sabbath of rest, an holy convocation; ye shall do no work therein: it is the sabbath of the LORD in all your dwellings.

Deuteronomy 5:13 (KJV)

[13] Six days thou shalt labour, and do all thy work:

Ezekiel 46:1 (KJV)

[1] Thus saith the Lord GOD; The gate of the inner court that looketh toward the east shall be shut the six working days; but on the sabbath it shall be opened, and in the day of the new moon it shall be opened.

Luke 13:14 (KJV)

[14] And the ruler of the synagogue answered with indignation, because that Jesus had healed on the sabbath day, and said unto the people, There are six days in which men ought to work: in them therefore come and be healed, and not on the sabbath day.

We must keep in mind that having Sunday or the "first day of the week" as a day of Worship and Rest is a pagan idea and not a biblical idea. We must always obey The Most High God rather than man.

Acts 5:29 (KJV)

[29] Then Peter and the other apostles answered and said, We ought to obey God rather than men.

WHO CHANGED THE SABBATH DAY TO SUNDAY?

According to the scriptures it doesn't appear as if the Most High God himself had anything to do with the changing of his holy day. Neither, The Messiah or the disciples are involved in the changing of the Sabbath Day (Saturday) to the first day of the week (Sunday).

If the bible doesn't support this change then some investigation is warranted to find out when and who changed it. Roman Emperor Constantine changed or made it legal to worship on Sunday. This happened in 321 AD.

Constantine was a Roman Emperor who reigned during the 4th century from 306 to 337 AD. He was responsible for changing The Most High God's Sabbath Day. This change took place in 321 AD solely for political gain. Constantine was a sun worshipper and he adapted his belief system into Christianity by changing worship from Saturday to Sunday in honor of his pagan sun god.

The Roman Catholic System in general has made many changes to the doctrines of Christianity since the very beginning. This Apostasy started way back in the days of the disciples and continues to this day.

---

2 Thessalonians 2:7 (KJV)

[7] For the mystery of iniquity doth already work: only he who now letteth will let, until he be taken out of the way.

The Roman Catholic Church (The Mother) and the other harlots (The Children of Other Denominations of Christianity) of the Roman Catholic Church are solely responsible for changing the Sabbath Day to the first day of the week (Sunday).

There are many confessions from the Roman Catholic Church along with and other Christian denominations admitting the fact that they had the authority to change the Sabbath to the first day of the week (Sunday), although the bible does not support such a claim.

Roman Catholic Church Confessions

Peter Geiermann, C.S.S.R., The Converts Catechism of Catholic Doctirne (1957), P. 50

> "Question: Which is the Sabbath day?
> "Answer: Saturday is the Sabbath day.
> "Question: Why do we observe Sunday instead of Saturday?
> "Answer. We observe Sunday instead of Saturday because the Catholic Church transferred the solemnity from Saturday to Sunday."

James Cardinal Gibbons, The Faith of our Fathers, 88th ed., pp.89

> "But you may read the Bible from Genesis to Revelation, and you will not find a single line authorizing the sanctification of Sunday. The Scriptures enforce the religious observance of Saturday, a day which we never sanctify."

Peter R. Kraemer, Catholic Church Extension Society (1975), Chicago, Illinois.

> "Regarding the change from the observance of the Jewish Sabbath to the Christian Sunday, I wish to draw your attention to the facts:

"1) That Protestants, who accept the Bible as the only rule of faith and religion, should by all means go back to the observance of the Sabbath. The fact that they do not, but on the contrary observe the Sunday, stultifies them in the eyes of every thinking man.

"2) We Catholics do not accept the Bible as the only rule of faith. Besides the Bible we have the living Church, the authority of the Church, as a rule to guide us. We say, this Church, instituted by Christ to teach and guide man through life, has the right to change the ceremonial laws of the Old Testament and hence, we accept her change of the Sabbath to Sunday. We frankly say, yes, the Church made this change, made this law, as she made many other laws, for instance, the Friday abstinence, the unmarried priesthood, the laws concerning mixed marriages, the regulation of Catholic marriages and a thousand other laws.

T. Enright, C.S.S.R., in a lecture at Hartford, Kansas, Feb. 18,1884.

"I have repeatedly offered $1,000 to anyone who can prove to me from the Bible alone that I am bound to keep Sunday holy. There is no such law in the Bible. It is a law of the holy Catholic Church alone. The Bible says, 'Remember the Sabbath day to keep it holy.' The Catholic Church says: 'No. By my divine power I abolish the Sabbath day and command you to keep holy the first day of the week.' And lo! The entire civilized world bows down in a reverent obedience to the command of the holy Catholic Church."

Martin J. Scott, Things Catholics Are Asked About (1927), p. 136.

> "Nowhere in the Bible is it stated that worship should be changed from Saturday to Sunday .... Now the Church ... instituted, by God's authority, Sunday as the day of worship. This same Church, by the same divine authority, taught the doctrine of Purgatory long before the Bible was made. We have, therefore, the same authority for Purgatory as we have for Sunday."

Catholic Virginian Oct. 3, 1947, p. 9, art. "To Tell You the Truth."

> "For example, nowhere in the Bible do we find that Christ or the Apostles ordered that the Sabbath be changed from Saturday to Sunday. We have the commandment of God given to Moses to keep holy the Sabbath day, that is the 7th day of the week, Saturday. Today most Christians keep Sunday because it has been revealed to us by the[Roman Catholic] church outside the Bible."

The Catholic Mirror, official publication of James Cardinal Gibbons, Sept. 23, 1893.

> "The Catholic Church, . . . by virtue of her divine mission, changed the day from Saturday to Sunday."

James Cardinal Gibbons, Archbishop of Baltimore (1877-1921), in a signed letter.

> "Is Saturday the seventh day according to the Bible and the Ten Commandments? I answer yes. Is Sunday the first day of the week and did the Church change the seventh day -Saturday - for Sunday, the first day? I answer *yes* . Did Christ change the day'? I answer *no!*

Daniel Ferres, ed., Manual of Christian Doctrine (1916), p.67.

> "Question: How prove you that the Church hath power to command feasts and holy days?

> "Answer. By the very act of changing the Sabbath into Sunday, which Protestants allow of, and therefore they fondly contradict themselves, by keeping Sunday strictly, and breaking most other feasts commanded by the same Church.'

John Laux, A Course in Religion for Catholic High Schools and Academies (1 936), vol. 1, P. 51.

> "Some theologians have held that God likewise directly determined the Sunday as the day of worship in the New Law, that He Himself has explicitly substituted the Sunday for the Sabbath. But this theory is now entirely abandoned. It is now commonly held that God simply gave His Church the power to set aside whatever day or days she would deem suitable as Holy Days. The Church chose Sunday, the first day of the week, and in the course of time added other days as holy days."

Stephen Keenan, A Doctrinal Catechism 3rd ed., p. 174.

> "Question: Have you any other way of proving that the Church has power to institute festivals of precept?

> "Answer: Had she not such power, she could not have done that in which all modern religionists agree with her-she could not have substituted the observance of Sunday, the first day of the week, for the observance of Saturday, the seventh day, a change for which there is no Scriptural authority."

Protestant Confessions

Protestant theologians and preachers from a wide spectrum of denominations have been quite candid in admitting that there is no Biblical authority for observing Sunday as a Sabbath.

Anglican/Episcopal

Isaac Williams, Plain Sermons on the Catechism, vol. 1, pp.334, 336.

"And where are we told in the Scriptures that we are to keep the first day at all? We are commanded to keep the seventh; but we are nowhere commanded to keep the first day .... The reason why we keep the first day of the week holy instead of the seventh is for the same reason that we observe many other things, not because the Bible, but because the church has enjoined it."

Canon Eyton, *The Ten Commandments*, pp. 52, 63, 65.

"There is no word, no hint, in the New Testament about abstaining from work on Sunday .... into the rest of Sunday, no divine law enters.... The observance of Ash Wednesday or Lent stands exactly on the same footing as the observance of Sunday."

Bishop Seymour, Why We Keep Sunday.

We have made the change from the seventh day to the first day, from Saturday to Sunday, on the authority of the one holy Catholic Church."

Baptist

Dr. Edward T. Hiscox, a paper read before a New York ministers' conference, Nov. 13, 1893, reported in New York Examiner, Nov.16, 1893.

"There was and is a commandment to keep holy the Sabbath day, but that Sabbath day was not Sunday. It will be said, however, and with some show of triumph, that the Sabbath was transferred from the seventh to the first day of the week .... Where can the record of such a transaction be found? Not in the New Testament absolutely not.

"To me it seems unaccountable that Jesus, during three years' intercourse with His disciples, often conversing with them upon the Sabbath question . . . never alluded to any transference of the day; also, that during forty days of His resurrection life, no such thing was intimated.

"Of course, I quite well know that Sunday did come into use in early Christian history . . . . But what a pity it comes branded with the mark of paganism, and christened with the name of the sun god, adopted and sanctioned by the papal apostasy, and bequeathed as a sacred legacy to Protestantism!"

William Owen Carver, The Lord's Day in Our Day, p. 49.

"There was never any formal or authoritative change from the Jewish seventh-day Sabbath to the Christian first-day observance."

<u>Congregationalist</u>

Dr. R. W. Dale, The Ten Commandments (New York: Eaton &Mains), p. 127-129.

" . . . it is quite clear that however rigidly or devotedly we may spend Sunday, we are not keeping the Sabbath - . . 'Me Sabbath was founded on a specific Divine command. We can plead no such command for the obligation to observe Sunday .... There is not a single sentence in the New Testament to suggest that we incur any penalty by violating the supposed sanctity of Sunday."

Timothy Dwight, Theology: Explained and Defended (1823), Ser. 107, vol. 3, p. 258.

" . . . the Christian Sabbath [Sunday] is not in the Scriptures, and was not by the primitive Church called the Sabbath."

Disciples of Christ

Alexander Campbell, The Christian Baptist, Feb. 2, 1824, vol. 1. no. 7, p. 164.

"'But,' say some, 'it was changed from the seventh to the first day.' Where? when? and by whom? No man can tell. No; it never was changed, nor could it be, unless creation was to be gone through again: for the reason assigned must be changed before the observance, or respect to the reason, can be changed! It is all old wives' fables to talk of the change of the Sabbath from the seventh to the first day. If it be changed, it was that august personage changed it who changes times and laws *ex officio* - I think his name is Doctor Antichrist.'

First Day Observance, pp. 17, 19.

"The first day of the week is commonly called the Sabbath. This is a mistake. The Sabbath of the Bible was the day just preceding the first day of the week. The first day of the week is never called the Sabbath anywhere in the entire Scriptures. It is also an error to talk about the change of the Sabbath from Saturday to Sunday. There is not in any place in the Bible any intimation of such a change."

Lutheran

The Sunday Problem, a study book of the United Lutheran Church (1923), p. 36.

"We have seen how gradually the impression of the Jewish sabbath faded from the mind of the Christian Church, and how completely the newer thought underlying the observance of the first day took possession of the church. We have seen that the Christians of the first three centuries never confused one with the other, but for a time celebrated both."

Augsburg Confession of Faith art. 28; written by Melanchthon, approved by Martin Luther, 1530; as published in The Book of Concord of the Evangelical Lutheran Church Henry Jacobs, ed. (1 91 1), p. 63.

"They [Roman Catholics] refer to the Sabbath Day, a shaving been changed into the Lord's Day, contrary to the Decalogue, as it seems. Neither is there any example whereof they make more than concerning the changing of the Sabbath Day. Great, say they, is the power of the Church, since it has dispensed with one of the Ten Commandments!"

Dr. Augustus Neander, *The History of the Christian Religion and Church* Henry John Rose, tr. (1843), p. 186.

"The festival of Sunday, like all other festivals, was always only a human ordinance, and it was far from the intentions of the apostles to establish a Divine command in this respect, far from them, and from the early apostolic Church, to transfer the laws of the Sabbath to Sunday."

John Theodore Mueller, Sabbath or Sunday, pp. 15, 16.

"But they err in teaching that Sunday has taken the place of the Old Testament Sabbath and therefore must be kept as the seventh day had to be kept by the children of Israel .... These churches err in their teaching, for Scripture has in no way ordained the first day of the week in place of the Sabbath. There is simply no law in the New Testament to that effect."

Methodist

Harris Franklin Rall, Christian Advocate, July 2, 1942, p.26.

"Take the matter of Sunday. There are indications in the New Testament as to how the church came to keep the first day of the week as its day of worship, but there is no passage telling Christians to keep that day, or to transfer the Jewish Sabbath to that day."

John Wesley, The Works of the Rev. John Wesley, A.M., John Emory, ed. (New York: Eaton & Mains), Sermon 25, vol. 1, p. 221.

"But the moral law contained in the ten commandments, and enforced by the prophets, he [Christ] did not take away. It was not the design of his coming to revoke any part of this. This is a law which never can be broken .... Every part of this law must remain in force upon all mankind, and in all ages; as not depending either on time or place, or any other circumstances liable to change, but on the nature of God and the nature of man, and their unchangeable relation to each other."

Dwight L. Moody

D. L. Moody, Weighed and Wanting (Fleming H. Revell Co.: New York), pp. 47, 48.

The Sabbath was binding in Eden, and it has been in force ever since. This fourth commandment begins with the word 'remember,' showing that the Sabbath already existed when God Wrote the law on the tables of stone at Sinai. How can men claim that this one commandment has been done away with when they will admit that the other nine are still binding?"

Presbyterian

T. C. Blake, D.D., Theology Condensed, pp.474, 475.

"The Sabbath is a part of the Decalogue - the Ten Commandments. This alone forever settles the question as to the perpetuity of the institution . . . . Until, therefore, it can be shown that the whole moral law has been repealed, the Sabbath will stand . . . . The teaching of Christ confirms the perpetuity of the Sabbath."

Resource:

The Bible Sabbath Association
Promoting Co-Operation and Understanding Among All Sabbatarians
Roman Catholic and Protestant Confessions about Sunday
https://www.biblesabbath.org/confessions.html
[March 2, 2019]

HOW TO KEEP THE SABBATH

The keeping of the SABBATH DAY is not a grievous task (I John 5:3) and can be obtained. The true descendants of the true children Israel are commanded to keep it because it is a perpetual covenant throughout their generations (Exodus 31:16).

Once the Most High God opens the eyes of his people the Sabbath Day must be kept. The majority of True Israel has been trained to have a holy convocation on the first day of the week (Sunday) instead of the Sabbath (Saturday). The first thought that usually comes to mind when one eyes are open is How to keep the Sabbath Day and what to do on the Sabbath Day.

1. **No Servile Work:**
The Sabbath day is a day of rest and there should be no work performed on this day unless it is absolutely unavoidable. Those who are bible believers should recognize we only have six days of work and one day of rest. Servile work could be defined as work of a physical nature that is forbidden on the Sabbath Day. In other words, there should be no heavy manual labor, needless work of business and no housekeeping etc. This Sabbath day of rest includes everyone (sons, daughters, maidservants, animals and strangers).

No Servile Work / A Day of Rest	
Genesis 2:2-3	God rested from all his work
Hebrews 4:4	God rested from all his work
Exodus 16:30	People rested on the seventh day
Exodus 20:10	No one should work
Exodus 23:12	No one should work
Exodus 31:15	No work or be put to death

Exodus 34:21	On the seventh thou should rest
Leviticus 23:3	Rest and have a holy convocation
Deuteronomy 5:13-14	No work should be done on the Sabbath
Jeremiah 17:22	Do no work but hollow the Sabbath
Luke 23:56	The women rested on the Sabbath day

2. No Buying, Selling or Trading:

On the Sabbath Day there should be no buying, selling or trading of any kind. An example of that would be in the book of Nehemiah 13:15-22. Nehemiah needed to shut the gates of Jerusalem because there were other nations of people selling fish to the children of Judah which was forbidden to do on the Sabbath Day. In other words, we should not go shopping, on line or in person spending money causing others to work, buy and sell, profaning the Sabbath day.

No Buying or Selling	
Nehemiah 13:15-22	Nehemiah encounter with Buying & Selling
Nehemiah 10:31	Don't buy on the Sabbath Day
Amos 8:5	Cannot sell until Sabbath is over

3. No Cooking or Burning of Fire:
The Most High God do not promote burning fire for the purpose of cooking

No Cooking or Burning Fire	
Exodus 16:23	No baking / cooking on the Sabbath
Exodus 35:1-3	Kindle no fire on the Sabbath day

4. Don't Do Your Own Pleasure:

Don't Do Your Own Pleasure	
Isaiah 58:13-14	Turn from your own pleasures

WHAT TO DO ON THE SABBATH DAY

The scriptures describe the Sabbath Day as a day of rest and this is exactly how the Sabbath Day should be observed. In this day of rest there are things that could be accomplished and still be legal in the sight of the Most High God.

1. **Holy Convocation or Worshipping:** The Sabbath Day is a day of gathering with others or believer's that will embrace the hearing or reading of the scriptures. Fellowship with those who desire and are willing to be taught the scriptures (Acts 13:13-16, Acts 13:42-44, Luke 4:14-16, 31).

2. **Personal Study of the Scriptures:** The Sabbath Day could be a day to personally spend time in the scriptures to learn

3. about the Most High God. This is a perfect opportunity to learn about his instructions concerning his law and other topics of interest of his doings (Psalm 77:12).

4. **Praying and Meditating:** Praying and meditating on The Sabbath Day is a great way to develop a closer relationship with The Most High God. The scriptures support meditating day and night on his laws of instructions (Joshua 1:8, Psalm 1:2).

5. **Listening to Uplifting Music:** Listening to music that edifies The Most High God (Ephesians 5:19).

6. **Current Events or a Day of Learning:** The Sabbath Day could be a day used to also study the current events that are happening around the world and compare how it relates to prophecies in the bible (Matthew 24:6-7, Matthew 24:15-16, Mark 13:14-19, Daniel 12:11, Daniel 9:27, Daniel 11:31, Jeremiah 30:7, II Thessalonians 2:3-4).

7. **Good Deeds:** Good deeds are allowed to be done on the Sabbath Day. If someone is in distress and it's a matter of life or death, it is perfectly lawful to help and or assist (Luke 14:5). Good deeds could include healing, satisfying immediate hunger or any other emergency that could cause for immediate action or the need for attention. (Luke 14:3, John 9:14, Matthew 12:1-8). We must remember The Sabbath Day was made for man not man for the Sabbath (Mark 2:27).

8. **Day of Rest:** Someone may choose just to rest for part of the day. Remember The Most High God did rest on the Sabbath day (Genesis 2:2-3).

In conclusion The Sabbath Day (Saturday) is the day according to the biblical scriptures is the day required by the Most High God to be observed as his holy day and should not be profaned. This day should be totally focused on him. The Sabbath Day changing to the first day of the week (Sunday) is just a tradition of men and should have never been implemented (Colossians 2:8, Mark 7:7-9). Blessed is the man who holds on and keeps the true Sabbath Day (Isaiah 56:2).

Isaiah 56:2 (KJV)

[2] Blessed is the man that doeth this, and the son of man that layeth hold on it; that keepeth the sabbath from polluting it, and keepeth his hand from doing any evil.

CONCLUSION

This book is just a summary and a reference of the notes I've taken upon my awakening to the truth concerning "TRUE ISRAEL", who are the African Americans or people of color around the world who has been scattered to the four corners of the earth.

The take away from this book is to encourage those who are seeking the truth and this book is just a remnant of information to jump start your own research work. Believe me when I say the rabbit hole goes a whole lot deeper than this book has explored.

Since I wrote this book, I've learned much more facts about the scriptures of the bible concerning the way "TRUE ISRAEL" should be living in order to re-connect with the God of Abraham, Isaac and Jacob. There is much to be gained when "TRUE ISRAEL" awaken and began following the Laws, Statutes and Commandments of the Most High God of the scriptures, along with having the faith in our savior required to live it. He stated repeatedly, "if a man do, he shall even live in them". (Ezekiel 20:11, 13, 19, 21).

Be encouraged "TRUE ISRAEL", our journey has just begun and our deliverance is near.

Let us hear the conclusion of the whole matter: "Fear Yah and keep his commandments: for this is the whole duty of man. (Ecclesiastes12:13).

Henry W. Barton

www.ingramcontent.com/pod-product-compliance
Lightning Source LLC
Chambersburg PA
CBHW070549100426
42744CB00006B/249